Leah Spanover, née White or Whitman, Mizocz, c.1921. Courtesy of Laurence Broun.

Memorial Book of Mizocz
(Mizoch, Ukraine)

Translation of
Mizocz; sefer zikaron

Original Book Edited by: A. Ben-Oni

Originally published in Tel Aviv 1961

JewishGen
מרכז עולמי לגנאלוגיה יהודית
The Global Home for Jewish Genealogy

A Publication of JewishGen
Edmond J. Safra Plaza, 36 Battery Place, New York, NY 10280
646.494.2972 | info@JewishGen.org | www.jewishgen.org

MUSEUM OF
JEWISH HERITAGE
A LIVING MEMORIAL
TO THE HOLOCAUST

Memorial Book of Mizocz

Translation of *Mizocz; sefer zikaron*

Copyright © 2024 by JewishGen. All rights reserved.
First Printing: September 2024, Elul, 5784
Second Printing: October 2024, Tishrei, 5785
Editor of Original Yizkor Book: A. Ben-Oni
Project Coordinator: Laurence Broun
Cover Design: Nina Schwartz
Layout and Formatting: Jonathan Wind
Name Indexing: Stefanie Holzman

Library of Congress Control Number (LCCN): 2022952289

ISBN: 978-1-954176-69-0 (hard cover: 338 pages, alk. paper)

About JewishGen.org

JewishGen, is a Genealogical Research Division of the Museum of Jewish Heritage - A Living Memorial to the Holocaust, serves as the global home for Jewish genealogy.

Featuring unparalleled access to 30+ million records, it offers unique search tools, along with opportunities for researchers to connect with others who share similar interests. Award winning resources such as the Family Finder, Discussion Groups, and ViewMate, are relied upon by thousands each day.

In addition, JewishGen's extensive informational, educational and historical offerings, such as the Jewish Communities Database, Yizkor Book translations, InfoFiles, Family Tree of the Jewish People, and KehilaLinks, provide critical insights, first-hand accounts, and context about Jewish communal and familial life throughout the world.

Offered as a free resource, JewishGen.org has facilitated thousands of family connections and success stories, and is currently engaged in an intensive expansion effort that will bring many more records, tools, and resources to its collections.

Please visit https://www.jewishgen.org/ to learn more.

Vice President for JewishGen: Avraham Groll

About the JewishGen Yizkor Book Project

Yizkor Books (Memorial Books) were traditionally written to memorialize the names of departed family and martyrs during holiday services in the synagogue (a practice that still exists in many synagogues today).

Over the centuries, as a result of countless persecutions and horrific atrocities committed against the Jews, Yizkor Books (Sefer Zikaron in Hebrew) were expanded to include more historical information, such as biographical sketches of famous personalities and descriptions of daily town life.

Following the Holocaust, the idea of remembrance and learning took on an urgent and crucial importance. Survivors of the Holocaust sought out other surviving residents of their former towns to memorialize and document the names and way of life of those who were ruthlessly murdered by the Nazis. These remembrances were documented in Yizkor Books, hundreds of which were published in the first decades after the Holocaust.

Most of these books were published privately, or through *Landsmanshaftn* (social organizations comprised of members originating from the same European town or region) that still existed, and were often distributed free of charge. The languages used to document these crucial histories and links to our past were mostly Yiddish and Hebrew. JewishGen has undertaken the sacred responsibility of translating these books into English so that the culture and way of life of these communities will be preserved and transmitted to future generations.

In 1986, a group of farsighted JewishGenners started a project to pool their efforts together in groups based upon their ancestors' towns and donate funds to translate the Yizkor books of their ancestral towns into English. As the translated material became available, it was made accessible for free at https://www.JewishGen.org/Yizkor . Hardcover copies can be purchased by visiting https://www.jewishgen.org/Yizkor/ybip.html (see below).

It is our hope that the translation of these books into English (and other languages) will assist the countless Jewish family researchers who are so desperately seeking to forge a connection with their heritage.

Director of JewishGen Yizkor Book Project: Lance Ackerfeld

About JewishGen Press

JewishGen Press (formerly the Yizkor Books-in-Print Project) is the publishing division of JewishGen.org, and provides a venue for the publication of non-fiction books pertaining to Jewish genealogy, history, culture, and heritage.

In addition to the Yizkor Book category, publications in the Other Non-Fiction category include Shoah memoirs and research, genealogical research, collections of genealogical and historical materials, biographies, diaries and letters, studies of Jewish experience and cultural life in the past, academic theses, and other books of interest to the Jewish community.

Please visit https://www.jewishgen.org/Yizkor/ybip.html to learn more.

Director of JewishGen Press: Joel Alpert
Managing Editor - Jessica Feinstein
Publications Manager - Susan Rosin

Notes to the Reader

The original book can be seen online at the Yiddish Book Center website:

https://www.yiddishbookcenter.org/collections/yizkor-books/yzk-nybc313895/ben-oni-asher-mizots-sefer-zikaron

OR

at the New York Public Library Digital Collections website:

https://digitalcollections.nypl.org/items/23a975e0-5b07-0133-f0c8-00505686d14e

To obtain a list of Shoah victims from **Mizocz (Mizoch, Ukraine),** the reader should access the Yad Vashem web site listed below; one can also search for specific family names using family name option. These lists are continually updated by Yad Vashem, so it is worthwhile to periodically search them.

There is more valuable information (including the Pages of Testimony, etc.) available on this website: https://yvng.yadvashem.org/

A list of all books available from JewishGen Press along with prices is available at: https://www.jewishgen.org/Yizkor/ybip.html

Cover Photo Credits

Cover Design by: Nina Schwartz

Front Cover:

Top:

Mizocz, c.1925. Courtesy of Mizoch City Library.
White (or Whitman) family; believed to be the family of Leah White Spanover's brother, c.1925. Courtesy of Laurence Broun.

Background:
Letter from Chasia Spanover Wygrajzer to her sister Sarah Spanover Cotel, 1936. Courtesy of Laurence Broun.

Back Cover:

Clockwise
Sonia, Michel (Henry-Michael) and Hinda (later Adah) Fishfeder, 1926. Courtesy of Beatrice Batt-Behar and Nancy Sarvet-Haber.

Perel Fishbein Mulman, c.1927. Courtesy of Beatrice Batt-Behar and Nancy Sarvet-Haber.
Gregori (Gersh) German, 1927. Courtesy of Joseph Oks.

Extended Langer family in Grandma Zissel Langer's backyard, Mizocz, c.1937. Left to right, back row: Arye Firer, Abraham (Bernshteyn?), Tammy Firer (née Langer), unknown hidden woman. Front row, three unknown (Firer?) children, Abraham Firer (in cap), Zissel Langer, Malka (Bernshteyn?) née Langer, Clara Langer (baby), Anna (Encia) Langer, Chava Firer, unknown boy, Miriam Langer. Courtesy of Claire, Sari, and Joseph Boren, and Tzvia Lifshitz.

Geopolitical Information

MAP OF UKRAINE AUGUST 2022

Russian annexed or separatist area

Map of Ukraine showing the location of **Mizoch**

Mizocz

Mizoch, Ukraine is located at 50°24' N 26°09' E 192 miles W of Kyyiv

	Town	District	Province	Country
Before WWI (c. 1900):	Mizoch	Dubno	Volhynia	Russian Empire
Between the wars (c. 1930):	Mizocz	Zdołbunów	Wołyń	Poland
After WWII (c. 1950):	Mizoch			Soviet Union
Today (c. 2000):	Mizoch			Ukraine

Alternate Names for the Town:

Mizoch [Ukr, Rus], Mizocz [Pol], Mizotch [Yid], Mizach, Mizoc

Nearby Jewish Communities:

Ozeryany 7 miles NW
Zdolbunov 9 miles NNE
Varkovychi 9 miles WNW
Kuniv 14 miles SE
Rivne 16 miles NNE
Mezhyrichi 16 miles ESE
Ostroh 17 miles ESE
Hlynky 17 miles NE
Dubno 18 miles W
Rakhmanov 19 miles S
Shums'k 20 miles S
Horynhrad 24 miles NE
Oleksandriya 25 miles NNE

Verba 25 miles WSW
Mlyniv 25 miles WNW
Klevan 25 miles NNW
Muravytsi 26 miles WNW
Olyka 26 miles NW
Hoshcha 27 miles ENE
Tuchin 28 miles NE
Kremenets 28 miles SW
Podlesnoye 29 miles SSW
Kornytsya 30 miles SE
Katerynivka 30 miles SSW
Bilohirya 30 miles SSE
Mochulki 30 miles NNW
Yampil 30 miles S

Foreword to the English and Ukrainian-language Translations

The Yizkor Book of Mizoch was published in 1960 as a remembrance of the 1,700 Jewish inhabitants of that town who perished in the Holocaust. It serves as a literary memorial, documenting a way of life that disappeared in unfathomable horror with the barbaric mass murder of the community on October 12, 1942. The original publication was coordinated by Asher Ben-Oni and his *landsmen*, Former Residents of Mizocz in Israel, a mutual aid society sharing hometown roots. To compile the book, the editors solicited essays from those born and raised in Mizoch who had emigrated to safety in decades before the war, and from the handful of Jews from that town who remained and survived.

When the volume was published in 1960, the editors enjoined the reader, "Remember! Pass before the eyes of your soul the images of the precious names of those who are of your own flesh and blood. They will return and live before you and their memories will be etched in your heart."

I discovered the existence of this book with hopeful anticipation of learning about my family roots and the place my grandparents were raised, and also with immense and overwhelming trepidation regarding the horrible fate that become their siblings, nieces, nephews and cousins. Because the original book was published in a mixture of Hebrew and Yiddish languages, translation of the material was a barrier for me, my relatives and others in the English-speaking world who seek to understanding this rich and wrenching heritage.

Two very amazing things unfolded in the journey to translate the Yizkor Book of Mizoch, and each, in its own way, gives new life and relevance to the lost Jewish community of Mizoch. First, rather than raise funds and hire a professional translator as has been done for other yizkor books, I turned to language professors and students at universities across the United States, and the result was amazing. The commitment of these young people to immerse themselves in the testimonials of the original authors became a labor of love. As they translated, in their minds they walked the streets and fields of Mizoch, joined youth groups, hid in the forests and witnessed unfathomable tragedy.

With their professors, the students crafted every word of the translation to be faithful to the original text while being understandable in modern English idiom. Four generations later, in many ways, these young people developed a profound bond with the authors they translated. The translators are now part of the story and will carry this history within them during their own lives. I apologize to them all for any sleepless nights reliving these stories, but it is our common burden and responsibility to remember, and to them I say, you too are all now Mizochians.

Second, the other unexpected part of this journey is a story my grandparents could never have imagined, the story of how Ukraine has changed in the decades since the Shoah. During my grandparents' lifetime, Mizoch was part of the Russian empire, then Poland, and after the war, Ukraine. Yet, they never imagined themselves as Russian, Polish or Ukrainian. In these ethnocentric places, my grandparents were -- first and foremost -- Jews. My grandparents could never have envisioned a multi-ethnic democracy in Ukraine, let alone one that would elect a Jew as its President.

As the Yizkor Book of Mizoch was translated into English, it was also being translated into the Ukrainian language. History Professor Roman Mykhalchuk, Rivne State Humanitarian University, hails from Mizoch and has made preservation and understanding of the lost Jewish community of Mizoch a passionate focus of his career. Together with his colleague Professor of Languages Dmytro Aladko, a variety of material including my own family story have been translated into the Ukrainian language for use in programs to promote tolerance and to combat anti-Semitism, xenophobia and racism. Their work underscores changes in modern Ukraine, the emergence of an independent, multi-ethnic democracy.

As you read this book, I share a passage remembered from childhood, a passage from the Passover Haggadah. The Haggadah said, "In every generation, each person must look inward as though they personally were among those who went forth from Egypt." In the same way, I ask the reader of this Yizkor Book to embrace this book as though they were personally a part of this tragedy. It is *our* story. This Haggadah also teaches, "In every age, the concept of freedom grows broader, widening the horizons for finer and more ethical living, and that each generation is duty-bound to contribute to this growth, else humankind's ideals become stagnant and stationary." While the authors of these essays righteously condemn the horrible misdeeds of many of their neighbors during the Holocaust, it is a grievous error to visit the weaknesses and sins of these forbearers on anyone alive today.

May we all learn from the saga of Mizoch and find strength to fight tyranny and to protect the meek and defenseless in our own age. Never again.

Acknowledgments

It is with profound gratitude that I thank the following professors and students for their dedication in making these materials available to the English-speaking readers. Their commitment to this project has been an inspiration to me and I will be forever grateful to see the story of Mizoch perpetuated by their work and carried by another generation in their hearts:

Professor Orian Zakai, George Washington University, Washington, DC, with students Corey Feuer and Yonatan Altman-Shafer.

Professor Itzik Gottesman, University of Texas at Austin, with student Clair Padgett.

Professor Naomi Sokoloff, University of Washington, Seattle, Washington, with students Nida Kiali, Eiden Harel Brewer, Caleb Bilodeau, Noa Etzyon, Ofir Horovitz, Adam Lamb, Gabrielle Cooper, Shira Zur, Jonah Silverstein and Professor Hadar Khazzam-Horovitz. Also sincere thanks to Professor Or Rogovin of Bucknell University for his support to the University of Washington team.

Danielle Shwartz, Denver Jewish Day School, with students Isaac Makovsky, Joshua Metzel and Samuel Rotenberg.

In Ukraine, I profoundly thank Professor Roman Mykhalchuk, Rivne State Humanitarian University, for his vision in suggesting the translation of this book into the Ukrainian language, and for his unceasing efforts to combat anti-Semitism, xenophobia and racism. He has kept the memory of the Jewish community alive with his ongoing professional and humanitarian work.

With immense gratitude, I thank Professor Dmytro Aladko, Rivne State Humanitarian University, for his professional skill and commitment in translating the Ukrainian-language version. Much of his work took place at the same time Russia launched its savage attack on Ukraine. As chapters appeared in my e-mail, he included updates on missile attacks in Rivne, descriptions of death and destruction in the region, and stories of daily air raid alerts. I imagine he completed many of the translations during endless hours in a bomb shelter, peering into the glow of his laptop computer. I also thank him for his friendship and providing his reflections about modern Ukraine.

None of this work would have been possible without the support of the JewishGen organization. This non-profit group provides a framework for translating Yizkor Books, infrastructure for posting materials to the internet, and publishing completed translations in the form of hard-copy books.

I sincerely thank Lance Ackerfeld, Yizkor Book Director, for the guidance he provided to bring this project to completion. Working with JewishGen volunteers Max G. Heffler and Jason Hallgarten, each document in this book was precisely formatted for posting on the internet. Also, thank you to Sondra Ettlinger for extracting the pictures from the original book, enabling their addition to the online project.

I also extend my gratitude for those working and volunteering at JewishGen who translated before I assumed took responsibility as project coordinator. Yocheved Klausner translated the Table of Contents, Nathen Gabriel translated captions and the List of Photographs, Beryl Baleson translated the List of Martyrs from the Mizoch Ghetto and Derman, and when I spotted my grandfather's family name in the photo captions, Yitzvchok Tzvi Margareten kindly translated the vignette about the family of my grandfather's uncle.

Conventions for translating Hebrew and Yiddish names into English have evolved over the years. It became necessary to standardize the spelling of surnames used across various essays in this book to generate an index of family names for the printed book. I profoundly thank Professor Bella Hass Weinberg, St. John's University Division of Library and Information Sciences, a pre-eminent expert on the indexing of Hebraic materials, for determining the most appropriate spellings of surnames, using the spellings genealogists are likely to find in family documents from this period.

Finally, and with much pleasure, I acknowledge the dedicated labors of the volunteers at the JewishGen Press Publication Team, who are responsible for production of the printed book. These efforts were deftly guided by Susan Rosin, who organized and managed the many tasks needed to produce this volume in book form. I thank Jonathan Wind, who took responsibility for book formatting and layout, and Stefanie Holzman, who toiled with great dedication over multiple iterations of the index. Graphic artist Nina Schwartz volunteered her talents to wrap the printed volume with a most attractive and meaningful cover, and to enhance the photographs in this book to display greater detail for the reader.

Additional Information

Readers interested in additional information about the Jewish community in Mizoch will be interested in the JewishGen KehilaLinks website at https://kehilalinks.jewishgen.org/Mizoch/, where several additional family stories are posted that were not published in the original Yizkor Book.

The list of victims included in this translation is taken from the original Yizkor Book. Since 1960, additional testimonies have been submitted and compiled at Yad Vashem, the world holocaust remembrance center. The central database of Shoah victims' names can be found at https://yvng.yadvashem.org/ where the user may enter the place name of Mizoch to view an updated list of records.

Laurence Broun
Washington, DC.
August, 2022

Table of Contents

Preface #		3
Mizocz – its Life and its Annihilation *	Asher Gilberg	4
The Holocaust Period		
How I Was Saved from Death in Mizocz *	Max Weltfreint	26
In the Ghetto, in Forced Labor, and in the Forest *	Nahum Kopit	30
The Forest Girl *	Kayla Goldberg–Tzizin	45
Memories of a Partisan +	Yankev Mendiuk	50
The Judenrat in Mizocz Had a High Moral Standard, But... *	Yehuda Braunstein	68
Bits of Memories from the Holocaust Period *	Miriam Kashuk-Szprync	72
The Horrible Days #	Ida Eisengart-Pliter	75
The Struggle for Life #	Yona Oliker	80
Dovid Fliter Tells His Story +		86
Dreams are Not False Omens #	Baruch Fliter	93
Father Saved My Mother from Death with a Speech #	Asiya Braz	99
The Partisan Izya Wasserman ^	A. Ben-Oni	104
The Zionist Organization		
Memories from Hashomer Hale'umi (Zionist Youth) in Mizocz	Lisa Nemirover	114
Gordonia #	Reuven Melamed	117
The "Gordonia" in Mizocz #	Yosef Ben Gedalyahu	120
The Gordonia Movement in Mizocz #	Moshe Feldman	126
The Beitar Movement and the Youth in Mizocz #	Moshe Perliuk	128
The Mute Beitar Member #	Asher Ben-Oni	136
Teaching and Education in Mizocz during Polish Rule #	Moshe Feldman	138
Toward the History of the Revisionist Movement in Mizocz #	Arbi	140
Memories and Impressions		
The 17th of September 1939 #	B. Asher	144
A Family in Mizocz #	Sara Shoham-Fleisch	148
Mizocz – the Place of My Happiness #	Soniya Polchik	151
Mizocz– A Town Where Guests Were Always Welcome #	Sarah Biber-Golick	152
Impressions, Memories and Evaluations #	Reuven Melamed	153
Derman, the Village #	W. Sudgalter	156
Life and Folklore #	Mordechai Scheinfeld	158
Pages from My Diary * #	Isaac Braz	165
How I Made Aliya #	Noah Stein	180
A Lieutenant General -- a Champion Collector ^ +	Asher Ben-Oni	183
Thoughts about the Holocaust Era #	Moshe Perliuk	187
The Last Jew of Mizocz Has Arrived in Israel #	David Dratva	191
Impressions and Memories of My Childhood in Mizocz #	Adah Fishfeder-Teichner	192

Figures, People, and Personalities

This is a Memorial *		195
Memorial for Mizocz (A Poem) *	Yoseph Koppelman	196
The Holy Rabeinu Natan Netta Lerner, May God Avenge his Blood *		196
The Teacher David Koppelman of Blessed Memory *	Reuven Melamed	198
Shmuel Gentzberg of Blessed Memory *		201
Shlomo Kopelman of Blessed Memory *		202
Reb Yitzhak Berez *		203
Reb Yechiel the Butcher of Blessed Memory *	A"BA	205
The Grandmother Leah Reznick *	Chaya	207
Yitzhak Port *	Chaya Reznick (Altman)	209
My Father's House *	Rachel (Ilka) Brisker-Nemirover	210
The Wound that Will Never Heal *	Liza Nemirover-Shtelong	212
In Memory of my Parents *	Asher	214
Reb Yitzaak Pliter and his wife Esther *	Baruch Pliter and Zev Gilberg	215
Baruch Pliter *	Baruch	217
Itzchak Shochet the Teacher *	Arbi	218
Siyuma (Sammy) Olicker *	Ben	219
Reb Yeshayahu Mayer Kotel of blessed memory #	Chaya Goldman–Kotel	220
In Remembrance of the Shwarzman Family #	Eliezer Shwarzman	222
In Remembrance of the Tentzer Family #	Braindel Shwarzman-Tentzer	222
Kaddish (Flitner-Shwarzgorn) #	Baruch, son of Zalman and Leah Fliter	223
My Father R. Shmuel Eizengart, May God Avenge his Blood #	Ida	225
An Eternal Flame in Memory of the Progeny of Chone the Rabbi of Mizocz #	Shmuel Mandelkorn	228
Golda Moshe-Hayyim Yossis (z"l) #	Reuben	229
Berko Iosilevich Street #	Chaya Murak	230
Acknowledging the Feldman Family #	Moshe Feldman	231
A Soul in the Breizman Family, May God Avenge His Blood #	Sarah Biber-Lukick	231
Without Graves… #	Moshe Perliuk	234
Our Mother Sarah Goldberg (née Truchler) #	Kayla and Mordechai	235
Leiber, Golob, Sudobitzky and Sizak #		237
In Remembrance of Our Little House that was Destroyed #	Nachum Zeev bar Yerachmiel Kopit	239
In Remembrance of My Brother Yosef Wolfman, z"l #	his sister, Tova	240
On the Grave of Our Friends Michael Nemirover and David Genzberg #	Yosef Carni and Yacov Gelman	241
My Parents, Yitzchak and Rivka Yasin #	Esther	243
In Remembrance of the Family of Eliahu Olicker #	Yona	243
Additional Family Photographs #		244
List of Martyrs from the Mizocz Ghetto		264

List of people from Derman', who were annihilated in the   311
Mizocz Ghetto in 1942
Last Name Index   313

* Translated by Hebrew language students, George Washington University
+ Translated by Yiddish language students, University of Texas at Austin
# Translated by Hebrew language students, University of Washington
^ Translated by Hebrew language students, Denver Jewish Day School

Memorial Book of Mizocz
(Mizoch, Ukraine)

50°24' / 26°09'

Translation of *Mizocz; sefer zikaron*

Editor: A. Ben-Oni

Published in Tel Aviv 1961

Acknowledgments:

Project Coordinator

Laurence Broun

Student Translation Project Coordinators – Hebrew Chapters

Orian Zakai
The George Washington University

Naomi B. Sokoloff
University of Washington

Danielle Shwartz
Denver Jewish Day School

Student Translation Project Coordinator – Yiddish Chapters

Itzik Gottesman
The University of Texas at Austin

This is a translation of: *Mizocz; sefer zikaron* (Memorial book of Mizocz),
Editor: A. Ben-Oni, Former Residents of Mizocz in Israel, Published: Tel Aviv 1961 (H 317 pages)

מ י ז ו ץ'

ספר זכרון

מיזוץ'-ספר זכרון

בעריכת אשר בן'אוני

הוצאת ארגון יוצאי מיזוץ' בישראל

תל-אביב. תשכ"א.

[Page 3]

Preface

The editor

Translated from Hebrew by Naomi Sokoloff

The Mizocz Book is a modest monument, a tombstone on the grave of this small, holy community, on the grave of our dear ones who were cut down while they were flourishing, tortured and killed by wild beasts, and their bones scattered to all the winds of Mizocz.

This memorial book has been created *ex nihilo*. It is the fruit of a blessed initiative, hard work, love for the town and its inhabitants, longing for its vibrant, interesting Jewish way of life, and a desire to leave for coming generations a vestige of this dear town in which we were born, grew up, and were educated, and from which we imbibed dedication to our people and love for the ancient Hebrew homeland.

This book was neither made nor written by people who are professionals at such craft. The editorial board had no historical, literary, or other sources. The material was collected and assembled with much labor, from the surviving sons of Mizocz, who saw with their own eyes the worst of catastrophes and felt on their own flesh all its cruelties, and from the few who succeeded in arriving at a safe harbor in the Land of Israel before the storm of destruction hit.

We recognize and acknowledge the defects, deficiencies, and errors in the book. It has not escaped our attention that the material gathered is incomplete and many gaps clamor to be filled. However, we are proud that in our circumstances -- when no material about our town remains anywhere in the world, and when we number no more than 50 families, all of limited means -- we nonetheless, with remarkable volunteer effort and tireless labor, knew how to make a monument to our loved ones who were not fortunate enough to find Jewish burial. We have put in place a memorial for them.

It is my pleasant obligation to acknowledge the dedicated, faithful contributors and express here my thanks to Moshe Feldman, Nachum Kopit, Baruch Fliter, Yacov Gelman, Liza Shtellung and Chaya Altman, who worked hard gathering material and producing the means to publish the book. To Moshe Perliuk who advised us and edited the book, and to Reuben Melamed who spared no effort in collecting testimonies and gathering material. To Mordechai Scheinfeld and Yosef Karmi, who devoted their time and energy to the book. To Menachem Shtellung and Aharon Altman, whose connection to Mizocz came to them by way of marriage to women from our town; they lent a hand and aided us passionately in realizing our goal. Similarly, my thanks go to all who contributed their writing to the book. Blessings on them all.

[Page 4]

Mizoczers in Israel on the eve of the memorial for the martyrs of the shtetl in Tel Aviv

[Page 5]

Mizocz – its Life and its Annihilation

by Asher Gilberg

Translated from Hebrew by Yonatan Altman–Shafer and Corey Feuer

In the heart of western Ukraine, in the triangle between the cities of Rivne, Dubno, and Ostroh; in a wide–open ravine, surrounded by dense forests, blooming villages, and the most fertile spaces – sat the esteemed town of Mizocz.

The time of its founding and the names of its founders are shrouded in mist; in the literature of tears of the Cossack riots of the seventeenth century there is not even a trace of the name of Mizocz, even though it lies on the path of the bloody journey of the ataman Khmelnytsky, may his name be blotted out.[1] The name of the town is also not found in Hasidic literature, despite the town's proximity to the cities of the Hasidic cradle: Velyki Mezhyrichi, Ostroh, and Korets.

The town was young, there were no antiquities there. Even the pedigree of the Polish count Karwitzky, the landowner of the town, is short lived and is almost unknown among the nobility.

The town's cemetery was small and only after the thirties did people start to distinguish between its old plot and new plot.

Of all the above, it should be noted that the age of Mizocz is not more than 200 years, and that Mizocz was established out of necessity, in order to serve as an administrative center and repository for the rich crops of the fields, the gardens, and the forests and for the overflowing produce of the barn and the coop.

Factories, Trade, and Services

The first to recognize the importance of the town was the Jewish industrialist Horenstein, who built a large sugar factory on the northeastern edge of the town, and next to the sugar factory, a farm for fattening cattle with beet waste.

This factory over time fell under the control of the famous Jewish sugar magnate Brotzky, and he expanded and refined it until it became a big factory with considerable productivity and exquisite output.

The count Karwitzky set up a factory for beer and a large flour mill, and the Jew Isaac Braz set up a factory for coarse woolen fabrics for the farmers. Thanks to the sugar factory, a track was laid for a train that connected Mizocz to the larger world via the Kyiv–Lviv railway line. Apart from these, many workshops and small industries were established, such as: the oil press houses of Avraham Bronstein, Bozai Mizocz,

[Page 6]

Temah Berman, and other smaller ones; two sawmills belonging to Kaput and Meislitsch; a dairy belonging to Meir Braz; and many workshops of all kinds.

At first, the sugar factory employed few Jews and only in clerical positions, but over time, thanks to the influence of Zionist youth movements, their numbers increased to many tens who worked in all departments. The extensive trade of the town was originally dominated by a few big grain merchants, who were buying the crops from the farmers before harvest and were sometimes paying for crop yields years in advance. Each merchant had farmer–suppliers that lived in the villages in the domain under his near–exclusive influence, and the transactions that amounted to considerable sums were usually only done verbally without any written commitment. These merchants made trade connections, not only with grain stores in the country, but also with distant countries abroad, and hundreds of wagons loaded to maximum capacity with various grains were exported, which indirectly led to the opening of the train station in the town. When they realized the industrial value of the plant called hops, which requires certain knowledge and specific treatment, they knew how to convince the Czech farmers to grow the plant and export it in large quantities.

When the industrialization of Poland began and a large shipyard, which required a lot of oak wood and a special type of brick, was built in the city of Gdynia, the authorities eyed the virgin forests surrounding Mizocz, and they set up a lumber industry in the city and the surrounding area. The wood trade required significant expertise, professional knowledge, and a great deal of wealth, and therefore only the local brothers Tekser and Leib Gurewitz dealt in it. The rest of the merchants and expert clerks were mostly non–

local Jews and came to the city especially from Rivne, Warsaw, Vilna, Danzig, and also from outside of the country.

A number of years before the Holocaust, several of the locals learned the profession and made a decent living from the wood trade. The gentlemen Kopit, Kleinman, and Gantzberg, managed with modest financial means to establish wood–trade partnerships and become players in the market.

Mizocz was overflowing with an enormous selection of the most exquisite fruits of the species with which Ukraine was blessed. However, until the beginning of the thirties, only the close city of Rivne enjoyed them. This is because the peddlers in their wagons did not go beyond it [Rivne]. The fruit trade was conducted until then in a primitive manner and on a small and narrow scale; the peddlers would buy several seasonal fruit trees from a farmer, load them in bulk on a cart harnessed to a horse, and move them to a shop in Rivne. There, they sold them to the fruit stalls for no matter the profit and sometimes, when the market was flooded with fruit,

[Page 7]

they would come out of the transaction with a great loss. Generally, these fruit merchants worked hard from morning to evening and their livelihood was meager. At dawn they went out to the villages to pick the fruit, working all day to load the cart, and at night they would transport the fruit on rickety paths in order to make it to the market in the city by dawn of the next day. In Rivne, they would stay for some hours until they sold their goods, and at the end of the day, they would return home in their empty wagons in order to start anew the next day. Some of them learned to store fruit in the cellars and to sell it at winter for good prices. A few families in our town made meager and austere earnings from the fruit trade.

At the beginning of the thirties, some Jewish fruit merchants from Warsaw and western Poland "discovered" Mizocz. From then until the town's destruction, the fruit trade included most of the city's residents. Directly and indirectly, all of the residents benefited from it. They no longer transported fruit in janky carts, but rather in train cars, with hundreds and thousands loaded at the train station, and the exquisite fruit transported to Polish cities as well as to cities across the border. An entire industry of packing tools and materials developed. The Jews learned the science of storage, familiarized themselves with the markets of the greater world, and adapted to the tastes of the residents of the big cities. The fruit trade that had until then been considered a disgrace to its dealers started occupying an important place in the town, and everyone benefited and profited from its success.

The developed trade in grain and wood and in fruit and in cattle on the one hand, and the sugar factory and the rich villages surrounding it on the other hand, brought great prosperity to the town. Mizocz was thus one of the sole cities in Poland – if not the only one – that did not know scarcity and poverty at the verge of the war. Some of the residents became rich and affluent, while others only earned a living at a profit, but no person knew paucity. In Mizocz, there were businesses and stores that could have glorified any main street in one of the largest cities in the country. It happened occasionally that merchants and salesmen from the timber and grain industries came to the town at the same time, along with those seeking to buy cattle, poultry, and eggs. Together with the fruit merchants that were in the town nearly all year, they filled every hotel and hostel and brought great abundance to the place.

Gradually, the small and ugly houses disappeared from the horizon. In their place, beautiful multi–leveled houses from brick were built, the roads were paved and expanded, and quality of life in the town rose dramatically. The town's name spread far and wide, and white–collar professionals, students, and other workers came to live there.

On the verge of the war, Mizocz stood at the peak of its material success. The authorities began to encourage Polish settlers to trade in the town and planned the construction of a row of factories for the preservation of meat, fruit, and vegetables. The Polish businesses developed,

[Page 8]

View of Mizocz

[Page 9]

though they could not hurt those of the Jews, which were more experienced and competitive. The Ukrainians and the Czechs also tried to infiltrate trade in different ways. The space was not narrow and provided opportunities for everyone.

After the fall of Poland and its division between Germany and the Soviets, the occupying Soviet army found goods and materials in Mizocz that could satisfy for about a whole year a huge army of soldiers, officials, and party functionaries from Soviet Russia, who were hungry for consumer goods of beautiful and high quality.

Religious Life in the Town

Mizocz was a traditional town, tolerant and far separated from religious zealotry. It is doubtful there was a single house in Mizocz that did not follow Jewish law and respect the Jewish tradition. Still, it was common among many of the youths to visit a Christian restaurant, and no one stopped them from doing so. During Saturdays and Jewish holidays, commerce halted fully and absolutely, and even a free–thinking Jew from out of town would not dare to desecrate the Sabbath in public. During holidays, everyone went to a house of prayer with almost no exceptions. On Saturdays, however, it was common for the bachelors to skip the prayers. Married men, conversely, could not shirk the duty of visiting the house of prayer.

There were three houses of prayer in the city; a *beit midrash*, the *kloyz* of the Trisk Hassidim, and the big synagogue.[2][3] Next to this last one was a small house of worship, intended for *Mincha* and *Ma'ariv* during weekdays for worshippers of the big synagogue, although over time it became an independent house of worship.[4] Each chapel was always full of worshippers and in the *beit midrash* and the *kloyz* several *minyanim* were held every day.[5] During the High Holidays and the Days of Awe, the houses of worship were not able to contain all those seeking to pray in public, and so several temporary houses of prayer were prepared. They were especially populous during *Simchat Torah*.[6] The prominent and permanent of the *Simchat Torah minyans* were those of the Jewish National Fund and the Revisionist Tel–Chai Foundation.[7] In these *minyanim*, they always used to speak of matters of the day before the Torah reading and would preach to the worshippers to donate generously to the foundation. After the services were held, there was a great *kiddush* for every *minyan* that usually lasted for many hours.[8] Among the private *minyanim*, the minyan of my uncle Baruch Fliter's house especially excelled. For *Simchat Torah kiddush*, they prepared at his house many days before the holiday, and it would last until the evening hours. When they were blissfully inebriated, the participants of this *kiddush*, who were all friends of the master of the house,

[Page 10]

were ordered to bring kugels and delicacies prepared by their wives, and there was no end to their delight. Three years before the Holocaust, the private *minyanim* were canceled, and their members went to pray in *minyanim* of the foundations.

Initially, every house of worship had a certain different class of worshippers; the rabbi, the slaughterers, the scholars, the holy vessels, and the respected homeowners prayed in the *beit midrash*. The pious and Hassidic congregated at the *kloyz*, and the craftsmen and the masses of the "simple folk" prayed at the big synagogue. In the last ten year of the town's existence, due to the great prosperity that befell the town, the partitions between the classes dissolved and the status of the big synagogue rose. The sugar factory owner, the great Jewish philanthropist Halbmilion, donated a considerable sum of money to renovate the synagogue. He brought artists from outside, and with their help, the synagogue turned into a little temple. The inauguration of the synagogue was held in all of its splendor and was attended by officials from the nearby city. Whenever Halbmilion was in town during a holiday, he would pray at the synagogue. The pharmacist Finkel, the doctor Liebster, and other guests who were in town for business quickly followed him. Since the synagogue was spacious, beautifully decorated, and very comfortable, and dignitaries such as Halbmilion and the like prayed there, many of the young people began to purchase seats in the synagogue. The permanent cantor there was rabbi Yechiel Reznik the butcher. After his death, his only son Tzvi Reznik took his place.

There was one rabbi in the town who lived close to the synagogue. The last to serve in this role was Rabbi Neta Lerner, who was a great student of the Torah, pure and god–fearing with a strong affinity for the Zionist movement. He inherited the position of Rabbi from his father–in–law, the Rabbi Michael Lerner, and he was accepted by every section of the population.

The slaughterers and checkers in Mizocz were four in number: the brothers Reuven and Yosef–David Milhalter, Rabbi Yechiel Reznik and the yeshiva student Yehoshua Langer.[9] After the death of Rabbi Yechiel, three butchers remained, because Yechiel's successor, his son Tzvi Reznik gave up the position. The sons of the brothers Milhalter also did not train as slaughterers and checkers, and only Yaakov, son of Rabbi Reuven, learned at the yeshiva, but he wanted to be a rabbi rather than a slaughterer and checker.

Some of the respected landlords supported the rabbi in addressing the religious needs of the town. They were responsible for the matter of the purity of the family and kept the bathhouse and the *mikvah*.[10] The number of people in need of material help in the town was zero, and if the opportunity arose to help someone, everyone was happy to fulfill the mitzvah of "and let your brother live with you".

Rabbi Yechiel Reznik served as *mohel* of the town until the day of his death.[11] He was an artful *mohel*, and doctors would marvel at his agility and expertise.

[Page 11]

After his death, a *mohel* was brought in from outside.

Shmurah matzah was baked at the *kloyz*, and Mordechai Gnipoler provided matzahs for all the people of the town.[12] The home–baking that was called "tolka" in the dialect of the area stopped completely a number of years before the destruction.

The religious and social lives centered around the houses of prayer. Each house of worship chose its own *gabbayim* on *Simchat Torah* night, before the *hakafa*, and they conducted the business of the community for the course of a year.[13] The "*chevra 9ahrzei*" was connected by its members to the big synagogue.[14] Its assemblies and the traditional feast fell on the 7th of Adar which according to tradition is the same day Moshe Rabbeinu passed away.[15] A special committee headed by the rabbi took care of the bathhouse and the *mikvah*.

Weddings customarily took place on Fridays in Mizocz. The *kiddush*in was handled by the rabbi, who was usually accompanied by Yosef David the butcher and his sons or Yechiel Reznik with or without his son Tzvi.[16] The two butchers had embroidered chuppahs of their own, which were placed under open sky, and Jewish couples stood under them in order to enter the marriage covenant.[17] It was customary to put up a chuppah inside only for a second marriage.

Religion played a very important role in the Jewish life of Mizocz until the day of its destruction. Every private joy and every public event was connected to the synagogue. Memorial services for important figures, announcements of a new factory or fundraiser, jubilee celebrations, or the marking of an important date — all were held within the walls of the synagogue. The *gabbayim* did not discriminate between the different groups and let everyone use the synagogue according to their needs. It should be noted that only the big synagogue and the *beit midrash* allowed the Zionist movement to operate within their walls. In the *kloyz*, Zionist operation was limited despite most of its worshippers being Zionists. Out of all of the houses of worship in the area, only the *kloyz* was also used as a place to study Torah, and after the hours of worship, there were always people there engaged in Torah study. The rabbi's house, the houses of worship, and the bathhouse were all located nearby to each other. Only the *kloyz* was located a bit of a distance from the rest, seemingly not only in place but also in time.

Institutions and Organizations

The oldest committee in town ran the "Wheat for Money" campaign, collecting donations of matzah and wine for Passover to give to the poor of the town. This institution was very active until the town's bitter end. In its last years, when there were nearly no more needy in the area, they brought the donations to the center of the yeshivas. The committee–members I remember were Rabbi Yoel Mulman, the grandfather Rabbi Yitzchak Fliter and Rabbi Yonah Nemirover.

[Page 12]

The Hebrew kindergarten in Mizocz

The Committee for the Orphans

The Committee for the Orphans did wonderful and beneficial work. The committee was organized in 1927 and was constantly supervised by the Central Committee in Warsaw and the Provincial Bureau in Rivne. The committee received much monetary and material support from the center, and together with the money collected in the area, was able to provide assistance to every orphan and widow. At the head of the committee were Mrs. Wasserman, secretary Avraham Gantzberg, and as treasurer,

[Page 13]

Mrs. Esther Fliter. In times of need, the Committee for the Orphans was able to mobilize people for large and lucrative projects. The glorious masquerade dance was especially memorable, conducted by the committee in the winter of 1928, with many guests from nearby cities as well. Because there were no more needy orphans, the committee dispersed at the end of the 1930s.

The "Bestowing Chesed" Fund

The "Bestowing Chesed" Society was founded in town at the start of the 1920s.[18] The basic capital was received from the American committee for the aid of Jews who were wounded in the war. Among the first committee members were Yitzchak Fliter, Yonah Nemirover, and Yehoshua Bar Gantzberg. The fund gave no–interest loans to all who needed, and it consistently operated until the Soviet occupation. Among the committee members, Moshe Mendyuk, who is currently in Uruguay, stood out in particular. The fund's money was confiscated by the Soviet authorities and the society dispersed.

Banking

The cooperative bank, founded in Mizocz with the encouragement of the center in Warsaw, developed into a major financial institution, ultimately employing ten workers. The first manager of the bank was pharmacist B. Finkel. However, when the institution developed and needed a real salaried manager, they chose Asher Schapira for the job. At the beginning of the 1930s, a second Jewish bank called "The People's Bank", whose majority shareholder was manager Isaak Kashuk, son of Tuvia, was opened. This was because of the growth of business conducted in the town. The existence and development of both banks was assured. And indeed they both conducted their operations up until the Soviet occupation.

The Merchants' Association

The heavy taxes, the various harsh sanctions, and the explicit policy of the Polish government that encouraged Polish trade at the expense of the Jews necessitated contact with the authorities and constant protection of those affected by the policy. Consequently, the Merchants' Association was founded, headed by former teacher Yitzchak Schochet. On behalf of this organization, participants were vetted and selected as representatives by the authorities at the District Tax Office in Zdolbuniv. Some time after its establishment in 1932, a second organization of small business owners was established, led and managed by Moshe Rudman. Both organizations provided legal assistance to their members and helped them overcome their difficulties.

The Fire Department Society

The Fire Department of Mizocz was a veteran and respected institution with many members and a lot of property.

[Page 14]

It was housed in a spacious cabin not far from the synagogue. Many of the town's youth were members, and strict discipline was maintained. At the head of the society was Baruch Fliter with his deputy Binyamin Halperin, son–in–law of Moshe Mirmelstein. The organization would perform maneuvers from time to time and demonstrate their capabilities and equipment to the great joy of all the children in town. They would always participate in the processions on May 3rd and November 11th, the two national holidays, as a few of the members of the society were Christian neighbors. Those Christians knew how to speak the Yiddish tongue well, due to all the meetings and exercises (with the possible exception of special professional terms) that were conducted in that language. All of the members were given special clothes and shiny helmets, and they were required to train frequently. The Christians had a separate yet similar organization, associated with the fire department of the sugar factory. During fires, there would be competition between the two societies, and the Jewish organization always proved its effectiveness.

The Municipal Zionist Library

The library was founded at the dawn of Zionist activism in the country by Yisrael Koppelman, Gisiya Kestenberg, and Hava Teller. At the management level were Shmuel Gantzberg, Yosef Kleinman, Shlomo Koppelman, Laivish Melamed, Yehuda Braunstein, and Reuven Melamed, all leaders of the *Hitahadut* party.[19] The library included 2,000 books in Yiddish and Hebrew from the best and most beautiful literature, in both original and translated editions. There was also some scientific literature. Additionally, there was a reading hall next to the library. There, aside from books, were daily and weekly newspapers and magazines, both from the land of Israel and from other countries. This library was open to the12ahrzec three days a week and board members took turns working there. On Saturday nights they would sometimes hold *iton chai* as well as lectures or readings.[20] The editor of the *iton chai* was Shmuel Gantzberg, an experienced and very cultured journalist. All the town's luminaries would contribute to the newspaper and would read pieces they wrote on all sorts of topics. Hava Teller would write gentle, sentimental pieces about nature and the cosmos. Laivish Melamed often wrote about the history of Mizocz and created interesting pieces about the town, the people, and their livelihoods (a shame that he perished and his work was lost). The editor Shmuel Gantzberg was always brilliant, especially in his main article on current events. He wrote and read about subjects at the forefront of current events, and Yonah Firer would always close the evening with a humoristic feuilleton, making everyone burst into laughter.

[Page 15]

Admission to the *iton chai* nights was typically by reservation, and the hall would fill up completely. When rival parties to the *Hitahadut* formed and created separate libraries for themselves, the municipal library was dissolved and its activities discontinued. Some of the books stayed with their borrowers, and the remainder went to the authority of the *Hitahadut* party. The Beitar movement established a great library for themselves, and the National Guard had their library too.[21] All of the libraries operated up until World War II broke out.

The Kindergarten

The members of the *Hitahadut* party founded a kindergarten in town in the early 1920s. This matter didn't come easily; they had to invest a lot of effort and work into it. The first kindergarten opened in Gedalya Kornik's house, and was initially supported ideologically and financially by the Zionists. Over time the kindergarten developed, purchasing suitable equipment in line with their mission. The kindergarten was run entirely in Hebrew and hosted plays and dances independently. The teacher was typically socially involved and active in JNF and the Zionist movement.[22] A large part of the organization of the kindergarten should be credited to Yitzchak Meir Tekser, who helped guide it through its first steps.

The Drama Troupe

Many twists and turns underwent the Drama Troupe in Mizocz: they began at the end of World War I. Among the first of its members were Mirmelstein (from the village of Holchi), Batsheva Kopit, Avraham Scheinfeld, Yisrael Koppelman, who died at a young age, Shimon Kestenbaum, Avraham Fliter, Sarah Oliker, Fulia Schenrik, Asher Schapira, and others. The plays were performed in the fire department's cabin, the hall in the sugar factory, or in Lieba Atlas's warehouse. They put on all kinds of shows, and all proceeds went to orphans and refugees. However, with the *13ahrze* of Sarah Oliker, the death of Koppelman, and the marriages of the rest, the troupe's work began to lull.[23] In 1925, Asher Schapira restarted the troupe from scratch and performed his own dramatic piece with great success. There were many attempts to reorganize the troupe with talent from the girls' choir, like Liza Melamed and Tehila Schochet, but after only a few performances, the choir came to an end. In 1928, a dental technician named Abba Fidelman settled in Mizocz, and he renewed the activities of the troupe which continued on even under the Soviet occupation. Fidelman tracked down the right people and encouraged them to return to the stage. The troupe performed plays by Gordin,

[Page 16]

Sholem Aleichem, Sholem Asch, and plays from the world repertoire. The plays were of high quality and always attracted a large audience. Later, during the Soviet occupation, they performed Gordin's "The Slaughter" to great acclaim. Many others were in this play: Abba Fidelman, Baba Bakast, Celia Kashuk, Asher Gilberg, and others. The authorities of the occupying forces were present at the play, along with most of the Communist Party, as well as a massive crowd. After the show, the authorities demanded a ban on the repertoire and ordered the performances of the Soviet play "The Chimney Sweep" ("Der Koimenkerer"). The veteran members of the troupe were pushed aside, and Fidelman, with endless zeal, brought in young new members. In the ghetto, the troupe did not perform.

The Zionist Movement

Zionism never had to be brought to Mizocz; the town's Jews were Zionists from birth and the children were raised on the love for Zion from infancy. In the teacher Koppelman's *cheder*, all the children learned Hebrew, Tanach, history of the Jewish People, and love of Zion.[24] They all knew how to recite and sing Bialik's poem "To the Bird" by heart, up until the line "The land where spring never ends." Intense longings for the ancient homeland had laid dormant in the depths of their young souls, and every little spark would set their souls alight.

I remember in the tender years of my childhood learning in Koppelman's room. Someone brought the Gospel of Svoboda and the Balfour Declaration to Mizocz.[25] The older students stitched together a blue and white flag, beautiful and grand, and organized a *Lag B'Omer* procession for students in the Sosenki Forest.[26] Many young people participated in the procession, and of those walking at the front, I remember Nunek Idsis, Reuven Melamed, and Aharon Kleinman. With song on our lips, we marched joyously and cheerfully, and proceeded into the forest. Someone would lead the song "*She'u Tziona Ness v'Degel*", sung with great intent, until we reached Teller's house.[27] There, we were blocked on the road by large Gentiles who wanted to steal the flag. I remember Nunek Idsis tried to coax them and explain that the Svoboda now allowed Jews to hoist flags. I don't recall precisely how the incident ended; I only remember that I never reached the forest, and that I decided then and there to leave the diaspora. I was not yet ten years old.

In those days, around the years 1920/1921, the first of the pioneers that had escaped from the terror of the Communists arrived in Mizocz, stopping on their way to the land of Israel. The pioneers were all educated and enthusiastic idealists. In town, we thought of them as lunatics and shook our heads at them. They worked all sorts of jobs to make a living— from

[Page 17]

cleaning cowpens and chopping lumber to giving music classes to the wealthy children. They were with us for a few weeks and planted within Mizocz the first seeds of the Labor Zionist party.[28]

I remember that the first Zionist gatherings were held in Koppelman's *cheder*, where I went to school when he was alive. His oldest son Yisroel and his good friend Shimon Kestenbaum were the main speakers in these meetings. I was able to attend the gatherings because I had organized a children's play and given the proceeds to the benefit of the JNF. I received a print receipt from their headquarters and kept it forever. This was the era of the Russian civil war, and the town passed from the Bolsheviks to Petliura's army, after which the Bolsheviks returned, and then came the antisemitic Hellerchiks from the new Polish army.[29] With great joy, the Jews were mentally preparing themselves to make *aliyah*. A few wealthy, esteemed men decided to bring a new Hebrew teacher to Mizocz in place of the late Koppelman— a teacher who would fill his predecessor's shoes and be able to establish a "Tarbut" Hebrew school.[30] They decided and so they did. They traveled to Rivne and announced that the new teacher would be coming soon. And one day towards the end of the summer, the long–awaited man arrived in town. The teacher was named Yitzchak Schochet; he was tall and handsome with beautiful horn–rimmed glasses, dressed majestically and in all means respectably. He only had ten students who paid very high tuition for the time period. He arrived with his wife Tehila and their little daughter Hadassah, who only spoke Hebrew with the Sephardic pronunciation. Their house became *the* Zionist center of the town. His first public appearance was in the *minyan* of JNF on *Simchat Torah*. He spoke Hebrew and Yiddish and enchanted the crowd with his speech. He was a "General Zionist", and he successfully founded a branch of the party, and brought in the pharmacist Finkel, Dr. Liebster, and other esteemed Jews.[31] Members of the *Hitahadut* party brought to town another teacher, in addition to Yitzchak, by name of Leib Dayan. The two teachers had known each other from earlier days, and despite the fact that they had different political views, found for themselves a shared language, to collaborate on expanding Hebraic and Zionist education and to bring it to an appropriate level. Their influence was very deep in the town, and they left their mark on the place for years to come. Thanks to them there was a common vision to see young Jews conversing in fluent Hebrew. Eventually, Mr. Schochet left the profession of teaching, and his friend Dayan moved to Argentina. In their places, many new teachers arrived; however, the impact of those two remained in Mizocz up until our generation.

[Page 18]

There were no non–Zionist movements in Mizocz. To the town's credit, this remained so during the Soviet occupation.

The first attempt to organize a Zionist youth group for "*Hashomer Hatza'ir*" in Mizocz was conducted by Yosef FoigelStein of Rivne in 1927.[32] FoigelStein came to stay with his brother, the son–in–law of Yehoshua Katz. The branch was formed and listed more than fifty youths as members. They organized a few gatherings and worked on plans of action, but immediately after FoigelStein's departure from Mizocz, the center was dispersed amid disputes over power and roles within the group. Learning from the experience, another attempt to open a branch of the youth movement was made in 1928 by Asher Gilberg and Moshe Perliuk, rebranded as "*Hashomer Haleumi*," with the encouragement of the teacher Yitzchak Schochet.[33] This organization was, in fact, the first Zionist youth group in the area. After many great efforts, they managed to include within the organization a significant portion of the town's children, who willingly accepted the discipline imposed upon them. Thanks to the modest dues and the work of the adults, they rented a meeting space in Aharon Schenrik's house, and created connections with the main leadership in Warsaw and the *Galil* leadership in Rivne, and the organization became a major player in town.[34] The drama troupe of the youth movement and the choir under the leadership of Siome Oliker performed with great success and attracted people to the ranks of the movement. Rabbi Yonah Nemirover, father of Liza, a member of the leadership, provided much assistance to the movement.

Members of the *Hitahadut* began to organize the "Gordonia", both for young children and teenagers, successfully recruiting some of the unaffiliated youth to the group.

After the split of "*Hashomer Haleumi*" and the departure of the Revisionists from the General Zionist movement, Moshe Perliuk, a student from the gymnasium in Rivne, joined the Beitar movement. During the summer break of 1931, when Moshe returned home to Mizocz, he founded the town's Beitar chapter. Beitar began its activities with great momentum and soon cut off the other groups, taking its place as the foremost youth movement. They had great success with recruiting Siome Oliker to their ranks. Aside from being popular in town, he also had significant organizational skills. With *aliyah* of Perliuk to the Land of Israel, Siome was appointed as commander of the chapter, and under his leadership, Beitar of Mizocz became one of the best, most magnificent, and largest branches in the entire country.

In the days of the formation of Beitar, a branch of *Hatzohar* and a branch of the Soldiers' Alliance also opened up, which involved circles that were previously not engaged with the Zionist movement.[35]

Here are the Zionist organizations that were active in Mizocz:

a. The *Hitahadut* party and its youth group "Gordonia", and the Women's League for the pioneering work in the land of Israel
b. *[Page 19]*
c. The General Zionist Party and its youth group "The National Guard" (a Zionist group)
d. *Hatzohar* and its youth group Beitar, and the Soldiers' Alliance
e. The Political Zionist Party (*Judenstatler* or *Grossmanists*)

Only in the last few months before the outbreak of the war, when the horrors of doom and destruction loomed over our heads, the relationships between the movements stabilized. Up until then, there had been tense relations between the groups, with frequent eruptions. The quarrels and struggles were especially fierce between the strongest groups: *Hatzohar* and the *Hitahadut* . When the fights were related to raising funds, distributing shekels, or some shared cultural activity, they were very productive. However, when Arlosoroff was murdered, or at the time of competition between JNF and Tel–Hai Foundation, the struggle between groups took on a new form that damaged the general Zionist vision.[36]

The activists of two of the groups, all friends since birth, would not even greet one another, as they saw each other as not just political opponents, but personal enemies. In the middle of the 1930s, Gordonia and Beitar founded two training camps for their members. With the revocation of the certificates from Beitar by the Zionist leadership, and of intensification of the illegal immigration operations, the Beitar camp came to its end, while the Gordonia's camp continued on.

Only when it came to sports was there consistent collaboration between the movements. The sports club Z.S.C. (the Żydowski Sports Club) was made up of the best soccer players from all the Jewish youth groups, and managed to successfully face off against the Christian sports clubs. Oftentimes, they even won against the local Polish army's strong team. The club only appeared united against non–Jewish groups; within their organizations, they continued to maintain their unique character.

The Jewish National Fund

Until the split with the Revisionist camp, the Jewish National Fund was the only institution that everyone accepted. It was considered a privilege and an honor to be a member of the local JNF committee. Not a single household in the town refrained from hanging the blue box on its walls. The special projects of the foundation, its benefit banquets, were always successful and were a major event in the city. Activists and unions fought for the right to collect money for the JNF.

[Page 20]

The best activists from all of the parties and organizations participated in the local JNF committee, and Shlomo Koppelman served all those years as a JNF treasurer.

Keren Hayesod

Keren Hayesod rarely operated in the city.[37] While there was a committee of dignitaries, it would only start operating when an emissary from the headquarters arrived. They would then go out to raise money, which would continue for a few days, and some lectures would be delivered, and with the departure of the emissary, the action almost completely halted. *Keren Hayesod's* efforts centered on a small number of donors and the activists involved were mostly the same as those who worked at the JNF.

Keren Tel Hai

This fund became a factor in the city after the boycott announced by the Revisionists against the JNF and the establishment of the New Zionist Organization.[38] Its projects enjoyed considerable success and the new proceeds from emptying the boxes caught up with the JNF's proceeds. Baruch Fliter headed this fund and most of its activists were members of Beitar, *Hatzohar*, and *Brit Hahayal*.[39] The Jews eventually got used to the competition between the JNF and *Keren Tel Hai*, and many contributed to both of the foundations.

Incidents, Events, and Special Occasions

Life in the town was usually quiet and gray. But sometimes — however rarely — there were occasions and events that left their marks for days.

The Murder of A.S. Langer

An event that shocked the community and haunted it for a long time was the murder of Avraham Shmuel Langer. It happened during the war between the Bolsheviks and Petliura's army. He was slashed with a sword in broad daylight in the middle of the road for no particular reason. After this incident, a secret defense force with firearms was organized. The rioters heard about this, and from then on, throughout all the upheavals, nobody harmed the Jews and their property.

The Death of Kashuk

On one of the Sabbaths during which *Rosh Chodesh Menachem–Av* is celebrated, the elderly Kashuky left his house in good health to go to synagogue to serve as *hazzan*.[40] When he lifted the Torah and reached the words "and give us long lives" in the prayer *Birkat Hachodesh*,

[Page 21]

he collapsed and died with the Torah in his hands.[41] The event was the talk of the day, and it also received a lot of publicity in the mainstream press of those days.

The Committee for Orphans' Masquerade Ball

The magnificent masquerade ball held in 1928 by the local committee for orphans was a source of great pride for Mizocz. The masquerade ball was held in Meislitsch's silo hall, which two decorators and an outside painter decorated for weeks. The masks were a great success and marveled everyone with their original designs. The organizer of this masquerade ball was Avraham Fliter, who was a man with a well–developed sense of beauty, and who was well–versed in the art of decoration and make–up. He arranged for an orchestra, a bountiful and tasteful buffet, and for guests from the cities of Rivne, Dubno, and Ostroh. The masquerade ball brought in a lot of money for the organizers and justified all of the investments put into it.

The Inauguration of the Big Synagogue

The owner of the sugar factory, the Jewish philanthropist Halbmilion, donated a large sum to the renovation of the synagogue. He himself took care of finding suitable painters and he spared no effort nor expense to give the synagogue an elegant look. When the work was completed, the synagogue committee organized a glorious inauguration inspired by the benefactor. Thanks to Halbmilion, the ceremony was attended by all the high officials of the district with the *starosta* in the lead, army representatives, the Pravoslavie and Catholic priests, the prince Karwitzky, and lots of other curious people from all denominations.[42] The synagogue shone with beauty and it raised the reputation of the Jews and their religion in the eyes of the authorities and the population.

The Inauguration of the Beitar Flag

The inauguration of the flag of Beitar Mizocz was held when the movement was at its peak in 1934. The local chapter invited to the celebration all of the parts and factions of all the movement's branches near and far. Consequently, several hundred Beitar followers and soldiers from the *Brit Hahayal* came to town in full uniform. The officers of *Brit Hahayal*, who came wearing their swords and symbols of rank, made an unforgettable impression on the town's residents. The military procession of all those gathered made a significant impression on all who saw it, and the Poles had said that Mizocz was occupied for a day by a Jewish army. And indeed, with every step taken, they would run into a Jewish military man. The flag inauguration took place in the big synagogue, with participation of Dr. Chertok — who presented the Beitar center — the local rabbi,

[Page 22]

Parade of the "Beitar" group in Mizocz

[Page 23]

representatives of all of the Zionist parties of the area, the institutions, and government representatives. During this event, Dr. Chertok revealed the flag and guests stuck silver pegs into the flagpole. In the evening, a magnificent ball with lots of guests was held. It should be noted with satisfaction that although the celebration was partisan, it brought great pleasure to all of the Zionists.

The Immigrations to the Land of Israel

The departure of the first immigrants to the Land of Israel had a significant impression on the town. The departures of Yaakov Gelman and his family and those of Sarah Oliker and Mordechai Scheinfeld were accompanied by banquets, parties, speeches, and large crowds. Women and children came to say goodbye to them, and all of the residents gave them blessings for their journeys. As time went on, people got used to this sight. Nonetheless, each departure caused excitement in the town. Nobody left Mizocz for the Land of Israel without a banquet and a crowded farewell.

Dr. Liebster's Suicide

The old bachelor Dr. Liebster was admired in the town and was considered a quiet, level–headed, and most decent person. He was a member of the General Zionist Organization, donated routinely to foundations, was acquainted with the pharmacist Finkel's family, and had connections with Christian high society. He never fought with anyone, and he never involved himself in conflicts, gossip, or murmurings – – none of which were lacking in Mizocz. This perception of him was shattered out of the blue when Dr. Liebster killed himself. He got up one summery Saturday morning, washed himself, shaved, put on clean underwear, lay down on the couch, and shot himself through the mouth with a gun in his possession… I do not think since the founding of the town a suicide had ever occurred there. The town was therefore in turmoil for many days. Everyone talked about the incident, theorized about the content of the suicide letter left to the pharmacist, and finally decided that the surest death was that of a shot through the mouth and not through the temple like normal.

Relationships with Neighbors

The relationships between the Jews of Mizocz and their Ukrainian, Polish, and Czech neighbors were exclusively related to trade. There were no social relationships between them. Only a few individual families established social relationships with their Christian neighbors in the town. That being said, a large part of the Jewish population, whose livelihoods were at the village, had sincere, mutual friendships with the Ukrainians, Czechs, and Poles. The Czech teenager Lyuba Bachan, for example, spoke Yiddish like she was one of the Jewish girls,

[Page 24]

visited the youth Zionist clubs, and was good friends with the Jewish girls her age. Thanks to respectable relations between these neighbors, the city did not face suffering from Petliura's army during the wave of disturbances that befell Ukraine throughout his reign, nor did it face suffering during the war between the Poles and the Bolsheviks. The murder of Yerachmiel Langer was at the hands of foreign and distant rioters who were immediately stopped by local Ukrainian leaders. Even when the Nazis were in control, many of the town's Christian population tried to maintain friendships with the Jews. Here is the problem, though: these friendships misled the residents and community leaders and planted the dangerous illusion that the town of Mizocz would yet again be the exception and that it would be saved from annihilation and extermination. And indeed, when it came time to put this to the test, all of these "friends" stood over the blood of the Jews and broke their promises to notify in advance what was about to happen to them, to provide shelter to them, and to rescue the ghetto residents. About half of the Jews of Mizocz managed to escape on the day of the destruction through the fences of the burning ghetto. Most of them, however, later died at the hands of their neighbors and acquaintances. Of the many hundreds of survivors, only 19 lived to see the defeat of the enemy. Most of them are in Israel and only a few ended up in America.

The Soviet Occupation

Upon establishing itself in the town, the Soviet government immediately introduced significant fundamental changes both to Mizocz's appearance and its way of life. The expansive, flourishing trade industry stopped in its tracks. The town's private businesses were shut down one by one, and their owners and managers tried to squeeze their way into jobs as clerks and workers in the government factories established in the town. The rich people who were afraid to stay in the town settled successfully in cities near and far while concealing their backgrounds.

The town's Zionist organizations shut down on their own the day war broke out between Germany and Poland. Young people from all of the Zionist organizations joined *Komsomol* in order to hide their Zionist backgrounds and to be saved from expulsion.[43] Because there were no Jewish communists in Mizocz under Polish rule, and the Jews who rose to prominence among the Bolsheviks were all active in one way or another in different Zionist organizations — the Zionists did not suffer any particular harassment. In secret, many Zionists continued to congregate to dream together about Zionist work and making *aliyah* to Israel.

The residents of the town, who under Polish rule had flaunted their beautiful and elegant

[Page 25]

clothing as well as their gorgeous and neat apartments, adapted immediately to their new situation and altered themselves beyond recognition. Everyone knew how to speak Russian and Ukrainian and they at least seemed to integrate completely into Soviet life.

The population of Mizocz swelled due to the many refugees arriving from Nazi–occupied Polish territories, who found residence and work in the town. Everyone knew, however, that the authorities were plotting against a large portion of the Jewish population. This was evident through the mass and frequent deportations of Poles, refugees, and some Jews and Ukrainians. Investigations into the pasts of all of the town's residents did not bode well for the Jews and robbed them of any sleep, although, unfortunately for them, the Soviets did not get to massively expel them. And so in their blindness, the majority stayed in their places instead of fleeing from the Nazis deep into Russia on the day of the Red Army's retreat. And everyone knows how that story ends.

It i' worth noting that the few Communist Jews in Mizocz who rose to prominence only under the Soviet rule not only did no harm to the suspects, but also attempted to protect them and prevent harsh rulings against them.

Indeed, Misha Vigoda, an educated guy who spent eight years in a Polish prison for Communist activity, tried at the beginning of his government career to harass the Zionists and to mention their crimes at every opportunity; luckily for us, however, he quickly fell out of favor and was dismissed from his government position. I remember that during the first days of Soviet rule in Mizocz, he did not respond to my greetings and always turned his head away from me, even though we knew each other well and spent time in the same circles during the days of Polish rule. During one of his public appearances at a mass rally, he viciously attacked the Zionists, and, pointing at me standing on a balcony in front of the stage, promised to hamper the Zionists. For some reason unknown to me, however, he quickly fell out of favor with the authorities and he lost his high standing.

Since then, he always sought my company and greeted me first… Among the new leaders were a few influential Jews. I especially remember Scheinman, the director of the sugar factory. He was a talented and lively young man, an avid Communist with a warm Jewish heart. We talked a lot, and at night we freely discussed politics. He tried to get me to write an anti–Zionist statement. Naively, I opened up my heart to him and passionately defended the Zionist ideology. I note here with appreciation that he did not turn me into the authorities and only insisted that circumstances had changed and warned me to be careful. Our relationship became distant from then on and we no longer met for friendly chats. When I tried to ask him for a job at the factory,

[Page 26]

as he had at one time promised, he denied me work under various pretexts, ultimately advising me to work as a menial laborer and to keep to myself. From then on, I knew I was a candidate for deportation.

During the Red Army's retreat from Mizocz, I walked next to him for some time while escaping deep into Russia. He gave me many pieces of advice as to how to act in Russia and hinted to me that the war had saved me from deportation. We parted at Pitovka and I never heard from him again.

Under Nazi Rule

The Nazi occupation began with a pogrom against the Jewish population. Miraculously, the pogrom ended with two or three casualties, a few wounded and some store looting. It should be noted that it was not the Germans who initiated the pogrom. The Ukrainians began it on their own accord, and had it not been for the quick intervention of the German army, it would have ended up much more tragic.

For a long time after the German takeover of the area, Jews were not harmed. Furthermore, even after the order to establish the ghetto, the authorities took into consideration the Judenrat's opinion regarding the determination of the ghetto's borders, and in fact, the ghetto was open even after its establishment.[44] Jews were able to exit it, Christians were able to enter it, and many of the residents worked at factories outside the ghetto and came into unrestricted contact with the Gentiles.

The Judenrat was comprised of experienced and veteran community dignitaries: Abba Shtivel— head chairman, Shmuel Bonis, Melech Gusack, Moshe Berez, Yonah Nemirover, Avraham Weinstein, and Hersch Goldbrenner as representative of the refugees. Moshe Rudman took the role of secretary. Because of disputes over authority and interactions with the Germans, he got into conflicts with the Judenrat, and the Germans expelled him from the town. After a few days, his wife Sonia and two sons were also taken. Nothing is known about their fates. At the head of the Jewish police was a member of the Judenrat, Goldbrenner of the refugees. The police's job was to make the deserters from forced labor return to work and to collect the various levies imposed by the Judenrat, in order to satisfy the German demands for money, clothes, dishes, jewelry, etc.

Not once did the police ever act violently or abusively. A few of the Jews, mainly from the professionals among them, even succeeded in endearing themselves to the Germans, thanks to the free services they provided. This deluded the ghetto's prisoners with false hopes and empty promises that Mizocz would be saved from extermination due to its usefulness to the Germans, and if the worst comes, they would save the Jews who are essential to them. Abba Fidelman, for example, was a very effective dentist for the Germans, and he believed that this would save him and his family, up until he was led naked to the slaughter pit.

[Page 27]

He left the bunker where he was hiding with his father–in–law Mr. Scheinman, when he heard that anyone who would be found hiding would be shot on the spot. Scheinman warned him that the Germans should not be trusted, but Fidelman took his family and settled in the market square, at the front, so that his German acquaintances would notice him. One of them indeed approached him and advised him to give him his watch and all of the valuables in his possession for deposit. He promised to return them to him immediately after his release to continue his work for the Germans. It is interesting that Mr. Scheinman, who was hidden with Fidelman in the bunker, survived and is currently in Israel, whereas Fidelman was among the first to be shot.

At the time of the ghetto, aside from the aforementioned Rudman, the Germans also took Reuven Gelman, as he had gone out to the villages to trade with the farmers and told them that according to information in his possession, the Germans were being beaten on the front. It is possible he would not have been punished for simply leaving the ghetto, but there was no saving him from being punished for spreading rumors of German weakness. Due to a small monetary dispute, the butcher Shlomo Kniever tipped off the Germans about Zeide Gelman (the brother of the aforementioned Reuven), who had slaughtered a cow in the ghetto, and the Germans hanged him in the town square in front of his wife, children, and elderly mother.

Throughout its entire existence, the Mizocz ghetto never suffered from need or hunger. The Jews knew how to get by. Flour, fruit, vegetables, and even meat aplenty were smuggled into the ghetto. The environment was as bountiful as it always had been; even in the ghetto, nothing was missing. No wonder, then, that the Jews of Mizocz believed that God would not bring any evil onto them. Even when survivors of nearby cities, who had begun to flee death, (Verkovich, Yaziorni, Dubno, etc.) came to the town, and told them that all hope was lost and that the days of Mizocz were numbered — and also that they must flee immediately into the forests — the residents of Mizocz did not believe them. They continued to sit beside their pots of meat, quite literally, and believe that "it won't happen to us."[45]

It is possible that if at the time there had been courageous and wise leadership, they would have warned the residents of Mizocz in time, and most of them could have scattered among the nearby forests and thus been saved from extinction. A battalion of partisan fighters also could have been established from among the excellent youth of the town, as all the optimal conditions for success existed. But this illusion was their downfall. Only in the last days did the youth start to dream of escaping to the forest, weapons in hand. Yet time worked against them and they were too late.

On Tuesday, October 13th, 1942, all of the Jews were summoned to the market square and led to pits prepared by armed soldiers. Before they left for their final journey,

[Page 28]

they managed to set their homes and property on fire so that the oppressors would not be able to benefit from their belongings. Although the firefighters immediately went into action, they were unable to quickly get the massive fire under control, and most of the town went up in flames.

Details about the last days of Mizocz are found in the records and memories of the few survivors who experienced the Holocaust in the flesh, who fought with bitter Death and defeated him.

After the fall of the Nazi oppressors, I visited the remains of my beloved Mizocz. The Banderite gangs, who endeavored to complete the destruction started by the Germans, still roamed the area. Some loved ones, who managed to escape from the German predator, fell at their hands. The home of the sole Jew in Mizocz, Mr. David Dratva, resembled a fortress under siege; sandbags in the house, barbed wire against the windows and doors, grenades in hand, and constant vigilance. The town was terrifying in its shocking destruction, and it was as silent as a graveyard everywhere.

Now, with the *aliyah* of the Dratva family, not a trace of the Jewish people is left in Mizocz. And only in the Ukrainian houses can evidence of the roots of rich and vibrant Jewish life be found in the form of clothes, dishes, furniture, and jewelry. Jewish life in Mizocz was cut off prematurely when it was still in full bloom; cruelly and treacherously, it was destroyed.

**The "Gordonia" Hachshara (kibbutz preparation) group in Mizocz
(1934)**

Translator's Footnotes:

1. In 1648, a series of pogroms led by Cossack rebels were launched against the Jews in what is now Ukraine; thousands of Jews were killed. Bhodan Khmelnytsky led the Cossack uprising responsible for the pogroms.
2. A *beit midrash* is a Jewish study hall in a Jewish institution.
3. *Kloyz* refers to a Hassidic prayer house; the Trisk Hassidim were a Hassidic dynasty in Eastern Europe.
4. *Mincha* and *Ma'ariv* refer to Jewish prayer services; the former is during the afternoon and the latter is during the evening.
5. *Minyanim* (singular: *minyan*), are quorums of ten Jewish men that are needed for traditional prayer.
6. *Simchat Torah* is the final High Holiday of the Jewish month of *Tishrei* celebrating the finishing and restarting of the reading of the Torah.
7. The Jewish National Fund and Tel–Chai Foundation refer to prominent Jewish organizations. Revisionism is a branch of Zionism that advocated for territorial maximalism in the Land of Israel.
8. *Kiddush* refers to a communal reception or meal held after Saturday morning services.
9. A yeshiva is a traditional Jewish seminary.
10. *Mikvah* refers to a Jewish ritual bath that is used for spiritual purification.
11. A *mohel* is someone who performs Jewish ritual circumcisions.
12. *Shmurah matzah* is an unprocessed form of matzah (unleavened bread).
13. *Gabbayim*, plural (*gabbay*, singular), are the assistants to the rabbi in running the synagogue, typically tasked with calling readers up to the Torah. *Hakafa* refers to a Jewish ritual in which congregants walk

in circles around an object, usually the table upon which the Torah is read, and/or dance with the Torah on the holiday of *Simchat Torah*.

14. *Chevra kadisha* is a group of Jewish men who prepare a body for burial according to Jewish law.
15. Adar is a month of the Jewish year that typically falls around February or March of the Gregorian calendar. The term Moshe Rabbeinu is an Hebraic epithet meaning Moses our Rabbi.
16. A *kiddush*in is the Jewish ritual for engagement.
17. A chuppah is a Jewish marriage canopy that the couple stands under during the ceremony.
18. Chesed is a Jewish value of kindness and compassion towards others.
19. *Hitahadut*, a branch of the Zionist labor movement.
20. *Iton chai*, literally translating to "live newspaper" from Hebrew, refers to briefings on current events.
21. The Beitar movement was a youth branch of the Revisionist Zionist movement.
22. JNF, or the Jewish Nationalist Fund, is a Jewish fundraising organization aimed at the development of the state of Israel.
23. *Aliyah*, literally translated as 'ascent', is the Hebrew term for moving to Israel; it has a connotation of spiritual homecoming.
24. The term *cheder*, literally 'room', refers to Jewish school.
25. The Balfour Declaration was a British public statement in 1917 supporting the establishment of a Jewish state in the British Mandate of Palestine.
26. *Lag B'Omer* is a Jewish holiday that occurs on the 33rd day in between the Jewish holidays of Passover and *Shavuot*, often celebrated with parades and bonfires.
27. *She'u Tziona Ness v'Degel* was a song composed by Polish–Jewish journalist Noach Rosenblum following the First Zionist Congress.
28. Labor Zionism is a socialist branch of Zionism that promoted the Jewish working class.
29. Petliura was a leader of the Ukrainian army.
30. "Tarbut" schools were secular Hebrew–language schools in the Pale of Settlement that were administered by the "Tarbut" (literally, culture) movement.
31. General Zionism was a centrist branch of the Zionist movement.
32. *Hashomer Hatza'ir*, literally 'the young guard', is a secular and socialist Zionist youth movement.
33. *Hashomer Haleumi*, literally translates to 'the national guard'.
34. A Jewish administrative region within Poland.
35. Hatzohar was a right wing revisionist Zionist organization.
36. The *Tel Hai* Foundation was a Jewish organization that focused on fundraising for the Land of Israel.
37. *Keren Hayesod*, literally 'the foundation fund', is a fundraising organization that currently operates in Israel and works with the Israeli government.
38. The New Zionist Organization was founded in 1935 as an extension of Revisionist Zionism.
39. *Brit Hahayal* was a Revisionist Zionist organization comprising of Jewish reservists from the Polish Army.
40. *Rosh Chodesh*, literally 'the head of the month', is observed as a monthly Jewish holiday; *Menachem–Av* refers to one of the twelve Hebrew months of the year. A hazzan is the man leading a given service at a synagogue.
41. *Birkat Hachodesh* is a prayer uttered on *Rosh Chodesh* wishing for a good month ahead.
42. *Starosta* is a Slavic word meaning a community elder who administers a clan's assets. Pravoslavie refers to the Eastern Orthodox Church.
43. The *Komsomol* was a Communist youth group in Russia.
44. The Judenrat was a council of Jews that were appointed by Nazis to oversee their brethren. They were very unpopular and hated by both groups.
45. 'Sitting beside their pots of meat' is an idiom in Hebrew denoting Jews living in wealth in foreign countries; originating from the Book of Exodus.

[Page 29]

The Holocaust Period

How I Was Saved from Death in Mizocz

by Max Weltfreint

Translated from Hebrew by Corey Feuer and Yonatan Altman–Shafer

Our permanent residence was in Katowice, and our livelihood was in Mizocz; my father was a prominent fruit merchant, and he supplied fruit not only to the major Polish cities, but also to foreign countries.

Mizocz was a major source of fine fruits that were praised far and wide. Naturally, fruit sellers from all edges of Poland were attracted to it, and Dad was one of the first who opened a branch in the surrounding economy. Starting in the early '30s, Mizocz became our second home, and Dad and I spent most of the year there. We went back home to Katowice only for holidays. During the summer months, the entire family would come to Mizocz, which was like a retreat with its charming scenery and excellent atmosphere.

On September 1st, 1939, the date on which Germany invaded Poland, our family as usual was in Mizocz. The disintegration of Poland and the annexation of Katowice by the German Reich prevented us from even thinking about returning to Katowice, and Mizocz became our permanent home.

We chose Mizocz as our residence not just because of the mercantile roots we had in the area, but particularly because of its kind–hearted residents and comfortable social environment. For the same reasons, dozens of other refugee families from Polish territory occupied by Hitler went on to live there.

* * *

Two days before the Mizocz ghetto was wiped out, Mr. Goldbrenner, a Judenrat member on behalf of the refugees, told us that the Sonderführer hinted that the days of the ghetto were numbered, and we needed to flee. I turned to Yaakov Grossblatt, told him what I heard, and suggested fleeing to the forests. He hesitated and postponed the decision for a day or two. And while I was hesitating and was considering what to do,

[Page 30]

the ghetto was surrounded, and its residents were ordered to gather in the town square.

At this point, without thinking much, I headed towards the ghetto fences. I was not the only one involved in the effort to flee the encirclement; there were dozens of bold men among us. The guards shot at us, sent dogs after us, and even chased us. Some of the escapees were killed, some were wounded and apprehended, and I, after running intensely, barely made it to the village of Horvy.

Horvy village was located within thick forest and its residents were Polish. Some acquaintances in the village gave me something to eat but refused to allow me to hide among them for a few days. I wandered from place to place, from one acquaintance to another, until I made it to Zelinsky, a Baptist acquaintance.

Zelinsky agreed to hide me, and I stayed at his house for 10 days. I sat closed off in my room, only looking through a crack in a hidden window. I saw individuals from Mizocz walking around looking for places to hide or disappearing into the thick of the forest. I also saw Jews being led from the forests by the Ukrainian or German police. Among the apprehended was the pharmacist Finkel's family. I saw them all sitting cramped in a cart being guarded by police officers. Zelinsky told me after a few days that the whole family killed themselves with a potent drug while riding in the cart.

* * *

I learned from one farmer that Jews were living on the sloping mountain in the forest. I went there, and I indeed found the Berman family — all three brothers and the sister. Over the course of two weeks we would see each other every day. I was not able to live with them because their dwelling was incredibly filthy.

During one of our meetings, Ukrainians surrounded us and began shooting at us. We all scattered in different directions. A few days later I found out that only a guy named Schimonowitz and I were spared from the shooting. All of the rest of the participants at the meeting, including all of the Berman family, were killed.

I wandered from village to village and from forest to forest. I met with every survivor of the Mizocz ghetto who was living in the area, but I did not find for myself stable companionship.

Fate had it that I witnessed the murder of the Wasserman family at the hands of a farmer in whom they had placed their trust: I happened to go into the house in which they were hiding to ask for bread. I did not know that the Wasserman family was being hidden there. Suddenly Kraszewska the neighbor barged in, shouting in panic that the Germans were nearing the house. I hurried to escape and hid in an open space not far from the house.

[Page 31]

After a few minutes I saw the Wasserman family led by the master of the house to the fields.

I lay still for a long time and did not see the Germans come, so I got up and went off towards a distant house. The Wassermans' son Yitzhak arrived a few days later with his partisan group. He called me to him and told me that that night he would avenge the blood of his family, who were murdered in the most treacherous way by the farmer with whom they were hiding; I learned from him that the story of Kraszewska — bursting into the house and calling that the Germans were coming — was staged and calculated. Immediately after the scream of "the Germans are coming", the farmer took the whole family to the field, and, with the help of some acquaintances, murdered them. Only the son–in–law, Moshe Meislitsch, escaped. All of the family's gold, money, and jewelry of course fell into the farmer's blood–stained hands.

Yitzhak suggested I join his squad and participate in their quest for vengeance that night. Since Yitzhak, who led the squad, was its only Jewish member, and the rest of the squad consisted of Poles, and also because their demeanor did not mesh well with my character — I refused.

That night, Yitzhak and his squad surrounded the house of the Polish murderer, woke everyone, and stood them up against the wall. After killing them, they lit their house on fire.

The actions of Wasserman's squad brought us respect among the Gentiles, and Yitzhak was feared by everyone in the area. I was once caught by a group of unfamiliar partisans. After interrogation, they imprisoned me in a room in which the Rosenblatt brothers and Yisroel Erlich were also found. Meir Roseblatt told the commander that he owned a weapon, and if they released us, we would bring him the weapon in order to be accepted to the group. The commander agreed. We went off and returned in the morning with a weapon. The partisans, however, were not there, and to this day we have no idea who these partisans were.

From that point on, I lived in the forest. I was saved from death countless times by unexplainable miracles. Many Jews from Mizocz and the surrounding area fell before my eyes and our numbers became very small.

One time, two young guys caught me, took my belt off, and bound my legs with it. They bound my hands with a rope. They tried to kill me with what was either a piece of a tin or a knife blade, but they could not do more than wound me with a "tool" like that. I was bleeding, but I was still alive. One of the guys went to get a knife and the other stayed to guard me. I collected all of my strength and with my bound up legs I kicked the guy guarding me forcefully in the stomach. He fell over moaning and I undid the binding around my legs and escaped. To my great fortune, I immediately ran into the Fliter brothers, who dressed my wounds and brought me to a quiet, safe corner.

Meanwhile, there was a change in morale and in the situation on the frontline. The defeat of the Germans

[Page 32]

was certain and fast approaching. In exchange for promising that we would pay in full for every kindness the farmers extended to us, a few of the farmers agreed to provide us with shelter and food. To be safe, we wandered from village to village and frequently changed our place of residence until we finally saw the first soldiers of the liberating Red Army.

The pharmacy in Mizocz (built in 1935)

[Page 33]

In the Ghetto, in Forced Labor, and in the Forest

by Nahum Kopit

Translated from Hebrew by Yonatan Altman-Shafer

That day, Sunday, the 22nd of June, 1941, I will remember until the end of my days. That day, I spent time with my sister Gisiya away from our parents' house, with our close family that lived in the city Slavuta in Soviet Russia; these were very pleasant days, sitting with our formerly estranged relatives, bringing up memories as well as plans for the future. Early in the morning we got up to visit an aunt (our mother's sister whom we didn't know) in the city of Izyaslav. That summer was extraordinarily beautiful, with blooming gardens and intoxicating scents in the air. A gentle breeze blew as we strolled happily to the train station. On the way, we encountered a young Russian man who told us that war had broken out. We lingered, puzzled, not understanding the full meaning of the news. The echoes of nearby explosions began to reach our ears, and then we saw the first horrors [of the war]: houses going up in flames, crushed corpses, panic and terror. We returned immediately to our aunt's house and found everyone healthy and whole.

After Molotov's speech to the Soviet people that afternoon, and after the initial recovery [from the attack], our relatives began to plan their evacuation at home into the depths of Russia. They wisely tried to convince us to join them, but we wanted to be with our parents in Mizocz. We parted emotionally and in low spirits, we left for the train station for the second time to return home. However, the possibility of going home seemed very faint then–the repeated bombings generated a terrible panic. People were running around crazed; there were signs of doom and destruction, of death and bereavement, at every turn. The regular transportation was stopped or just broke completely, and the roads were flooded with military and civilian vehicles, to the point that it was impossible to pass through, and the train station was much more chaotic than even expected. Everyone was being pushed; yelling, crying, begging, and pouncing on every train heading east. We were among the few that were trying to go west; nevertheless, it still took us three days to get there instead of the usual three hours. We traveled slowly, with frequent interruptions and bombings, until we arrived in Zdolbuniv. In this city, which was an important crossroads in the days of the Poles, the Germans caused great damage to the train station,

[Page 34]

and with the last of our strength, we arrived in Mizocz utterly exhausted.

Mizocz was then also gripped by panic and anxiety. Members of government and those close to the state had already left the area and fled to Russia. Many of the Jews wanted to follow in their footsteps but were not allowed to do so. Only on the fifth day of the war was the border opened, and it was possible to leave the country. In our houses, it was decided that the youth would flee, and only the elderly would remain with the youngest children, and when it was all over, the youth would come back to Mizocz. We began to separate. The parents could hardly hold back their tears – it was difficult for them to see their children off. When my niece Tzipkela approached me to say goodbye, I broke down. I loved her above all; she was cute and innocent and I was unable to leave her. So we all stayed together in order to bear our hardship as one to the end. In the first days, we took solace when many of those who fled returned due to hunger, the horrors of war, and hardships of the road, but the consolation did not last.

The Germans' Arrival in Mizocz

On Friday, June 27th, 1941, the Germans arrived in Mizocz. They came in riding motorcycles in perfect formation, very polished, in shiny new clothes the likes of which we had never before seen. They filled the town and asked very politely if they could bathe. The Jews were amazed by this kindness, and suspected that all of the stories of German cruelty were lies. And so their vanguard remained with us in town for two days without any harm coming to us. They left and a steady stream of army vehicles passed through the town, and the situation began to worsen by the hour. The Jews sat in groups in basements and hiding places, scared of the Germans and terrified of the bombings. The first victim of the bombings was Feibel Fishbein; at his funeral, we felt the oncoming storm, because then was the first time the Ukrainian neighbors stoned the Jews for no reason, audaciously and with insulting provocation.

The second victim in town was the wife of Baruch Trochler–Chana. She was killed by drunk Ukrainian rioters after the Germans gave everyone free beer that they had confiscated from Matzak's brewery. Around nearby villages, the rumor spread that the Jews' property was now unclaimed, and they came in droves to take advantage of the opportunity. After they got drunk, they began to rampage in the streets of Mizocz. They broke into stores, shattered windows, trampled, destroyed, and robbed, and desecrated the great synagogue, throwing the Torah scrolls outside. Some Jews, including my father, bless his memory,

[Page 35]

put their lives on the line and brought the Torah scrolls to a secret location.

A few anarchic weeks passed with us at the mercy of a raging mob, and only when Mizocz was selected the location of the district headquarters, did the district governor, the gendarmerie, arrive, and then the robberies and atrocities were committed by law of the authorities. The Jews were ordered to wear white ribbons that were 10 centimeters wide on their left arms, each with an embroidered blue Jewish star. They created a committee (the Judenrat), which was led by Abba Shtivel, who also served as town's soltys [head of village government] under the rule of the Poles. The Judenrat also had Jewish policemen at their disposal, armed with clubs. Every day, we were flooded with a stream of harsh and humiliating decrees, becoming increasingly hard to withstand. The Jews were forced to do all kinds of utterly pointless work; their only purpose was to make them despair. After 7:00 in the evening, it was forbidden for Jews to leave their homes, though the Ukrainian police would often come into their houses then… Eventually, the ghetto was established, and all the Jews of Mizocz, as well as the Jews from the surrounding villages, were forced inside.

Our house, as well as my sister Ita's home, fell within the territory of the ghetto. The houses [in the ghetto] were not very specious; they were barely enough for their owners. However, everyone tried to squeeze tight, and somehow every Jew found space with their brethren. Yaakov Rosenstein and his mother Tzivia stayed at our house, and the big Perlmutter family from the village of Fivcha, our good friends from before, went to my sister's. The Gentiles were ordered to eschew any contact with the ghetto, whose inhabitants were now forced to place yellow badges on the fronts and backs of their clothes. The Jews were also forced to give their valuables and jewelry to the authorities, and had to subsist on the meager rations that were allotted to the ghetto. The Jews' stockpile soon ran out, and the famine and general scarcity forced the Jews to break all of 'he rules at risk to their own lives. It was forbidden for Jews to eat meat or raise domestic animals and poultry, among other things… but meat was not missing from the ghetto. I remember this because once, when my mother was cooking a small goose, which was purchased through bartering, there was suddenly a random search in the ghetto. And when the Ukrainians were searching, they reached the pots on the stoves. Consequently, Mom quickly spilled the goose into the basement, which was then filled with water. I also remember a time when my father of blessed memory wanted to go over the weekly

Torah portion on Friday night as he used to do in previous times. All of the children went to bed, and he hid the light of the candle and sat down to do his pious work. Suddenly [the police] began to knock and demand entry to the house. Knees trembling with fear, Father approached the door and opened it. The cruel Ukrainian police came in, and Kalim from Mizocz stood out among them;

[Page 36]

a man who had, in the days of the Poles, always been eating from the tables of the Jews, living off of them, and now was a tyrant making their lives hard. In instances like these when a Jew was caught at night, bent over books by candlelight, he'd be accused of providing information to the enemy over the radio. But this time, the same cruel soul simply blew out the candle and ordered Father to go to bed. Perhaps he remembered the time when Father helped him with his job, and thus showed him mercy. However, miracles and acts of grace like this one did not always occur with the Ukrainians. Reuven Gelman, my cousin's husband, used to drive to the village of Bilishev to sell items. [During the occupation], he secretly continued to travel to the village, which was about three kilometers from Mizocz, and bring food supplies back to his home and family. The residents of Bilishev were all his old acquaintances. Many of them owed him money and others remembered him with grace, so every venture to the village was worthwhile.

During one of his visits to the village, he said offhandedly to his acquaintance that rumor had it that the Germans were retreating, and their end was imminent. His slip of the tongue reached the ears of the Germans, and Reuven was taken into interrogation, from which he did not return.

In Forced Labor

During this time, the Judenrat was ordered to provide workers for German factories. My fate was to be among the recruits for working on a train in Zdolbuniv. We lived in the local synagogue and our sustenance was provided to us by the Judenrat in Mizocz. The living conditions in the synagogue were terrible, and anyone who could afford it was allowed to rent rooms in the ghetto. I rented a place to sleep with the Singer family from Równe. The father was an accountant by profession, and he worked in construction with me. The work conditions were horrible. When I first saw the fellow townspeople, who were sent to forced labor before me, I felt hopeless. I especially recall the horrible sight of Mottel Sizak, father of two, breathing heavily as he pushed a wheelbarrow filled with soil. Walking with the wheelbarrow didn't allow for any stopping whatsoever, not even for a breath of fresh air, as when one person stopped, the entire circle halted immediately. And if someone was forced to delay because his strength had left him, he was taken next to the shed and cruelly beaten by the supervisors.

The factory we worked in belonged to "Jung Solinger," a railway building company. The head manager of the factory was an engineer named Gerber, who was rarely seen in the workplace. He was filled in for by a different engineer called Shmalier, who was in charge of the Schwab area, a man who was almost always present and watched over us with great scrutiny. The first was tall and wore glasses that covered a cruel face. He was a crazed animal in the form of a man. The second was middle-aged and similar in viciousness to the first. Both were

[Page 37]

capable of beating any person to death, especially Jews, and for any offense. For example, to them it was a serious offense to drink water while working. However, I was lucky enough to be transferred after two days to work in construction, where the conditions were much better. At my new workplace, we worked only until the afternoons on Sundays, and could spend time at home (an 18 kilometer walk, as Jews were forbidden from using transportation of any kind), as long as we started work on time the following day at

6 a.m. From time to time, we could get days off from the cruel engineer to visit home. However, such a request actually posed a great danger, as if the engineer was in too good or too bad of a mood, he could beat the applicant to the point of causing a lifelong deformity. Yet in spite of the ever-present dangers, people continuously took risks, solely so they would spend a single day with their families. I was never satisfied with the visits at home. At work there was never time nor a way to receive and process news. By contrast, at home there was information galore, and the news was always appalling: Moshe Rudman, who had served as secretary to the Judenrat, argued with his colleagues, and, as a result of mutual snitching, was taken by the Germans and disappeared. After some time, his wife Sonya was taken too, and no one knew what happened to his two sons. A more shocking event occurred with my childhood friend Zayde Gelman, may God avenge his blood. He was a butcher, and, with the knowledge of the Judenrat, would secretly provide meat from time to time to the Jews. Another butcher, Shlomo Kniever, reported him to the Germans, for refusing to give him fifty marks in hush money. It should be noted that this is the same Kniever who went to the Judenrat and warned them that if they wouldn't pay him off, he would tell everything to the Germans. Despite his threats, not a soul believed that he actually would do it.

This whistleblowing could have ended in a horrific disaster for the entire community, but Gelman accepted all the blame and did not implicate the Judenrat or the buyers. The Germans set up the gallows in the square, and gathered all the Jews as well as the Christian residents. The first person they brought to the gallows was the farmer who had given a cow to the Jewish butcher. They placed the rope around his neck and announced that he would be hanged for this offense. But afterwards they took the rope off his neck and set him free with a stern warning. After him they brought poor Zayde, and in front of his elderly mother, and in the presence of his wife and two children. Forcing the entire entire crowd to watch the appalling event, they hung him, jeering.

I was not present for this "performance"; I was in Zdolbuniv then, where a similar situation unfolded: one of the residents, Fliter was his name, fixed his house's fence that stood on the border of the ghetto. He was immediately accused of attempting to dismantle the ghetto. It was obviously a lie, a glaring libel, and the Jew publicly hanged for this "sin".

[Page 38]

A different Jew among the refugees, a young man, though thin and weak, was exhausted and miserable from hard labor and hunger. He was shot like a dog out in the open by an SS soldier, who was generally considered to be a good and compassionate man. After this action, the soldier burst into the Judenrat offices and announced that he shot the young man because "they should not waste bread", and ordered him to be buried. I myself was saved from certain death once by a miracle. When I went with Mrs. Singer, whom I lived with, to help her during the shopping hours that were reserved for Jews, I was late in taking off my hat before a gendarme who had appeared in front of me. He lifted his gun and was about to murder me over this transgression. I quickly took off my hat as Mrs. Singer began to wail, and he let go of me. This happened immediately after the liquidation of the Równe ghetto, so apparently his appetite for Jewish blood was satisfied by then. Incidentally, thanks to the German engineer Gerber, 50 of our people were saved from certain death, as we were in Równe precisely at the same time as the *Aktion*.

The local council building (the "Gmina") in Mizocz

That Gerber had hidden them, protected them and transferred them to Zdolbuniv as workers in his factory. This was when the absolute and final liquidation of all of the ghettos began. One by one, the surrounding ghettos were wiped from the face of the earth, and only three ghettos remained: Zdolbuniv, Ostrog, and Mizocz. My brother Levi of blessed memory lived in Dubno from the day of his marriage. When *Aktion* began there, his family hid him thinking naively that only men were needed for labor. However, when my brother left his hiding

[Page 39]

place after a few days, he was the only one that remained alive of his entire family. Among the holy martyrs in Dubno, his wife Kayla and daughter Miriam also perished, and all his property was looted, yet despite everything, being depressed and in shock, he arrived in Mizocz after all of his hardships. In those days, I had been away from the house for a long time. So I braced myself and, on Saturday, I went to the oppressive engineer and requested a day off on Monday, which happened to be Yom Kippur. I wanted that day so I could be together with my family, and to unite with the Creator alongside my community, in the synagogue that I had always prayed in, but the wicked man denied my request. On Sunday, I went to work as usual, and I arranged for my friends to clock me in on Monday; if my absence were to go unnoticed, it would all be well and good, and if they were to discover I was gone, they would give me some sort of punishment and send me home. This was the last Yom Kippur on the soil of Mizocz. The *Sonderführer* extended the curfew by two hours for *Kol Nidre*, so the synagogues were filled to capacity. We felt that this was happening because it was the last Yom Kippur for our community, and this was reflected in our heartfelt prayers. My absence from work went unnoticed, and after a while I was formally released from forced labor and returned home. In town, survivors of exterminated ghettos were wandering around, and they found temporary refuge with us, and the Germans did not notice them. This provided us another sign that our end was near. The delusions that our city would be saved, that her fate would not be similar to her sisters, had ended.

The Beginning of the End

Everyone was making rescue plans, and I, together with my cousin Eliezer, formed a bold plan to escape into the woods, weapons in hand. We said we'd buy a gun from sellers in Zdolbuniv.

On October 11th, 1942, Eliezer left for Zdolbuniv with his railroad worker permits, and I was ready to go the day after him with money to purchase the weapon. I arrived on time and found Eliezer in a despairing mood. Rumor had it that there was no possibility of buying weapons, as the Zdolbuniv ghetto was in its last hours. He returned home and I stayed back in hopes that I would potentially succeed in acquiring a weapon.

On Tuesday, October 13th, 1942, or in Jewish years, the second day of *Mar-Cheshvan*, 5703, the Zdolbuniv ghetto was besieged by the Gestapo and the Ukrainian police in an attempt to raze the ghetto. I, alongside the rest of the Mizoczians who were working in Zdolbuniv, tried to escape, but all those who attempted to use the convenient escape routes died trying. At daybreak, the Gestapo and police began to fire into the ghetto, and forcefully brought the remaining Jews to the pits that had been prepared the day before in "Kridova Gora". Following the advice of Lev Wiener, nine of us Mizoczians went into the small and rickety cowpen, which had cracked plank walls

[Page 40]

and was visible to all. I objected to hiding in this dangerous place,but Lev said that there was nothing to lose. Aside from us, there was Yosef Stefer, Yehoshua, Chaim Wiener**Error! Bookmark not defined.**, Yaakov Rosenblatt, a Polish refugee whose name I forgot, Yitzchak Wiener, and Moshe Likwornik.

Through the cracks, we saw all the atrocities of the Aktion. The Gestapo and Ukrainian police passed by the cowpen countless times in their pursuit of fugitives, but they never peeked into it. Around noon, silence finally won out in the ghetto; every once in a while, a few lone policemen would be spotted carrying valuables out of the homes of the deportees. Several officers stowed objects in a pile of stones in front of the cowpen, and Lev Wiener even suggested that we take the valuables, as they could be useful if we stayed alive, but we rejected his idea. At night, all the policemen returned to the ghetto. They brought a lot of alcohol and food with them as well as took whatever food and drinks had been left in Jewish homes. They were being rowdy and became very drunk, savoring the massacre of the Jews. We found that time ripe for leaving the cowpen and escaped one by one from ghetto. On side roads and across fields, over rivers and valleys, we headed home to Mizocz. After walking for hours, we realized that we were lost. Having no choice, we knocked on a window of one of the [nearby] houses and asked for directions. A woman came out and recognized us as Jews, explaining that we could not go to Mizocz, as the ghetto had already been demolished and the town had gone up in flames. While we pondered our fate, dawn broke and we arrived in the village Zlisi, which was inhabited by Czechs and lay around three kilometers from Mizocz. We separated into three different groups, three in each set, as we knew that a group of nine people would not easily find shelter even for one day. In my group was myself, Lev Wiener, and Yaakov Rosenblatt, who had many acquaintances in this village. One of Rosenblatt's Czech contacts brought us into his home, feeding us generously and also providing us with a place to live. He confirmed the woman's story that the Jews of Mizocz had been murdered, and told us that they themselves had set fire to the town, so that the Germans and the Ukrainians would not benefit from their property and work. We spent three days with this Czech man, and we wept over the fate of our loved ones who we'd never see again. On the fourth day, the

Czech man told us that he had been in Zdolbuniv, and there he saw large signs on behalf of the Germans warning that anyone who shelters Jews would be killed.

Wandering in the Shadow of Death

The Czech man requested that we leave the residence. The danger in those days was very great; gangs, extortionists, and flat-out murderers roamed the roads, not even including policemen and Gestapo. They all sought to destroy any [Jewish] survivors

[Page 41]

who had managed to escape the liquidation of the ghettos. We decided to hide for a few weeks in the surrounding villages in the residences of acquaintances, and then to take shelter in the woods. I had many contacts around the village Soime since my father owned a flour mill there, as well as a grocery store. I knew the area and its residents well; I had been in trade relations with them up until the breakout of the world war. But that night, to my amazement and our severe disappointment, not a soul answered our knocking on the windows as I identified myself. Some "acquaintances" didn't answer at all, and a few responded that they didn't know any Nachum… We fled for our lives from there and arrived at the edge of the great forest, where a few foresters' houses were scattered. We knocked on the window of my contact Kirili Filianiuk, and I identified myself. He opened the door, loudly expressing his happiness that I had stayed alive. He brought me and my friends into his home, feeding us and preparing a place for us to sleep on the threshing floor. From our hiding place in the granary, we often saw policemen, who were leading the Jews they'd capture from the woods to interrogation. The number of the apprehended was quite large, and we then realized that had the Ukrainians not completed the work of the Germans in exterminating the Jews–many tens of thousands would have been saved. After a week of relative calm, we had to leave the place and venture into the woods. We were not yet accustomed to lying on wet ground, but we did, without any soft surface or warm cover. We lived for consecutive days without food, and our suffering was great. We searched the forest for brothers in suffering and anguish, feeling sorry that we had parted from our fellow Mizoczians with whom we had been saved in Zdolbuniv. During the days we hid and rested, and at night we went on expeditions into nearby villages to obtain food. More than once we would return from our night work without a single slice of bread, but from time to time we would experience delightful revelations in people who felt our pain and tried to ease our distress.

During one of our visits to the village of Moszna, while staying with one of my acquaintances, the Czech Jozef Svoboda, I learned that my brother Levi and sister Gisia were in the village, alive and well. After many searches, we found them, and from them we first heard full details about the bitter storm that had overtaken our town of Mizocz. The cruelty and unwillingness of our Ukrainian neighbors to help was most painful. They had been reliable acquaintances of ours, but now they didn't listen to my sister's pleas to at least save her child, Tzipka'le. And there were also those who murdered their Jewish neighbors with their own hands. We now comprised a large group of five people, which involved considerable difficulties in obtaining shelter, food, and water, but we did not want to part from one another. In the village of Bilishiv a poor shoemaker helped us a great deal, putting his life in grave dange' for our sakes. From him, we learned that his rich neighbor, a devout Christian and church activist, told him he wants to help us. We went to him, and indeed he fed us and also

[Page 42]

The mass grave of the martyrs of Mizocz next to the Sosenki Forest

[Page 43]

provided a hiding place with him. Already the very next day, while serving us food, he began to preach the teachings of Jesus to us. He was sorry for our suffering to no fault of our own, but justified the situation, for the sin of our forefathers in murdering the prophet Jesus. His incessant preaching felt like rubbing salt in our wounds, so we left his home and continued our wandering.

In time, we had to turn to him again for help, but he refused to aid us with anything. He also told the shoemaker that we shouldn't be helped, due to the fact that it was a sin to help the insistent, infidel Jews. Once, entirely by surprise, we ran into Yaakov ben Yechiel Baruch Oliker, together with Tzvi Toharan, from among the refugees. They explained to us that they had made a shelter in the Lysa Hora forest, and lived there along with Yosef Wolfman. Next to their shelter was another pit, which could easily be turned into our own shelter. They gave us a detailed description of the location and then we parted ways with the hope we would be reunited soon. The next day, we headed to that location, and on the way, we ran into Yonah Oliker, who had been with Moshe Likwornik. He told us that one of his Ukrainian acquaintances had tempted Woltzi Klotzman, Shmuel Fisher, another refugee, and Yehoshua, husband of Tzivia Rosenstein, to come stay with him. When they came with him, he brought them to a pit and told them to wait there until he brought them tobacco and food. Germans then appeared who murdered them on the spot. He offered me a similar invitation and we fled for our lives from there. After endless wandering, we arrived at the designated place. We asked immediately if someone had seen our friends in the area. They replied that only Mikolaj from Mosznice knew about the location, and not only did he know but he also helped a lot with setting it up. The location was narrow, fitting for a caveman from the Ice Age, not for a person from today. However, since our predecessors had been there for a few months, without anyone harming them – we stayed there too.

Yosef Wolfman believed we would be saved by Purim. We prayed there, laying *tefillin*, as during his escape from the ghetto, Yosef had not forgotten to take his *tefillin* and *tallit* along with him, as well as an ax for self-defense. The surrounding area was populated with Poles, from whom we obtained our meager food supplies. We would thaw the snow and use the water for washing and cooking. There we learned that the brothers of Yaakov Rosenblatt were in the area, and over time we met up with them, as well as with Avraham Perlmutter from the village of Pivatasha. He and his daughter were nearly naked, wrapped in worn rags and terribly hungry. They told us that Shlomo Koppelman managed to escape from the ghetto and lived in Pivatasha until the Ukrainians murdered him and threw his body to the dogs for their consumption. I sent Avraham to my contact, whom I had smuggled clothes to from the ghetto, and asked him to give him

[Page 44]

one suit. After some time, when I met with this acquaintance, he told me that Avraham visited him and received a suit, but he had only worn it for a couple days before he was murdered. One day, Yaakov Oliker and I found ourselves at the place of the Polishman Oblowski. He fed us and told us about a Jewish boy who had been seriously wounded in his escape from the ghetto, and was wandering about the area. The child defecates without being able to properly move his hands and feet. Consequently, everyone refuses to let him enter their homes. This was the 12-year-old son of Aryeh Firer. His father found him, cleaned and healed him, but both eventually perished.

When we heard rumors about hidden Jews, potentially from Mizocz, we did not consider the possible danger and did not spare any effort trying to meet with them. Farmers informed us that there were Jews from Mizocz hidden three miles away. We started to search for the location, and with great efforts, we found their hiding place. There, we discovered Max Weltfreint, Yaakov Rosenstein and his wife Leah, Aryeh Lipshitz and his whole family, Ephraim Mulman with his son, and a few more Mizoczians. Meetings like this were sources of encouragement and joy in our unbearably difficult lives; they instilled a spirit of hope in and strengthened our faith in the Day of Redemption. During this encounter we heard additional evidence about the bitter annihilation of Mizocz, which we were desperate to hear more about. I was especially interested to hear from Yaakov Rosenstein about the last moments of my family, whom he had lived with until the end. My father of blessed memory, who had already been an old man, lacked the strength and courage to escape into the unknown, wrapped himself in his *tallit* and *tefillin*, said a prayer of confession, and accepted his fate. The dear mothers only worried about their children, hiding them, providing food for them, and praying for their lives. They themselves lined up for the death marches to the pits dug next to the sugar factory. Yaakov Rosenstein, his wife and his 2-year-old son, hid in a shelter that was built under their house's cowpen. His mother and my mother provided them with a great deal of food and covered the shelter in sand and hay. They stayed in the shelter for a few days until their child was sick from lack of oxygen. Then they left the shelter and headed towards the village of Ozirka. Their child died on the way, and after much wandering, they arrived at a cave, where they had lived until now. We discussed amongst ourselves about how the upcoming Shabbat was *Rosh Chodesh* of *Adar Bet*, so the men could come to us and form a halachic minyan. Life became more bitter and difficult than usual, as the Banderites had heightened their war against the Germans, and they had not forgotten about the remaining Jews and Poles. There was then virulent infighting, and scarcity became prevalent in the wealthy and established villages. Everyone was terrified of the Banderites; even the good and decent among the villagers were scared to give us any help. Thus, Leib Weiner and I decided to try our luck in a place far from where we lived. My brother Levi wanted to join us,

[Page 45]

but I was against this, as he was very depressed after everything that had happened to him: the liquidation of three ghettos in which he had lived and the loss of his entire family. Additionally, he was very weak and not fit for the long and hard road ahead. Although there was a shortage in the forest, the Jews were much safer there.

We were about 15 kilometers away from our lair in the woods when we reached the house of my Polish contact from the village of Svienta. He told us that not far his house laid the corpses of four Jews who were killed by an informant. He wanted to bury them but was scared of the Banderites. We asked him to prepare tools and promised that in one of the coming evenings, we would find the bodies and bring them to a proper eternal rest. However, things went completely differently than we had thought or wanted. In search of means of sustenance and livelihood, we arrived at the village of Bilishev and knocked on the window of the farmer Nachum, who had been the best and most honest of all the villagers. He quickly ushered us into his house, hiding us in a place no one could see. He warned us that we were now in great danger, as all roads were being watched by Germans for the Banderites. The latter are also following in the footsteps of the Germans to attack them, but neither of them have forgotten about the Jews. He volunteered to go to safe locations for us and bring us what he could, so we stayed for six consecutive days in the hiding place without seeing the light of day. Only after we knew that the things had calmed down did he kindly allow us to leave our hiding place. This was two days after *Rosh Chodesh* of *Adar Bet*. We left Bilishev loaded with food and made an effort to reach our lair in the forest before dawn. The journey was long and hard, but thanks to our lengthy rest, we arrived at the location in time. However, we immediately felt a suspicious change in the area. Everything was scattered around, and above all there was a very threatening silence. At nightfall, after some recovery, we started going over the disparate objects with our hands, and I came across the corpses of my brother Levi and my sister Gisia… I went to the other shelter where more friends had been hidden, calling out their names, but there was no response. I struck a match and opened the door, and discovered a horrible and shocking spectacle. Blood everywhere, congealed brains and a terrible stench. Yaakov Oliker laid dead with his five-year-old son on him. I left the pit and said to Leib that we needed to flee as quickly as possible from this place before daybreak as they had discovered the hideout. Before I had even finished speaking, out of the dead of night, a child's cry rose up from the pit: "Mommy, Mommy, it hurts." I retraced my steps and brought the child out of the pit, and we learned what happened from him. The man who had arranged the hideout brought the Banderites, and they tortured and murdered everyone. The child, seriously injured and suffering from great pain, survived because he knew how to pretend to be dead. And thus, he survived. When the morning dawned, we realized how horrific the abuse and robbery of the dead had been.

[Page 46]

Without wasting another moment, we fled from the place that served as a shelter for us for two months. The boy could not walk due to his wound bothering him, and was also deeply exhausted, so we took turns carrying him, and with great difficulty we reached a pit where 12 residents of Mizocz had once lived. The place was completely deserted and there was already full sunlight. We rested for a bit and then had no choice but to leave the boy in the pit with enough food. We promised him that we would come back for him later when we find a place for all of us. The boy, after spending two days among the dead, having been terribly lonely and surviving off crumbs he found in the pit, agreed to it all. So, the two of us sat on a felled tree trunk in the thick of the forest, looking for a way out of the situation. I remembered that I was once in this area with the father of the child at the home of the Pole Jan Orlovski, and was hospitable. We decided to find Jan and ask for his aid. We left all of the food we had with the boy and that was the first time that we went to find the Pole in the light of day. Luckily, we got to him without incident. I introduced myself and he immediately recognized me. Despite all of the dangers, he gave us shelter and sincerely helped us with our troubles. He especially mourned the loss of his friend Yaakov, and sent his son to the boy in the pit to console him and to bring him back to the house that evening. The young Orlovski returned from the pit with the boy, expressing his concern that there was no chance that the boy would survive, but I said I was certain that if the boy received care, he would live. That night, they brought the boy to the Pole's house, stripping and washing him in a warm and cleansing bath. His wool hat was stuck to his wound, but with the help of the hot water we were gently pouring over the wound, the congealed blood thawed and the hat slipped off. The boy did not say a word the entire time. The poor child had learned how to suffer. We cleaned his wound spiritedly, made him a clean bandage smeared with oil, and laid him down to sleep. The next day, the problem faced us again with renewed severity–what would we do with the boy? We could not leave him in the pit or the granary. In the house he posed danger both to himself as well as to us, not to mention the Pole. Consequently, we decided to offer the Evangelicals to adopt him, as they once expressed their interests in adopting a Jewish child and educating him according to their faith. However, this time they refused to even speak with us, as fear of the Ukrainians had fallen upon them. We turned to the Pole and he immediately informed us that while we were gone, the Germans destroyed his neighbor's house, as they had been providing shelter for a Russian prisoner who had defected. We discussed it and promised the Pole that we would leave that night.

The Pole was very saddened by our fate, and was happy along with us to see that after a few days of care the boy began to recover. The wound healed, he looked healthy, and we took him to our hiding place. It was then that Kayla Goldberg, along with one of the refugees who lived in the Mizocz ghetto, stumbled upon us.

[Page 47]

The encounter was, as usual, very exciting, and gave all of us great joy. Once again, memories of our beloved town arose, and we did not tire of hearing about its bitter end. Then we told each other about the miracle of salvation. Kayla informed us that a Ukrainian acquaintance whom I knew as a professional thief, crook, and man of the criminal underworld, hid her in times of danger and helped her tremendously. I could not believe these things and thought her description of this man was incorrect, but over time I also witnessed the strength of his character and goodness of heart. Despite his poverty and urgency, despite living a life of petty thievery and working for the rich, he shared his bread with us during the war at a time when others were afraid to even talk to us. Indeed, who can really understand a human soul?

At night, we all left together to find the Jews with whom we once promised to hold a minyan together. We found them and they told us that indeed they had come to us for the minyan, just as our hiding place was revealed to the murderers. They heard the shootings and screams of those being murdered but miraculously managed to escape for their lives. Ephraim Mulman was among them, and he agreed to try to arrange for our boy to be together with his son who was staying with an acquaintance farmer. We brought the child, whom we called Ben-Tzion, and Mulman succeeded in his mission in having the boy stay with his son, whose name was also Ben-Tzion. And from then on, we all lived together in the forest.

One night, seven of us men left to fulfill a sacred debt towards our slain brethren and bury them in a human grave. We buried them and formed a marker of sand over the graves in the hopes that maybe one day we would be able to return to the place and bring their bodies to a Jewish graveyard. Kaddish echoed through the depths of the forest, saturated with our tears of rage, though we felt a little relief from our hearts, as we had done a kindness of truth [*chesed shel emet*] for our precious people. We then decided that on the following Sunday we would also bury the four Jews who were murdered near the village of Svienta. And so we did. We arrived at the house of the Pole who had saved their lives and to whom we had promised at the time that we would bury them. We explained to him the reason for not having done so yet and he understood. After a few minutes, he brought us a Jew with a long beard, thin as a stick, and asked us to identify him. We could not. Only when he started to speak did we recognize him as the younger brother of

Leib. I have no words to describe the reunion of the brothers, who had each thought that the other was dead. Nor do I have words to describe the rescue of Moshe Weiner, who was hidden for six months on the roof of a farmer's house in the village of Derman, covered in planks and rags, his body shrunken from a lack of sunlight and insufficient oxygen. If not for the good food he received, he could not have stayed standing in his condition. It is therefore no wonder that it was impossible to recognize him. When he learned that his brother was alive, he left his hideout and went to the Pole's house with hope to find Leib. We were glad that the story resulted in adding another living Jew to our ranks. Together, we left for the place the Pole was leading us to, where the dead were. It was already impossible to recognize the place. We buried them, said Kaddish,

[Page 48]

and added markers to the graves so that we could find them in the future. The number of Jewish survivors we found in the forest grew steadily, so we separated into different groups, though we stayed in contact with each other. My group included Leib Weiner and his brother Moshe, Alter Gerber, Aryeh Firer and his daughter Chava'le, Lipa Langer, and others.

The holiday of Passover approached. We acquired 16 kilograms of wheat, and Chava'le ground it at an acquaintance's hand mill and baked matzah. On the night of the seder, we held a small bonfire in the thick of the forest. The eldest in the group, Rabbi Alter Gerber, read us the Haggadah from a siddur we had, and everyone repeated after him. Aryeh Firer's son Avraham'le asked the Four Questions. We reminisced about the seders we used to have in our homes and we wept bitter tears. The Haggadah became the lament of Tisha b'Av and the seder became a eulogy. On the first day of *Chol Hamoed*, Leib's brother Moshe passed away. We buried him according to Jewish law and envied him for dying by heaven's hand. In light of bitter past experiences, we learned to change hiding places frequently, constantly moving to another location. There we met Niona Langer, wife of Yosef Langer and her daughter Chaya'le, who found Gisiya, Aryeh Firer, and Lipa Langer by surprise. The child Ben-Tzion was also brought to us and our group became a large unit filled with women and children. The three or four brave men were given another heavy burden of obtaining food for everyone. The Ukrainians had destroyed the Poles and were persecuting them no less than the Jews. The Poles were fleeing their towns at night and leaving all of their fortunes behind. Repeatedly, they would give us the food stashes instead of leaving it to the Banderites, or they would tell us the location of food stashes of Poles who had fled the area earlier. We then encountered the Rosenblatt brothers with the family of Asher Schapira, along with Baruch Fliter, with Bronia Weinzweig from Zdolbuniv, who would visit Mizocz every year with her close friends and many others. The brothers Avraham and Eli Rosenblatt lost their lives when they ran into armed Germans. They tried to defend themselves with a weapon they had but could not stand against soldiers with automatic guns. On Sunday, the morning of the 25th of Iyar, the day after the demise of Avraham and Eli, we left to visit their group and learn how they lived. Aside from me, our group included Baruch Fliter, Lipa Langer, Leib Wiener, and Velvel Ochs and the lawyer Zatz from Dubno. Together, we were a very large group of 20 Jews; we were very happy and also mourned the death of the Rosenblatt brothers. The weather was fair and good and I fell asleep on soft grass.

[Page 49]

The screams of Mulman's son awoke me. And before I even realized what was happening, I saw Jews fleeing in every direction. And gunshots were heard. I stood on my feet and started to run away. I came across Germans who shot at me from the ground but missed. Later, after I left my hiding place, I became aware that there was a steady silence in the area. I wanted to know about the fates of my friends so I began searching in the place where the attack started. I was first to arrive; then came Baruch Fliter and the Meir brothers and Herschka Rosenblatt. We left together to check the area and found the dead: Shimon Feldman,

Lipa Langer, the son of Alter Gerber, Yaakov Rosenblatt, Leib Wiener, Asher Schapira, Chaya Lipshitz and her son Yehoshua, and Ephraim Mulman. In the morning, we dug a hole and buried everyone in a communal grave. Only the elder Gerber dug a separate hole for his young son, burying him and shedding a wave of tears over the grave. Still missing were Asher Mulman, the boy Ben-Tzion Oliker, Yaakov Rosenstein, one of Lipshitz's daughters, and the lawyer Zatz. Later we learned from the farmers that they had been caught alive and hanged in the forest.

After that, our lives in the forest were hard to bear. We could not stay in one place for more than a few hours. Sources of food supplies were inaccessible. We were afraid to light fires, and the distress in full swing. When we would return to a prior hiding place, we would always find traces of rioters who had demolished and destroyed everything. The only thing they did not find was us. Over time we learned how to harvest potatoes and vegetables from abandoned Polish fields and to collect mushrooms and berries from the forest; the only thing missing was bread and salt. And from time to time, we would get a bit of that too.

Following the Partisans

At that time, we first heard about the groups of partisans in the forests. But here was the problem. The Russian partisans did not treat the Jews as persecuted people; if they did kill them, they chased them away. Nonetheless, Nachum Poliak and his two daughters, Kayla Goldberg, a few refugees, as well as Yisraelik Erlich and Baruch, son of Hershel Trochler managed to stay around them. The last two were murdered by the partisans for some kind of an offense. Or just because they were Jewish. However, in spite of this gloomy information, we wanted to join the partisans, as we did not have anything to eat aside from potatoes. In the meantime, we managed to steal a cow from a cowpen and slaughter it. We were satisfied with the meat, but there was a lot of difficulty in covering the traces of the theft. One evening we came across a Ukrainian who was a member of a partisan group, and he told us that if we so desired, he would help us join them. Some of us were enthusiastic about it, but others said that he could be a spy and it would be good if we killed him. However, Jews are always prone to imagining things, and not only did we not kill the "Partisan" we also did not change our hiding place. Ultimately, he informed the Banderites about us, and they, disguising themselves as partisans, won the hearts of the women, who convinced the men that the partisans wanted to do good by us. They even brought us apples and good food

[Page 50]

and told us to gather on Sunday to go as a group to join the partisans. In the end, only the doubters among us survived, and the committee were shot or buried alive. Among the last survivors were, aside from myself, just the Meir brothers and Hershka Rosenblatt, Niona Langer and her daughter, the brothers Baruch and David Fliter, the two children of Asher Schapira, and one boy from Shumsk. These individuals constituted the sole survivors remaining in the forests. On my advice, we decided to leave the woods and to try to manage in the villages. I suggested this for one reason only: if we were killed in the forest we'd be eaten by dogs, but in the village, we would at least be buried...

Once Again in Mizocz

The chances of getting by in the village were then very faint. The Poles moved into town, the Ukrainians were scared of the nationalists, and the Czechs did not want to risk themselves for the sake of the Jews. In spite of all of this, we left in small groups to try our fates. I was with Yonah Oliker and we decided to knock on the doors of acquaintances that were known to help Jews. We wandered from acquaintance to acquaintance, but we could not stay with anyone for more than a single day. Ultimately, we decided to turn back to Mizocz to the Ukrainian Pochbula, whom we knew had hidden the Yehuda Braunstein. And indeed, he took us in and, in exchange for a suit, agreed to hide us for two months. His two sons were members of the army troops of the Banderites, but they were among the few who did not murder other peoples. They told us that in senior positions in the party there are now two opinions regarding the treatment of minorities. The extremists demanded the elimination of the Jews once and for all, as well as of the Poles and the Russians. The moderates were more in favor of occupying the land without war with the local residents of other ethnicities. They proposed to postpone coming up with a solution to the minority issue until after the war. And in the meantime, each group would act of its own accord, with the extremists killing any person who did not belong to the Ukrainian nation. Unfortunately, our days of rest with Pochbula did not last. After a few days, he came to us with the suit and requested that we, for our own sakes, flee from Mizocz that night, as the Ukrainian nationalist command decided to attack the Germans from here, and to turn Mizocz into their fortress, scrubbed clean of any foreign element. As soon as night fell, we left his house and saw many other residents of Mizocz leaving town. Of course, we could not afford to be discovered, and we climbed onto the roof of a pigsty and lay on it. We saw the Banderites banding together, heard their orders, and thought that our end was near. During the night they took over the Polish district and massacred its population. Afterward, they burned all the houses to the ground. The Germans were not able to be taken as easily, and their war lasted all night. Towards morning, the Ukrainians began to retreat in battle and the Germans burned

[Page 51]

all the areas of the town which were inhabited by Ukrainians. Fortunately for us, the pigsty upon which we hid was in a different part of the town that was intended to be saved, and thus we were not burned alive. We lay there without any food or water but we hardly felt this for three days. When things calmed down, the owner of the pigsty returned home and, without any choice, we called out to him as he came out and went around the pigsty. He was simply happy to see us and told us to dig potatoes out of the plot alongside the house for both the pigs as well as for ourselves. The residents of Mizocz who had fled because of the battles began to return to town and, due to the fact that most of the houses had been destroyed, many found shelter in the house where we were staying.

So, we were both pushed into a hole in the granary, without any room to move. The owner of the house who knew about us then located our hiding place, and subsequently invited all those who stayed in the house to a feast inside, while helping us out of the hideout and allowing our escape. We decided to go to the village Borshechibksi-Czechi, where Yonah Oliker had hidden with Liza Melamed and her son Yasha immediately following the destruction of the ghetto. The Czech Milak Dos could not hold everyone, so Yonah left while Liza and her son stayed. The Czech man was not among the wealthy so we knew that the suit in our possession would buy us shelter for a few days. The Czech was very happy with us, as his conscience constantly bothered him for sending Yonah away. And when he realized that he was still alive, he was truly content. To our question of whether or not Liza still lived, he answered that he hoped that all Jews will be in as good of shape as her. He added that she and her son remained under his wing, and that he would protect her until the end of the war, even if he would have to pay for it with his life. The following day we met with Liza and her son. This was the first time since the destruction of the ghetto that Liza had seen another Jew, and everyone was immensely happy. Liza and her son looked terrible. Though they were relatively secure, they were also dirty, skinny, and filled with lice, suffering from hunger and deprivation as the Czech was poor and lived in squalor, though he shared with them what he had. Also hidden in this village were the Rosenblatt brothers and Yisrael Oliker, Yonah's uncle. In those days, the village had different parties that were connected with the Ukrainian parties. Presumably they did so only to prevent the fate of the Poles and save themselves from extinction. Our Czech was the head of the local party, and his uncle Yosef Altman was the secretary of the party. The two of them were poor, but that did not prevent them from helping us. When we met with Yisrael Oliker, he told us that the Banderites had caught Yehoshua bar Trachtenberg alive, and when he told them that he resided in the Czech village Broshchivki, they sent him to the secretary of the local party, Altman, to ask for work and help on their behalf. And so it was. The attitude of the Czech village–where everyone knew about us–was more than excellent. For example, the wife of the man whose house we were in, did not agree to let us eat our meals in the cowpen,

[Page 52]

and more than once we had to eat at the table with everyone. We always preferred to eat in the dark, as when we sat at the table in the house, we were always expecting danger.

Under the Auspices of the Czechs

Due to the disruption of transportation, the mutual war between the residents, and the extinction of the Jews, there was a great shortage of clothes and salt. For simple salt, which used to have a near-zero price, you now had to pay a fortune. This situation was also caused by the fact that the Ukrainians were afraid to visit cities because the Germans would be suspicious that they were spies. The head of the party, the same Altman, therefore approached me with an offer: that if we had enough money, he would go to Zdolbuniv and bring salt and clothes from there. Of course, he promised me a share in the profits. I gave him ten dollars as well as a letter to a Czech contact who lived in Zdolbuniv and owed me money. That morning, he rented a cart and traveled, and we entered the granary to grind flour in the hand mill. The children and their mother were in the fields. Surprisingly, and without us noticing, a cart filled with armed Ukrainians entered the yard. They headed straight towards the pigsty where we were working. And they were very happy to see us, as one of them was an old acquaintance, even asking me to say hello to my parents. When I said that they had perished, he expressed his sorrow, and I do not know if this was about the loss of my parents or the fact that I still lived… Then he asked about the identity of my friends. I said that one was named Yonah and the other was Srul Oliker. When they heard that his name was Yisrael, they began to probe and determine if this was the Srul who owned a tavern in Mizocz. I realized immediately that this murderer had sinister intentions towards Rabbi Yisrael, but I could not back down anymore and claim otherwise. They did indeed move on without harming us, but we were already experienced in these matters and knew that we had to leave the place right away. Of course, the next day they returned, searching for us among the pigs, especially for Yisrael, but did not find anyone. Altman's journey was successful; he returned from his mission safely and collected my debt from the Czech. In Zdolbuniv he sold poultry and eggs that he bought relatively cheap in the village for high prices, as well as bought salt that had been purchased at a comfortable price and sold at a very fat margin. He was in a good mood and he decided to act cunningly. He went to the headquarters of his Ukrainian party and asked what he should do with the Jews coming to the village. To kill alone or to keep them alive? To his amazement, they said to him not to harm them, but rather to give them any help they could. So, he told them that the Ukrainian nationalist army had searched for Jews in order to kill them. The party told him in the clearest way that those who did that were merely robbers and they must be simply expelled from the village. And to reinforce the message–they gave him weapons

[Page 53]

for distribution among the members of the party for the purpose of this action. After that, our situation greatly improved. Altman got very rich and even brought me a pair of boots for the winter.

On the Verge of Liberation

Fall arrived. Due to the persecution, almost all those remaining from Mizocz were gathered in the village. The Czechs received and organized everyone. I was then already free from food-related worries.

Altman was earning a lot of money and provided for all of my needs. Good news began to fill the air. The Germans withdrew along the entire front and we already knew that the day of liberation was approaching; however, that was exactly when the danger increased and we did not want to die on the verge of liberation. The damned Banderites harassed us and threatened our lives. Night after night, we would have to change where we were living, occasionally fleeing into fields as well. I remember that one night, amidst an intense frost, it was rumored that the Banderites were coming to take us. I was transferred to Liza's hiding place, which for some reason was considered safe. As we lay half-naked in the "beds", we heard the footsteps of many people. We jumped out of the window with only the skin on our backs. All night, we lay in the snow in an open field, and in the morning, it turned out that it had been the Soviet vanguard. On December 2nd, the first of the regular Soviet troops entered the village. Our happiness had no limit, but we were not relieved at all. Mizocz and the surrounding villages were used as the center of the Ukrainian nationalist gangs. They fought the Soviets, shooting them down, and no Jew would come out alive. Herschka Rosenblatt, who had managed to get through all of the days of the German occupation, was murdered at the hands of the Banderites after liberation. Mizocz was left with nothing but the place where it once stood, so we could not return to live there, and the Banderites were in control there no less than the Soviets. Consequently, we left to live in Zdolbuniv. But before I left my damned and beloved birthplace, I visited the place twice more, in order to part from the remains of my loved ones' bodies. I saw the place where all of the holy people of the town were killed. I held with my own hands the bones of our dear children that we found after the rain had revealed the earth that covered them. I covered them in soil mingled with tears and silently parted from them, forever in burning pain.

[Page 54]

The Forest Girl

by Kayla Goldberg–Tzizin

Translated from Hebrew by Corey Feuer **and** Yonatan Altman–Shafer

The day of the Mizocz ghetto's destruction came unexpectedly and found all of the ghetto's residents surrounded by murderous soldiers.

Many of the Jews — myself included — knew that the days of the ghetto were numbered and decided to run away from the ghetto and to hide in either the forests or villages surrounding it, but they were too late. I even spoke with Gievski the Ukrainian, with whom I traded in the ghetto, and he gave me a solemn promise that when the time came, he would help me and hide me. The knowledge that the ghetto was surrounded and the destruction was commencing reached me in the wee hours of the morning before dawn.

Without thinking too much or consulting with anyone else, I headed towards the meadow behind the *kloyz* with my friend Mark Plinker, so that we could escape through it to nearby Krasnogora where my "friend" Gievski lived. When we reached the reeds, we saw Tuviya Kantor and Pontik Horowitz standing and consulting with each other as to whether to pass through and risk being shot or find another path. We too stood still and saw that they were shooting at every visible person that passed through the reeds. We also saw the first ones killed and were encouraged by the fact that quite a few people managed to escape without getting hurt. We ran forward. Whistling bullets flew over our heads and from all sides, and after a few minutes we found ourselves in the safe and sound in the garden of the Russian Orthodox priest. We rested for a few minutes and then taking a circuitous route, we made it to Gievski's house. I knocked on a window and I saw an unknown hand close the curtains. I continued to knock but nobody answered. There was no point in lingering by the house in the gentile neighborhood, and so we turned in the direction of the

Susinski grove. When we arrived at the grove, dawn was starting to break, and we could see the first farmers walking. With no other way to hide, we climbed a thick tree and hid between its branches. From atop the tree we saw very very many of the farmers of the surrounding area flocking to Mizocz to get a close look at our distress and to gloat. We became intensely fearful and decided not to come down from the tree until it was completely dark out. The farmers passed by the tree on top of which we were sitting and talked about the Jews being led to their deaths. We heard that everyone was praising the Germans and were happy about our misfortune, and our hearts told us that we would not be able to save ourselves from oppressors like those. But we heard other things being discussed as well.

[Page 55]

A few old farmers were shedding tears for our bitter suffering and were prophesying divine punishment for those involved. A glimmer of hope snuck its way back into our hearts and inspired us to fight for our lives, because the country was not yet devoid of honest people. Meanwhile, the day brightened and the traffic on the roads began to wane.

Terrifying screams, the rattling of machines, gunfire, and the cheers of drunken mobs met our ears. Every suspicious rustling in the forest made our blood freeze. Each gunshot tore a hole in my heart, each scream rattled my nerves, and the cheers of the crowd drove me mad. And as this torture and anguish carried on, day faded into the relief of the night. We descended from the tree and decided to go to the village of Horvi. I knew the directions to the village. I had never, however, been there before. I only knew that the village was populated by Poles, it was surrounded by sprawling forests — some quite large — and that in the ghetto, they said that it was a place where one could hide. It was dangerous to take the regular main road. Therefore, we went to the fields intending to reach the destination without being seen. The ground was wet; chunks of it stuck to my shoes, and walking was very difficult. The sky over our heads was red from the giant fire that engulfed Mizocz. We were tired, hungry, and broken, and we noticed we lost our way. We had no choice but to go the main road and ask for directions. We knocked on the window of one of the houses. To our great luck, we got a lot of help from this house. We received food and drink and precise directions for the rest of our journey. We continued down our path feeling reassured until we felt sand beneath our feet. We realized we had reached our destination. We immediately saw before us the forests we had heard about and the village itself. With the rest of our strength, we made our way to a forest, found ourselves a spot in the thicket, and, exhausted, fell right asleep.

When we woke up we were close to despair. The forest was very loud and its appearance was threatening to us. The trees and grass were covered with a thick layer of dew like after the rain. We were cold, and our hunger and thirst were beginning to get to us, when suddenly we saw close to us a young farmer with an ax. We did not know who he was and what his intentions were. Was he for us or against us? There was no point in running away. I gathered up my courage, approached him, and inquired about the way to the village of Horvi. He immediately said that he knew we were Jews, and that he would not cause us any harm. He said that he chopped wood in the forest and brought it down to the nearby valley. He was now waiting for his son who went to get a harnessed carriage for taking the wood to his house. As the conversation continued, he suggested we come over to his house for a few days, and he said that many of the people of Mizocz went to Horvi to hide. In the meantime, his son arrived with the cart and food. We then went with them to their house. In the evening, we arrived at a house that stood at the edge of the village. The farmer told us to stay next to the granary outside and that he would come to take us to the house after he put the children to bed.

[Page 56]

We sat next to the granary and waited. The hours passed by and the farmer was nowhere to be found. Different ideas popped into my mind. Who knows? Maybe he went to call the Germans in order to hand us over to them. Maybe he was sharpening an ax so he could murder us. But there was no choice. We did not have the strength to run away now. Finally, he appeared. We went into his house, had a big meal, and the farmer even set up sleeping space for us in the granary. We stayed four days in the granary and also got food. Eventually, it dawned on me that the farmer desired me and that Mark might pay with his life, so we decided to leave. On the fifth day, the farmer came and informed us that the "guys" were coming over that night and so it would be advisable to leave the village beforehand. We received from the farmer provisions for the trip, detailed instructions on how to get to the residencies of the Baptists, and a request to return to him any time we had difficulties. We kissed him and parted with him as friends. We found out later that the man was actually a dangerous horse thief, well–known from the underworld, but nevertheless, he treated us a lot better and nicer than the many others considered "decent".

On our journey, the Poles harassed us and threatened to rat us out to the Germans. I could not hold myself back and told them that they should at least, now that they had lost their independence to the Germans, treat us like human beings. The old Poles begged us not to argue with the young Poles and suggested that we escape quickly from the area. We returned to the forest, where we met Shlomo Steinberg with his two children, who were refugees in Mizocz. We were already five hunted people. Together we went to Kalinka and were joined there by the old Weltfreint couple from Katowice, who had been refugees in the Mizocz ghetto. Life, however, forced us to separate again. I met Shlomo Steinberg, who survived, after the liberation, but the Weltfreints were murdered. We heard from the gentiles in the surrounding area that not far from the town of Shumsk, there was a village called Andrushchovka populated with evangelicals who helped any Jews that came to them. We headed towards the village. One of the days we were at the village Feremarovka, we heard that the family of Mizocz's watchmaker was hiding in the nearby forest. This referred to Nahum Poliak. I found a farmer who knew exactly where they were residing, and he agreed to take me to them. My acquaintances wanted to dissuade me from going, but I decided to take the risk only so that I could meet Jews from Mizocz.

Incidentally, the guide felt at home in the forest. We walked a long way until we reached a cave. We entered the cave and found Nachum Poliak and his whole family. I hardly recognized them. Covered in soot, they were black like Africans. The cave was lit and heated with bonfires, and the family resembled people living in a grave. We spent the whole day sitting in the cave and telling our stories. We did not stop listening and storytelling until the farmer urged me to return to the village.

[Page 57]

During our wanderings, we met many of our acquaintances from Mizocz, and sometimes our group grew very large. We were especially invigorated by a group of refugees from Końskie who had been in the Mizocz ghetto.

One time, one of the Konskie refugees — his name was Ben–Zion — went with Mark to find bread for us and encountered Ukrainian murderers that killed them in cold blood. Our group dispersed out of fear, and I was left by myself.

Later, I once again met Nachum Poliak and his two daughters. He told me that their cave had been discovered and only he and his daughters survived the incident. I joined Nachum and his daughters and we hid in a village. One evening we were joined by two of the people from Konskie who had lived in the Mizocz ghetto, a man and a woman. His name was Gedaliya and her name was Bluma. A terrible storm was brewing outside and the farmer with whom we were hiding agreed that we would spend the night in his house. During the conversation, he told us that his son, who was a forest ranger, had adopted a Jewish girl that was found wandering the roads on the day of the destruction of the Mizocz ghetto. According to him, the name of the girl was Andazia, and she was from Konskie. Based on what the farmer said, Bluma understood that he was talking about her younger sister. And that was indeed who he was talking about. The farmer also told us that his son was visited by partisans, and we very much wanted to join the partisans. The farmer, however, did not easily agree to lead us all to the partisans. He first wanted to get explicit permission from the partisans' headquarters. We therefore decided to go to the partisans on our own. We went to the forest ranger and decided to trace his steps in order to find the partisans. During this period, Ukrainian Banderite partisans who also murdered Jews — not less efficiently and possibly more so than the Germans — also swarmed the forests, and great care was required in approaching the partisans. By chance, I happened then to meet with Miriam Trochlier. I learned from her that her son Baruch and his friend Yisroel Erlich were living in the forest and looking for weapons in order to join the partisans. According to her, the Rosenblatt brothers were also in the area. We eventually met, at the forest ranger's, with many Jews and also with the partisans. Among the partisans was a German officer called Stanislav who had defected from the army and joined the partisans. They said that he did so because of his communist opinions and views. The partisans, however, merely tolerated our presence near them. They did not allow us to join them, as they required in exchange for our joining many weapons, which we could not obtain. One bright day, the partisans disappeared and we were left alone and abandoned.

Once, when I stumbled again upon Feremarovka village and ended up at the house of an evangelist farmer, the farmer whispered in my ear that she was hiding another Jew. In the evening, we went to her pigsty, and answering her call, a terrible monster crawled out of a hidden hole. When he heard that I was a Jew, he stood up, began to stroke my hand, and in a strained voice mumbled incessantly:

[Page 58]

"You are a Jew! Another Jew is alive!" A revolting odor wafted from him, and he was dirty like the pigs in the pen. He told me that he was a ritual slaughterer from the nearby town and he had been living like this for several months. Then and there, I decided to take him with us. He caused us lots of trouble because he was not sound of mind and he prayed everywhere very loudly. He once went looking for Soviet partisans and ended up dying at the hands of Banderites.

On January 18th, 1944, the first of the Soviet soldiers arrived at the forest. On January 21st, we received a certificate from an officer of the regular army which said that we were Jews who were hiding in the forests of Slavuta and we were now being sent to the home front. They also brought us three horse–drawn wagons, provisions for the journey, and great relief. During those days, Shlomo Steinberg, with whom I had once hidden, joined us badly injured. The Soviet soldiers, who proceeded like a flowing stream, did not cause any difficulties for us during our journey. An officer once stopped us and told us to travel around a different path, as the path on which we were traveling was laden with mines. This thing — seemingly understandable and simple — brought me to tears; a few days ago we were like hunted animals and lo and behold, we were again human and there were people caring about our wellbeing. In the town of Krasnostav, we were stopped by an officer who told us to go to the school atop the nearby hill to see how a war criminal who had collaborated with the Nazis in the extermination of Jews was being tried for his crimes. When we entered the court, the mayor was testifying and he told of how the defendant with his own hands slashed the bellies of the Jewish children, crushed the heads of infants, and robbed and abused the Jewish civilians. He slammed the witness stand hard and shouted at the murderer: "how could you hand over our Jews to death for a kilogram of salt you got from the Nazis?" The murderer was condemned to death, and the sentence was carried out on the spot. We were present when he was hung, and we received much satisfaction from the death of the wicked man.

From there we reached Novohrad–Volynskyi. There was a serious military situation in the town. Nevertheless, the officer of the city provided us with a place to sleep. We could not and did not want to reach Kiev, as it was completely destroyed. We therefore went to Zhytomyr. We knew that a Jewish woman named Geskis lived there at 13 Snotzki Alley, and that many of the remaining Jews were living with her. We of course immediately went to this address and found an actual angel in the form of a woman. I had not seen a traditional Jewish home since the day we were imprisoned in the ghetto, and here, on a Friday, we had come to a house where candles were lit in gleaming silver candlesticks, the house was shining with cleanliness, and there were beautiful Jewish dishes on the table — and on top of all that, the house was full of Jewish survivors. In Zhytomyr, we underwent a medical exam. The badly wounded Shlomo was taken to a hospital and all of us received a little bit of money, clothes, and, most importantly, encouragement. After some time, jobs were also arranged for us. One time, I met Yaakov Gelman in the street. My emotions from the meeting ran high,

[Page 59]

even more so when I learned from him that my brother Mordechai was alive and that he was planning to head through Poland and Germany to the land of Israel. I immediately began to make preparations to go with the advancing Russian army to Poland. I enlisted with the army and made it to Berlin. Meanwhile, the war ended. I was discharged from the army and found among the living my relative Chaim Tzitzin. I married him and we got by in Germany. There, I connected with my brother who was in Austria, and after lots of wandering, we all met in our liberated country — in a Jewish nation.

The Sugar Factory in Mizocz

[Page 60]

Memories of a Partisan

by Yankev Mendyuk

Translated from Yiddish by Clair Padgett

I was twelve years old during the outbreak of the German-Polish war. At that time, I was in 5th grade at a Polish folk-school in Mizocz. My older sister Rokhl studied at the Tarbut[1] secondary school and my six-year-old younger brother, little Motl, was in kindergarten.

My parents had a nice manufacturing business in Mizocz, from which we earned enough money to take care of ourselves.

Soon after the fighting erupted, masses of refugees started arriving in Mizocz. We locals called them "*biezshentses*.[2]" Their numbers climbed day by day and we began to run low on basic products. The stores started running out and many of them closed. My father explained to me that we would also have to close our business since we could not travel to get more materials, given that all the trains were occupied by the military.

One Sunday, a rumor spread through town that the Russians were coming to aid Poland. People were saying that their troops were already in neighboring villages and that they would be in Mizocz at any minute.

There was a huge commotion. On hearing the news, everyone was out on the street and many went out to meet the Red Army with flowers in their hands.

My parents were among the few who were worried by the news, since they remembered well what happened in the 1920's, when, with the arrival of the Bolsheviks, Jews were beaten and their businesses ransacked.

But this time, the situation looked entirely different. The new Soviet regime disarmed the Polish police

[Page 61]

and declared that the war between Germany and Poland had ended, that western Ukraine would unite with Russia.

The Polish refugees then began returning to German occupied territories, and in their place, new Jewish refugees fleeing from German occupied Polish territories arrived.

The incoming refugees would tell horrific stories about how the Germans treated the Jews. They had recounted, among other things, how Jews were mugged by everybody. They were driven out of their homes and forced into hardship and agonizing labor. They had to wear yellow patches, could not come by basic goods, and were locked in ghettos. Jews were beaten and shot without rhyme or reason. The Jews of Mizocz received their fleeing brothers with open arms. And, although new refugees came to us daily, they all found shelter and work.

Meanwhile, the Soviets began to pillage the surviving businesses. They bought up everything possible and paid whatever price they were given. Watching them, old residents started hoarding too, and soon there was a general shortage. All of the businesses closed, and their owners started making efforts to acquire positions working under the Soviets. My father also liquidated his business and became an employee in the sugar factory, which had become nationalized.

In school, the Russian language replaced Polish. With the start of the school year, I became a sixth-grader. New teachers arrived and everything was re-arranged: a new language, new holidays, a new curriculum. Everything was new. In school, different social circles emerged. However, the children of business owners were not included. This caused plenty of anxiety for us children who were affected. In the midst of this, my father was establishing contacts with kinsmen in Russia and left Mizocz on a visit about three weeks before Germany invaded Russia.

[Page 62]

On Sunday, the 22 of June, 1941, for a second time a state of war was declared. This time, a war between Germany and Russia. Tuesday, the Russians started to evacuate Mizocz. The Jews, knowing what awaited them at the hands of *der daytch* (the Germans,) began to evacuate with the Red Army. Due to the hastiness of the Soviet's retreat and the resulting hardships, however, many of the evacuating Jews unfortunately returned to Mizocz. The Germans were upon us by Friday morning. The same day, the Russians heavily bombed the little town, and houses as well as the Orthodox Church were damaged. Some Jews, too, fell victim to the bombardment. The next Sunday, the Ukrainians began a pogrom against the Jews: masses of peasants came together from all of the surrounding villages, armed with axes, iron clubs, scythes and the like. They all inebriated themselves at the brewery and began to cut loose according to their custom. Houses were pillaged, several Jews were killed, and many more were wounded.

From that day on, we became strays. Not just the Germans, but the Ukrainians, too, did whatever they wanted with us.

Within a few weeks, the edicts began. First, the Germans ordered us to wear white patches on our right arms, then they changed the ordinance and told us to wear yellow patches. One in front on our right side, and one on our backs, between the shoulders. Children had to wear patches, too. I remember, as if it were today, how ashamed I was to walk out on the street with the patch, since my Polish friends would laugh at me and tease.

Before long the Germans established a Judenrat[3], with a Jewish police force armed with batons. Every day new taxes and laws were imposed on us. The Germans would make demands and the Judenrat would collect.

[Page 63]

The "HaShomer HaLeumi" on the day of the departure of Rachel Nemirover, the group's first immigrant to Israel

[Page 64]

Our family had remained together up to this point, except for my father, who was stuck with his kinsmen in Russia and could not come home.

In October 1941, I began to work in the sugar factory with several other Jews. We were tasked with the hardest work there was to do, and for this we were given 120 grams of bread, a few basic products and some money. Split among family members, we would get 30 grams of bread apiece.

At the start of 1942, the work at the factory ended and the Mizocz Ghetto was established. Our house fell within its boundaries. From all the surrounding hamlets, they gathered up the Jews and placed them in the ghetto. People lived in rooms, in attics, in cellars – it was cramped and stuffy everywhere. The Ukrainian police would often make searches in ghettos. They searched for arms and would take away anything they wanted. Meanwhile, they would beat and torment us. The 10th of January, 1942, the Germans ordered that 200 Jewish laborers be handed over. Before the workers had been supplied, they increased the number to 300. I was among those handed over. We were pushed 17 kilometers on foot towards Zdolbunov[4] , where there had already been a ghetto for over two months. Here we convinced ourselves that it was just like any other old town. In Mizocz, we had lived as though in paradise...

For work, we were organized in the middle street like horses. We were forbidden to go on the sidewalks. We had to remove our hats for every German and Ukrainian. With every mistake we were menaced with death. In the Zdolbunov Ghetto there were only women and children. The men were taken from them allegedly to work and had not returned. Those of us from Mizocz were located in the devastated and abandoned municipal synagogue, which laid within the domain of the ghetto. By night, we passed time on the wet stone in immense suffering and barely lived to see day.

6 a.m. after breakfast, which consisted of 40 grams of bread and a half-liter of black coffee, we left for work under the command of the German Joseph Jung. The working conditions were horrible.

[Page 65]

From 7 a.m. until noon, we had to work without stopping to catch a breath. Noon to 1 p.m. was lunch hour. Lunch consisted of a little bit of watery soup with some rotten, uncooked potatoes and 40 grams of bread. From 1 p.m. to 6 p.m. in the evening, we continued to work without resting, as if we were the worst of convicts. In the evening we had bread again, 40 grams of bread and a cup of black coffee. For pausing to catch a breath from work, we were given deadly blows.

Under the conditions, my sister Rokhl became terribly sick. The house was cold. There was no Jewish doctor there. A bit of fat or sugar was impossible to come by. Medicines were out of the question. My 8-year-old little brother would sneak out of the ghetto and go to work for a peasant in a village. For his work, he would bring home a bit of milk for sick Rokhl. We were sure that our Rokhl would not survive. But our neighbor, the old bonesetter Mr. Itzik Fliter, made a remedy for her and she became healthy.

I remained in forced labor far from home. In March, 80 Jews were driven from Zdolbunov to Rovne[5], and I was among them. In Rovne, we worked under the same command and the same doggish conditions as in Zdolbunov. In the once lively Jewish district of Rovne, over 6,000 Jews had lived in total. The majority of them were already liquidated. On "1 May Day" in 1942, the Gestapo ordered all the Jews to assemble at the regional commissioner's building in order to hear an important speech.

Various fantastic rumors soon spread in the ghetto. Some said that Hitler had reconsidered and was freeing the Jews from the ghetto, others said that something not so good was coming. Everyone waited for the uncertain morning. Our group was commanded at the time by the German engineer Grobe. He treated us decently and was generally not like other Germans. When the Jews from Rovne had to appear before the regional commissioner, he gave us leave and ordered us to go home.

[Page 66]

This had provoked suspicion in the Judenrat and they consulted with the Gestapo. Grobe got an order for us to immediately be called back to work and even before we arrived at home, we got the order immediately to return to Rovne. But we could not manage to follow this new order. We returned shortly afterwards, as the Rovne Jews were surrounded and loaded on railroad cars. The Gestapo and the Ukrainians were always after us, but Grobe defended us. The murderers succeeded in seizing only six Jews from our group. From our residence we saw how our Jewish brothers from Rovne were loaded into railroad cars like cattle. We heard their screams and cries, we saw and heard how they were shot and killed. We looked on as Engineer Grobe fought with the Gestapo for our lives. We saw the death before our eyes, and survived the resistance of the Rovne Jews.

The liquidation of the Rovne Jews went on the entire night, until they were driven away into the Kostopol forest[6] in the morning.

At 8 a.m. we were marched to work. Our group had grown a little larger and we were now numbered at a total of 100 men. We grew with the addition of 20 Jews saved from the slaughter in Rovne. Grobe transferred us back to Zdolbunov, since Jews were no longer permitted to be in Rovne: It was declared to be completely "*judenrein*.[7] "

I was put to work in Zdolbunov within four weeks. I lived at this time with a woman named Kitay. The Germans had taken her husband away as soon as they were inside Zdolbunov and she never saw him again. My strength began to leave me. The hard work, the awful diet, and the terrifying events I survived made a skeleton out of me. I was afflicted with a heart illness and I began to suffer from lethargy. My mother went to the Judenrat, and they gave them my father's holiday garments and obtained a month's leave for me. Afterwards, as they sent another to take my place, I was free to come back to Mizocz.

[Page 67]

The 24th of August 1942, soon after I came home, the Germans gave us a letter from my father. The letter had been sent out of the Russian state by the International Red Cross. At first, we were completely joyful, as this was the first bit of news we'd received from him since the war broke out. But soon anxiety and dread took the place of joy, and we began to live in permanent fear that the Germans would take us for communists and annihilate our family. However, they let us rest until the liquidation, which would come two months later. During my leave, fate had it that I would survive the denunciation of Zeyde Gelman by Shlomo Kniever, since he slaughtered a cow and sold the meat to the Jews. Gelman, as well as the farmer who had sold him the cow, were arrested, and both were threatened with death. There was a terrible panic in the ghetto. The peasants threatened everyone that if something happened to the peasant who had sold the cow, the Jews would never again get any kinds of basic goods from them. We soon raised money and the Judenrat proved successful in saving the peasant from the gallows. He got off with a little scare. Gelman, on the other hand, was hanged in the town square.

In early September, fugitive Jews from Dubno[8] came to us in the ghetto: Varkovitch and Yeziorani. Their ghetto was liquidated, and Dubno's borders were declared "judenrein." Zdolbunov now remained like an island in a raging sea, where Jews still lived for the time being.

At this time, the front was near Stalingrad[9] . We had no precise information about the situation. We only knew that if the Germans won, they would get drunk with victory and intensify their persecution of Jews. It was also bad when there were defeats at the front, since they would then take their anger out on the Jews.

[Page 68]

The High Holidays arrived unexpectedly. The situation turned hopeless. Not a ray of hope was left in the ghetto. Everyone came to the Rosh Hashanah prayer but no young people were seen there. All of them were working in foreign lands. Rabbi Lerner declared in his sermon that the work of the young people, who were not present for the prayers, was even more admirable than prayer since their labor saved the lives of many Jews.

On Yom Kippur eve, all Jews met in the synagogue, without exception. Even the small children and sick people. This time, people came to the synagogue at 3 p.m. because Jews were not allowed on the street after 6 p.m. Nobody really prayed – just sobbed and lamented. Everyone had someone to mourn or someone to plead for. I remember the sermon by the rabbi's son-in-law, Mr. Shimen Berkowski, as if it were yesterday. He compared us to a flock of sheep, some of which were marked with dye and did not know what the marks had in store for them. He also compared us to a cuckoo, who has no nest of her own and slips her eggs under other birds … we interpreted his words and were comforted a little. We believed that we could obtain salvation through pleading and prayer.

* * *

On the night of October 12 and 13, 1942, a powerful division of the German military and Ukrainian police surrounded Mizocz ghetto. That day, at 4 a.m., I needed to march with a group to work in Zdolbunov. However, they would not let us out. We immediately alarmed all of the residents, and within a minute the town stood weak on its feet. I remember how we were then covered by a thick fog. It seemed as though heaven was trying to protect us. Some Jews began to make for the ghetto boundaries to crawl out of the criminal siege. The fallen did not deter us because it was clear that, either way, death was unavoidable. Others, in turn, began to set fire to their houses so that they would not fall into the hands of the enemy.

[Page 69]

Around 8 a.m., the German police, S.S, Gestapo, and a great many Ukrainian policemen marched into the ghetto. They demanded that all Jews, without exception, should grab three days' worth of food and gather in the market, from which they would be marched to a train for "*relocation.*" Everyone already knew what *"relocation"* meant to the Germans. My mother gathered her children to her and said, with much pain, that we had to go with all the other Jews. But to me, a secret force whispered, "Don't give in. Fight for your life." I tried reasoning with my mother that we should hide. She didn't want to hear a word of it. I told her then that she wouldn't be so easy-going watching us as we were shot. Our father was alive in Russia and we children would try to save ourselves. With great effort I succeeded in changing the minds of my sister and brother so that they would come with me. I could not persuade my mother. We took my mother and went to my uncle, Hirsh Reznik, who was a cantor in the big synagogue. When we reached him, he was wearing his prayer shawl and tefillin, reciting psalms. Our great grandmother and her family were in his house. We said goodbye to all of them and looked upon our dear mother for the last time before going away to the hideout. Our hideout was in our house, well-hidden between two thick walls. The entrance was a concealed door in the corner of the attic. There were ten of us in there, almost all of us juveniles. There was no place to sit, and all of us stood pressed together like herrings in a barrel. In the streets, the wild cries of the mobsters came to our attention: the Ukrainian "*heyda!*", the German "*Jewish swine!*". Later, we heard the shooting, the weeping, and shuddered at the screaming of tortured Jews. That is how Tuesday, the 13th of October ended.

Wednesday the Germans started to pillage the remaining houses in the ghetto and stole whatever they wanted. We remained in the hideout. Thursday the Germans allowed the Ukrainians to finish the work of plundering the ghetto. These last ones came into the ghetto in big groups and, with crowbars and axes, hacked at the walls, ripped up the floors, and axed the furniture to find hidden Jewish property.

[Page 70]

Looking for things to steal, Ukrainian murderers found the hideout in the attic of our neighbors, the Branstein family. They soon brought Germans in, who blew the hideout up using grenades and strangled all of the survivors. We heard everything from our hiding place and stood terrified.

Friday the hunger really started to prey on us. Our legs were clabbered and we began to envy those who were already resting in their graves. That night two of us – a mother and a son – abandoned the hideout. I still don't know what happened to them. Saturday, the 17th of October, rain fell the entire day. Everyone's feet were swollen from hunger and from standing in splitting agony. At 1 o'clock my little brother and I abandoned the hideout. My sister was completely exhausted and could not come with us. The rain was still pouring. Creeping on all fours (we were afraid to walk like human beings) we crawled all the way to the river. Suddenly two Ukrainians appeared out of nowhere, as if they had popped up out of the earth. They had been lying in wait for Jews and blocked our way. I began begging them, weeping, trying to win them over, but nothing helped. They accused us of setting fire to Mizocz and said that we would have to go with them to the Germans. One grabbed me by the arm while the other held on to my coat and dragged me by force. I called to my brother telling him to escape to a farmer that we knew and try to save himself. However, he wanted to stay with me and share the same fate. I screamed at him and demanded him to run away. At this point, he threw himself into the river and began to swim. One of the thugs tried to catch my little brother and I tore myself away from the second, leaving a strip of my coat in his hand. Then both started to pursue me. With no other way out, I copied my brother and jumped into the water. It was already very cold and the thugs didn't feel like bathing.

[Page 71]

"Brit HeChayal" and "Beitar[10] " in Mizocz

[Page 72]

That is how I saved myself from their hands. I did not find my brother on the other side and have not seen him since.

I climbed up to a Ukrainian village not far from Mizocz. In the fields stood wet bales of grain. I crawled into one of them and collapsed like a corpse, exhausted. Sleep was impossible. The fate of my loved ones would not let me rest.

In the morning, farmers came with pitchforks to turn over the wet straw and drug me out half-dead. They led me into a small house where I came upon three more Jews from Mizocz. It was Hirshke Gantzberg and Ida Eisengart along with her brother-in-law. They had arrived here in a similar way. These Ukrainians loyally served the Germans and handed incoming Jews over to the Gestapo.

Our entreaties and arguments for them to free us had no effect. Only when we gave away the money and jewelry that we had managed to take with us did they let us go.

We escaped to the nearby forest and did not have time to hide before dozens of peasants came running after us. The thugs that had taken our money and jewelry in return for not denouncing us had still gone through the entire town spreading the word that four Jews were hiding out in the woods. Given that the Germans would give out salt and sugar for every Jew handed over, there was no shortage of enthusiastic volunteers ready to kidnap Jews. We were quickly surrounded and had nowhere to run. Hirshke Gantzberg and I risked our lives jumping into a deep trench where people crushed stones to make lime. Ida Eisengart and her brother-in-law were caught by the bandits. From the ditch we heard the murderers torture them to find out where we were. They searched for us for a long time. Only when night fell did they leave the woods. Late in the evening we got out of the trench with difficulty and headed for the Oyezdtse, a town with a Czech population.

[Page 73]

We had believed we'd find something to eat there, but unfortunately people did not want to give us anything, even when we offered them money. Here and there we were able to wheedle out a bit of bread. We only avoided dying of hunger thanks to the beets, potatoes, or little bit of fruit that we found in the fields and gardens. We slept on straw in the fields or out in the underbrush. After many days of that kind of living, we got used to it and adapted to the situation. We got our hands on an axe and a small cart. By night we would pry open warehouses and take bread, meat, fruit and other necessities. We didn't miss eating anymore, but we had to move around frequently.

When it became dangerous to go through Aynsbrukh near Mitlen we decided to go into Mizocz at night to find some of our valuables buried during our time in the ghetto.

After some due preparation, we got under way. Mizocz was a total of eight kilometers ahead of us. Late at night we cautiously entered the town and approached our house. Our apartment looked like a ruin. It terrified me; all of its doors and windows were torn out. An emptiness hovered in its rooms. The furniture was chopped to pieces, the floor ripped open, and the feathers from the pillows and bed covers were scattered everywhere. It was clear that the ransacking was exhaustive. However, we were successful in finding our jewelry and our silver tableware.

We left the town with our property. For the silver, we got six big rolls and spent an entire week laying in a field without having to move.

One day we were recognized by a farmer that we had known and he described to us exactly how our community had met its fate.

[Page 74]

He told us that the Jews from Mizocz had all been rounded up and forced into graves prepared for them near the pine grove and that the Germans had ordered them to undress and lay themselves out side by side. Once this was done, they were shot to pieces, and the Jews that were standing in line were forced to lay themselves over those that had already been shot. Those that were not shot to death were buried alive in these pits.

My teacher, the assimilated Jenia Schisel, had worked in the ghetto as a translator under the commissioner. Before her death, she had asked to be allowed to go into the grave not naked, but with her shirt on. But this last request of hers was refused. This farmer also knew how my sister and little brother met their end. According to him, my sister was successful in reaching Karp Parpeniuk, a farmer who still owed us money from before the war. She stayed in his house for a while and was eventually shot in his yard. After separating from me, my brother little Motl ran to some peasants that we knew, who hid him in a pig pen. When his legs became frostbitten and he could no longer walk, the peasants submitted him to a hospital. The doctor had immediately recognized that the child was Jewish and informed the Germans. When the police came to take him away, he resisted and begged them to spare his life. They promised him that he was just going to be driven to another hospital and would not be shot. He still did not want to go with them. At that point they forced him out into the hospital's courtyard and shot him.

The night I heard this story from the farmer's mouth, Committee persevered as I had on the night of the liquidation. The extermination of my little brother hurt most of all, and I wept long and hard.

The entire time we were in the woods, we had not changed our clothes or taken the boots off of our feet. Our feet became completely swollen and we often could not walk. With great difficulty, we reached a village.

[Page 75]

With my mother's jewelry, we got bread and fat. We turned back into the woods, crawled into a hole, took off our boots, and began to smear the fat over our swollen feet.

During the next few days, we were able to march. We heard from different sources that there was still a Jewish ghetto in Warsaw and we chose to head that way. We got to Zdolbunov by foot and snuck into a freight train that had to pass through our destination. We made it to Kovel safely and hoped that we would reach Warsaw. Unfortunately, we were discovered at the train checkpoint in Kovel[11] . They caught us and began to escort us to the Gestapo. On the way we both cursed the moment it had occurred to us to escape our destiny. We both said it would have been much better to die with everyone else in Mizocz than in some unfamiliar place after enduring so much pain. I was reminded of my mother's parting words to me, that trying to escape our fate would not be worth it ... and I chose, once again, to escape. I told this to Gantzberg and confessed to him that death could never arrive too late.

When we were over the railroad bridge in Kovel, I did not think long before jumping out. I took as much air in as I could with one breath. They shot and called out and tried to chase after me, but I escaped my persecutors. Now I remained alone. I lost my friend, who I had lived through so many hard days with. I was lonely, tired, and despondent in an unfamiliar place. Walking through the alleys of Kovel, people watched me go by, pointing, "There goes a Jew!". I don't look particularly Jewish, but my shredded clothes, my tired colorless face, and the terror that shone through my eyes had plainly unmasked me. I quickly understood that the town of Kovel was no place for me, and I went over to the nearby hamlets. I could pass for a Ukrainian and hoped to find work from a farmer. Nobody, however, wanted to take me in.

[Page 76]

Firstly, it was already late fall and there wasn't any work left. Secondly, people demanded documents, which I didn't have. I decided to wander around in the woods and wait for a miracle.

One day, walking through the forest, I heard the command *"Stoi, ruki vu vierch."* (Don't move- hands up!) It was the 24th of November, 1942. I turned around and saw that I was surrounded by 15 people, all armed with guns. I raised my hands and one of them immediately searched me. A thick snow had fallen and I trembled from dread and from the cold. I was sure that this time the end had finally come for me. One of them asked who I was, but I couldn't answer. My tongue was paralyzed. Before they blindfolded me, I could tell that my assailants were not people from any military unit, since they all wore different clothes. I was walking for a long time with my eyes covered, being led by two people. From their conversation I understood that they were partisans. We finally came to a halt. They uncovered my eyes and led me into an earth hut. An old man with a large moustache and small beard was sitting in the corner. He was clothed in an old fur coat, and wore a belt with a Lange pistol hanging off of it. He contemplated me for a moment and said loudly "Tell me who you are, you German spy".

"No!" I contested, "I'm not a spy. I'm a Jew from the town Mizocz, near Rovne. I escaped death. They murdered my elders, brothers and sisters. I saw them bury Jews alive and I went in search of the partisans so that I could take my revenge on the Germans." The commander thought a little and said to me "I'll take you in as a partisan, but remember, you are a Jew to me and nobody else".

I knew right away what he meant and I remained... as a Ukrainian. I knew the Ukrainian language perfectly well. I didn't look like a Jew and the performance proved successful. Given that I was the youngest in the detachment, they tasked me with working in the kitchen.

[Page 77]

From then on, I didn't want for any food, clothes, or place to rest my head. Our division was called *"Za Rodinu"* (For the Fatherland) and numbered 150 fighters. The commander was named Fiodorov, and the fighters had mostly come from defeated regiments of the Red Army. Some were also runaways who had been in German captivity. With time, I became familiar with partisan life and learned how to handle guns.

I liked the partisans and I really wanted to take part in the action. I wanted to avenge the innocent Jewish blood that had been spilt.

The commander did not want to use me for military undertakings, and only after pressure from my friends, did he relent and let me take part in partisan operations.

* * *

In the little town of Tseglov[12] , some German policemen pulled up to collect a consignment of goods. They compiled cows, pigs, grain and other products from the peasants. Everything was being brought together under the provision of the Polish clergy, from which mobilized peasant wagons had to drive everything to Kovel by morning. We got the job of liquidating the Germans and preventing the shipments from leaving town. A strong snowstorm was rampaging outside. It was almost impossible to move.

Following the plan, we marched in a group of 60 men to carry out the assignment. Coming into the hamlet, we split off into three groups. The first group was made up of 15 men and had the job of patrolling the town and its environs, cutting the telephone lines. The second group, which had 20 men, surrounded the place where the German unit was stationed. The third group, which was composed of 25 men, and was where I found myself, came close to their guard posts and left three soldiers dead.

[Page 78]

The Germans had not expected such a bold ambush and in a matter of minutes we commanded the warehouse and stalls. Meanwhile, the German unit, which found itself in the priest's house, realized what was happening and a heated fight broke out between our forces. We demanded the Germans to surrender and they answered with a heavy fire. This left us with no choice but to blow up the house together with the Germans.

Our commander Bandorenka turned to me then and said, "You are the youngest and smallest in our group. Here is a bottle of gasoline, matches, grenades, and a revolver. You need to crawl up close to the house, douse the walls with gasoline and set a fire. Then you can throw a grenade or two into the house. The revolver is for special situations." They adorned my ears with a white pelt, then I went over my task, took up the tools, and crawled over to the house. The house was built of wood, the walls were frozen and wet, and all over the doors and windows were shot up by the *"Fritzes."* (The Russians would call the Germans *"Fritzes."*) I was successful in crawling close to the house but soon realized that setting it on fire would not be easy. I pulled a grenade out of my pocket, removed the pin and threw it in a window. Seeing that my grenade had provoked confusion among the *Fritzes*, and that they had not even ceased shooting from one window, I crawled up to the house to sneak into an entryway, doused it well in gasoline and set it on fire. To my surprise, the entire house was soon engulfed in flames and the Germans were forced to abandon it. They then came up against our second group, who opened fire on them. Seeing that they were being attacked from both directions, and believing that we were everywhere in large numbers, they surrendered.

[Page 79]

That day seemed as though it were the best day of my life. I was glad and proud that I had managed to carry out the orders. The amassed goods set aside for the Germans were handed over to us by the peasants. Their losses totaled 18 dead, 24 wounded and 16 captured. In addition, we took eight machine guns, 20 rifles, 15 automatic rifles, 12 revolvers and thousands of bullets. In short, we returned to our base with valuable property and captives.

The military tribunal that the captives faced sentenced them to death for setting fire to the houses in Tseglov and for slaughtering a large part of the local population.

I had volunteered to be among those carrying out the sentence. When the commander gave the order "Fire!", I did so screaming out loud: for my sister, for my little brother, for my mother and for everyone in Mizocz I put several bullets in those Germans. And I shot them using their own gun.

* * *

From that day forward, an important change took place in my life. I started becoming a valuable member of the detachment. My partisan comrades started looking at me differently. They began to like me and take me into account. I started to feel less like an imposition and more like an authorized member.

The days ran by in a continuous struggle with the Germans. One day when Commander Fiodorov called us together, he told me: "you are Yankev Mendyuk, but everyone calls you 'Vanka.' Because you outwitted the Germans, I'll give you a last name, 'Makhliuk.'" Going forward, I was officially and unofficially named Vanka Makhliuk.

My single best friend during this time was either the automatic gun or the Luger pistol that I had taken from the Germans. I couldn't part with them for a minute.

[Page 80]

In springtime, 1943, our unit greatly increased in size. The German assault was broken in Stalingrad and Moscow. Their persecution became merciless and we created a new partisan unit with the name "Chapaiev".

On the 16th of April, 100 men from our unit (myself among them) received the orders to cross over into Poland in order to strengthen a local partisan branch called Dzerzhinsky. The group was led by a hero from the Soviet Union, who we called Charni (the black). We set out on our goal, losing 20 men on the way through side battles and joined the Dzerzhinsky unit, which was in the Rudnitsky woods near Vengrov[13] at the time. I knew Polish and fit in easily. They just changed my name from Makhliuk to Makhliak to sound more Polish.

I became involved in the intelligence group. Although it was much more difficult and dangerous than the military regiment, I put all my effort into carrying out my responsibilities.

Our task consisted of preventing German reinforcement along the Eastern front and recruiting more Poles into the partisan ranks. In my group, which was made up of 30 men, I passed myself off as a Pole. Our area of activity took up the Podlias territory and a part of the Lublin region. We had contacts and connections with people working for the Germans. Many of them used to help us, especially by laying mines in the roads. These were some of the same Poles who worked the railroads. I became interested in the fate of the Jews and came by different bits of information about them. There wasn't a ghetto any more. The Jews had all been deported. On rare occasions they were still found working, as so-called "useful Jews." I heard about the uprising in the Warsaw Ghetto. During the "deportation" of the Shedlits[14] Ghetto, the Germans handed over 180 Jews to work on the railroad.

[Page 81]

In May 1943, all of them were taken to the Jewish cemetery and massacred. A small group of Jews worked in Radzim[15] in the carpentry and lockmaking workshop under the local Gestapo. I was successful in establishing contact with them. Being aware of the fate of the Jews from Shedlits, I took great efforts and arranged for some of them to join us in our detachment. In Sokolov Podlaski[16], the Germans constructed an alternate railway which headed towards Treblinka. With this route they used to carry military cars full of "deported" Jews and drop them off in Treblinka. It was said that there the Germans had special facilities where they would kill thousands of people at a time. Afterwards, they removed the victims' skin and fat and made soap from it.

In late September 1943, our unit was stationed in the hamlet Karchov, 20 km from Sokolov. We were informed that a train carrying Jews had stopped at the Sokolov station. The train was decorated with flowers and was especially guarded. Various slogans were written on the sides of the train and it was headed in the direction of Treblinka.

Our members soon chose to hold up the train, liquidate the German guards and free the Jews. Afterwards we would inform them where they were being transported.

In order to execute this task, my unit went out in a group of 200 men. We stopped the train 20 kilometers outside of Treblinka by blowing up the rails with grenades. When the train came to a halt, a harsh battle broke out between the German guard and our unit. After the tough and bloody conflict, in which we lost 12 fighters, we took control of the situation. The transport consisted of 600 Jews, Czech citizens. It was very difficult to communicate with them, since none of them spoke any Polish or Russian. We quickly understood that they were all engineers and that they had been sent to the east in order to re-establish industries ruined by the war.

[Page 82]

The Polish Folk-School in Mizocz- almost all of the students are Jewish

[Page 83]

Interestingly, they were so fooled by the German propaganda that they had taken their instruments and technical manuals with them. They had even arranged an orchestra with a buffet in the car...

When we told them that only 20 kilometers away stood the death camp Treblinka, where Jews were murdered night and day and Germans made soap from their fat, they didn't believe us. Only when we told them to get a good whiff of the air and take in the smell of death did they begin to understand. They then set fire to the train and scattered as best they could. Some of the young people came along with our division.

After that bit of work, the Germans brought in the Ukrainian "Galician" Division, as well as Polish police, to stabilize the situation. They began a sweeping campaign to end the runaway engineers and exterminate the partisans. During the course of that week, we had endless clashes with larger German forces and many of our members were killed or wounded.

* * *

I remember a beautiful sunny day in July. We hid ourselves near the village Yablone, planning to wait it out there. However, we quickly realized that we were surrounded on all sides. There were 80 of us, many of which were wounded. An unbalanced fight ensued, for life or death. Our ranks were sparsely scattered and we no longer had anything to defend ourselves with. With superhuman strength we stood our ground until nightfall. Of the entire unit, only twelve managed to tear themselves out of the iron chain with which the enemy had encircled us. We went into Yablone and quickly blended in with the locals.

[Page 84]

I could have audaciously stayed in that village as a Pole and lived peacefully. I even had the right documents. My conscience, however, would not let me rest. My blood boiled and demanded revenge on the Germans, as much as possible. I met with my Polish friends and we chose to continue the fight in a new partisan unit.

We went into the Garvolin forest[17] and came across a partisan group which belonged to the A.K.[18] The commander, "Zhbik" welcomed us warmly as Poles who left the Soviet units and came together to fight with our Polish brothers.

After a few weeks of membership with the A.K., I was incorPorted into the second corps of military intelligence stationed in Lionke by Warsaw. My life became dangerous at this point. It wasn't the work itself that posed a threat, but the danger of being exposed by my comrades as a Jew. I was especially afraid that in my sleep, a Yiddish word might pop out of my mouth. A terrible hatred of Jews ran rampant in the A.K division, and the life of a Jew was not worth a dime. There were times when I discovered other Jews among the members, but I was scared of letting myself be discovered through association with them. It's possible that they felt the same.

Bit by bit we became the real sovereigns of the eastern part of Warsaw and its surroundings. Our influence was so great that we would attack the Germans in broad daylight.

At that point I saw the ruins of the Warsaw Ghetto. My hatred of the Germans was once again inflamed. Walking down the street, I always carried a gun and was ready for anything.

Once, walking in Praga down a street in Mokotow[19] with a suitcase full of literature, some Volks-Deutschen began harassing me, telling me to give them money since I was a Jew. My arguments and protests were of no use, and they began to drag me to the Gestapo. I hastily turned around, pulled out my revolver, and laid them out dead. I took off gladly, and left Esk(?) in peace.

[Page 85]

These money-hungry gangs, which were employed by the Germans, used to roam Poland, menacing Jews in hiding with the threat of death.

Something similar happened another time I was walking down Skarzhevski street in Prage[20] , across from the employment exchange, with a couple of comrades from my unit. Two girls, around 16 or 17 years old, were going to the employment exchange to enroll for work in Germany. They were detained by a German gendarme and a Polish policeman. Their documents were in order. One of them, however, looked like a Jewish kid. The policemen immediately stood them against a wall and shot two blanks at them. One screamed *"Oy vey iz mir!"* the other "Jesus and Mary!" The thugs, seeing their suspicions confirmed, executed the Jewish girl on the spot. We had stood by and watched the entire thing unfold. As soon as the girl collapsed, we took out our revolvers and laid the policemen out dead beside her.

My senses evolved drastically. I would detect a threat like a trained animal. In addition, I was careful never to forget the Sunday prayers in church and always wore a cross around my neck.

1944 was a year of heavy persecution by the Polish people. We received the orders to mercilessly liquidate the collaborators and informers working with the Germans and to recruit more men.

At the beginning of 1944, Gauleyter Kutchner, the well-known executioner and murderer from the Warsaw Ghetto, was assassinated on Unia Lubelska Square[21].

About a month later, we carried out a risky assault on an armored car which was carrying 10 million zloty from Krakow to Warsaw. The attack, which I took part in, occurred on Senatorska Street[22]. It made a strong impression on the entire country.

[Page 86]

The Germans promised a reward of 5 million zloty for information about the participants in the attack. Despite the frequent searches and arrests that the Germans were making in Warsaw, our activity expanded and intensified.

On the 17th of July, 1944, since I was born in Volhynia[23], I was moved to the Lublin station, the 127th Volyn division of the A. K.

The news from the front was very good: The Red Army was already standing at the gates of Poland. The invasion from the Allies in France had methodically unfolded and the Germans grew weaker day by day. We were also pursuing the retreating German army from the east and we caused serious losses.

On the 28th of July, 1944, the Red Army made it into Liubartov (Lubartow), which was 28 kilometers from Lublin.

Our unit, which numbered 250 men, was transferred to Lublin in order to take over the powers that be in the freed city. We were, however, disarmed by the Soviets there. A big part of our group took flight and the rest of us were arrested and put in the city castle, which had served as a jail during the German occupation. The Russians treated us as though we were enemies. They treated us very badly – they were brutal and pitiless.

I once called for Soviet officers to tell them that I was actually a Jew, and that I had only fought with the A.K. in order to save my life, but they paid no attention to me.

We were forced to carry out various difficult and unpleasant kinds of work. For example, exhuming people murdered by the Germans or, inversely, burying those that were killed during the German retreat and had not been buried.

In two weeks, a Polish committee under the direction of a major unexpectedly arrived in our prison in order to recruit volunteers among us for the front.

[Page 87]

The major was a Jew, and I told him how I came to be in the A.K. He took a strong interest in me and dispatched me to work in Lublin's district office. There, as an ex-partisan and worker with the U.B. (security service), I advanced as a second lieutenant.

At the end of August, 1944, I was dispatched to Shedlits (Siedlce), to the chief of the investigative service's office under the government's security division. There I had the opportunity to send hundreds of Jew-murderers and other German saboteurs and agents to rest eternally in their graves.

An important section of the ex-A.K. members, who were not happy with the new democratic order in Poland, became involved with the nationalist N.S.Z.[24] and they continued their underground fight. This time, however, it was against the new Polish order and the Red Army.

Though they had been successful in escaping German hands and surviving concentration camps, prisons, and cruel torture, respected democratic leaders fell by their murderous hands.

The first of November, 1944, an unsuccessful assassination attempt was carried out on me as well. I knew that I would pay for my office sooner or later with my life, and I realized the time was right to mobilize myself in the army, where I would offer my life in order to take the revenge that was due to all of the Jewish enemies and contemptible fascists.

The 3rd of January, 1945, I was admitted into the intelligence service of the second regiment in the third division and took active part in the fight in Warsaw.

The 11th of January, we received the order to fetch, for any price, a "tongue" (a living German captive.) On a pitch-black night, when it was difficult to see even up close, I went off with a group of soldiers to carry out the order.

[Page 88]

We put ourselves into two boats and, as quietly as possible, began floating through the Vistula river to the German shore. We moved very slowly, step by step. Every minute lasted an eternity and we were unnoticed approaching approximately 20 meters from the bank. Then, an accident occurred and one of our soldiers unwillingly let loose a grenade in the water. The German patrol heard the splash in the water and lit up our surroundings. It was the end of us. A fiery hail rained down over our heads and our sapper, who was sitting at the helm of my boat, had already fallen dead. Having no other way out, we went into the water. In one hand I held my rifle, and with the other, I fought against the strong January current.

Through some incomprehensible miracle, three of us made it to the bank completely frozen and utterly exhausted. The bank was in enemy hands. Within a few steps we stumbled upon the bodies of our comrades who had fallen on the first days of September 1944, trying to create a foothold right by Siski.

We quickly laid ourselves out among the dead and stayed there from dawn until late at night. As if to spite us, the night made itself bright and starry and there was no talk of going back. We had to wait another day. Perhaps the second night would make it possible to go back. Laying among the dead, we closely observed the Germans' movements. A strong wind blew and it was hard to keep our eyes open.

We nevertheless saw how a group of Germans moved forward carrying grenades. In front walked a sapper who cleared the way for them. Soon they were walking right next to us.

About an hour later we heard approaching footsteps. It was the German sapper, who had already brought the soldiers to their destination and was coming back.

[Page 89]

We remembered well our pledge to bring back a "'tongue" and we decided that this was the time to do it. As soon as the sapper came close to us, we used the last of our strength to throw ourselves on him, stop up his mouth, and told him that if he did not follow our orders, he would face a horrible death. He surrendered. We steered him to the shore and with his help made a raft out of planks bound together with wire. We then bound the German and laid him on the raft. We were the only ones in the water and we pushed the raft forward. When the water became deeper, we held on to the raft with one hand and swam with the other.

Our unit arrived half-unconscious but happy. They thought they had lost us and had even performed prayers for our soul. Our deed was highly praised and the eight of us (five dead and three surviving) were awarded with the "Virtuti Militari[25]" cross, 4th class.

The winter offensive on the eastern front began. Our regiment had progressed onward in endless battles. When we arrived in German territory, my pain was renewed, feelings of revenge were awoken and I paid the German murderers according to the old law: A tooth for a tooth. An eye for an eye…

While taking the city of Kolberg[26], our regiment endured heavy losses. Half a battalion fell, and among them many young Jewish men.

Here I want to mention and honor all of the unknown Jewish heroes who fell for the dignity of our people, taking vengeance on the German murderers. Their bones rest in the mass grave, together with their brave Christian friends. I would especially like to mention my good friend and hero Moyshe Klugman from 'Ianov Lubelski', who always remembered and served the Jewish people with honor. May the earth be easy on him.

The 4th of May, 1945, standing at the gates of Berlin, I was seriously wounded by shrapnel. I lost two fingers and was paralyzed in my left leg.

[Page 90]

For three months I lay in a hospital and when I was discharged in Lublin after the victory over Hitler, I was greatly disappointed that it was not destined for me to go into the nest of my enemies as a victor in the cursed, brown Berlin.

Footnotes:

1. Secular Hebrew language school..
2. A Yiddish word for refugees, implying they were bedraggled or in bad shape.
3. A Judenrat was a World War II administrative agency imposed by Nazi Germany on Jewish communities across occupied Europe, principally within the Nazi ghettos. The Germans required Jews to form a Judenrat in every community across the occupied territories. (Source: Wikipedia.)
4. Zdolbunov, a town near Mizocz. Current map reference Zdolbundiv.Ukraine.
5. Rovne, nearest city near Mizocz, 16 miles away. Current map reference, Rivne, Ukraine
6. Between July 13th and 14th, 1942, the last remaining 5,000 Jews in the Rovno Ghetto were gathered for liquidation, transported to the forest near Kostopol and murdered. In November, 1941, 15,000-18,000 Jews from Rovno were murdered in the Sosenski Forest. 2,000-3,000 Jews were murdered in the months following the German' arrival in June 1941. (JewishGen: Rowne Victims Killed in the Kostopol Forest
7. Nazi designation for areas cleansed of Jews, referring to areas in which the Jewish population was deported or exterminated. (Source: Jewish Virtual Library.)
8. Dubno, a town 18 miles west of Mizocz.
9. Stalingrad. Current map reference, Volgograd, Russia. The Battle of Stalingrad turned to tide of the war in favor of the Russians.
10. Betar is a Zionist Youth Movement founded in 1923. Members received paramilitary training in anticipation of the need to defend themselves in Palestine. In WWII, many Betar members joined British forces, and those remaining in their communities joined partisan groups.
11. Kovel is a town on the rail line leading to Lublin and Warsaw. The current map reference is in northwest Ukraine.
12. Tseglov, Current map reference Tsehiv, in northwest Ukraine.
13. Vengrov. Current map reference Wêgrów, in eastern Poland.
14. Shedlits. Current map reference Siedlce, Poland.
15. Radzim. Ccurrent map reference Radzymin, Poland.
16. Skoklov Podlaski. Current map reference Sokołów Podlaski, 80 km east of Warsaw.
17. The town Garwolin is 62 km SE of Warsaw.
18. A.K, Armia Krajowa (Home Army) was the dominant resistance movement in German-occupied Poland during World War II. (Wikipedia)
19. Mokotów is a district within Warsaw.
20. Praga. A historic area in Warsaw on the eastern bank of the Vistula River.
21. A square in Warsaw, plac Unii Lubelskiej.
22. .Senatorska , a street in Warsaw
23. Volhynia is the province within which Mizocz is located, also spelled Wolyn, Volin.
24. N.S.Z., Narodowe Siły Zbrojne.
25. The War Order of Virtuti Militari is Poland's highest military decoration for heroism and courage in the face of the enemy at war. It was created in 1792 by Polish King Stanislaus II Augustus and is the oldest military decoration in the world still in use. (Source: Wikipedia)
26. Kolberg. Current map reference Kołobrzeg, Poland, coastal city on the Baltic Sea.

[Page 90]

The Judenrat in Mizocz
Had a High Moral Standard, But…

(From Yehuda Braunstein's Letter to Reuven Melamed)

Translated from Hebrew by Corey Feuer and Yonatan Altman-Shafer

…Well done on your decision to commemorate our town Mizocz with a memorial book. You all are doing a great deed. I am not able to return to that period of horrors even in my thoughts, and to write memories means to return to and to relive those dark days – days of nightmares, anxiety, and humiliation. I will deliver only a few impressions and some knowledge on the last two or three years of the life of the beloved Mizocz:

The Soviet Occupation

As everybody knows, the Soviets conquered Mizocz without war; when the Polish army was crushed at the hands of the Germans and Poland's fate was already determined, battalions of the Red Army entered eastern Polish territory and took western Ukraine and western Belarus with almost no resistance. Many of the Jewish refugees that had fled from the Germans to cities surrounding us did not return to their homes and their cities, which were under Hitler's rule, and stayed to live among us. Our town Mizocz contained 3,500 Jews; during the Soviet occupation, it contained 5,500 Jews. This large growth came thanks to the many refugees who settled among us. A great many of the refugees were arrested after some months, while they were sleeping, as was usual among the Soviets, and they were taken to Siberia in freight cars since they refused to accept Soviet citizenship. This heavy punishment that the poor refugees suffered, however, saved them in the end from a life in hell on earth during the days of Hitlerite control. And about 50 percent of them from death.

Mizocz shifted and changed until it was unrecognizable; the stores disappeared, commerce went dead, the residents wore gloom on their faces, and worry gnawed at their hearts.

All the Jews managed to get a job with the authorities. They did it not so much for the salary as for the sake of obtaining the coveted status of being a decent citizen…

[Page 91]

After efforts, I too got an accounting position at the sugar factory as a talisman against imprisonment and expulsion to Siberia.

The occupiers treated the Jews with much more trust than they treated the Ukrainians because while the latter dreamed of national independence that they would achieve with help from the Germans, the Jews far preferred the Soviet rule to the situation of war, and some of them preferred the Soviet control even to the collapsed Polish rule.

Little by little, all the Jews adapted to the situation and integrated into the new life of the town while the Ukrainians plotted and watched for Hitler. And here their dream became reality. Germany attacked Russia.

The Days of Horror Under the German Whip

It is easy to imagine the panic that arose among us as a result of the new war. Us Jews were shrouded in gloom and worry while the Ukrainians were rejoicing and happy because here comes Hitler, and not only is he releasing them from the rule they resent, but he is also bringing them national independence. After a little while, they were indeed convinced that they were deceived and that it did not even occur to Hitler to grant Ukraine independence. Hitler kept his promise to them, however, with regards to at least one thing: the Jews were left at their mercy, and they were allowed to participate fully in the Jews' destruction.

Immediately after the German entry into Mizocz, the Gentiles from the surrounding villages organized a massacre of Jews. At the head of the rioters stood Yarmaliuk from the village of Darman. Yarmaliuk, who was known to be a communist, and during the time of the Soviets was close to the leadership, apparently wanted to atone for this sin with Jewish blood. He wounded with his own hands with an ax his acquaintance Eli Schindelhaus, who survived only by a miracle, and Chana Trochlier and some other Jews were murdered. Gershon Mossman, husband of Rachel Melamed, was gravely wounded in these pogroms. The joke of fate is such that we were then saved from horrible slaughter thanks to the Germans, who opened fire on the rioters and scattered them to the wind.

Leading the rioters did not save Yarmaliuk. His fellow Ukrainian nationalists remembered his collaboration with the Soviets and murdered him.

When things calmed down, the Jews buried their dead and washed the blood that had congealed, and … the decrees and harassment started. The Christian that just yesterday and the day before would bow to you and who was your friend no longer recognized you, as if he was seeing you for the first time in his life. And those who in their hearts secretly opposed the persecution of the Jews and wished them well had to act like everyone else and demonstrate their hatred for Jews.

The Jews slowly, slowly lost their security and with that their dignity.

[Page 92]

Poverty took its toll, morality declined, and division and suspicion amongst the Jews increased. We knew that in times of trouble and distress, unity increased among the Jews. Unfortunately, this time was different. You know, Reuven, of the terrible incident when Bernio Sannis's son-in-law snitched on Zayde Gelman that he slaughtered a cow in the ghetto and sold its meat to Jews. Bernio did it because he did not get his share from Zayde. Zayde was hung for his transgression in front of the whole community, and the snitch lived in the ghetto as if nothing happened. A similar incident happened in the Judenrat, which I will tell you about below.

The Judenrat

The Judenrat was established by the Germans for the further exploitation and easier eradication of the Jews. They would collect all sorts of contributions for the Germans; gather clothes, furniture, jewelry, silver, and gold for them; and organize labor groups for them. In exchange for this, Germans would promise personal safety and comfort to the members of the Judenrat. Of course, after these duties were fulfilled, the Judenrat members were killed together with the rest of the Jews and sometimes in a crueler manner.

I will note with satisfaction that with us the Judenrat members did not lose their humanity and even kept their morality and righteousness. Of course, we also did not exactly have it easy with the Judenrat, but the relationship we had with the Judenrat was ideal in comparison to that of other places. The role of the Judenrat was not at all easy because on the one hand, they had to fulfill all of the Germans' wishes, and on the other hand, they did not want to harm the Jews. And this could not be done. But relatively, our Judenrat was okay.

The Judenrat was officially headed by Abba Shtivel. He was, however, too weak for the role, and so Melech Gusack managed virtually all matters. In the Judenrat were experienced politicos like Yonah Nemirover and Mendel Dordick as well as some members from amongst the refugees.

When the time came to fulfill the Germans' demands for various items, the Jews of course did not want to part from their property. It was necessary to create a Jewish police force in order to prevent the activation of the Ukrainian police, and that is how the Judenrat turned into the lowest kind of hell. The members of the Jewish police believed, like their masters the Judenrat, that for their faithful service to the Germans, they would be saved from extermination. I must again note that we did not blame the Judenrat for taking advantage of their positions for their own self-interests, and I could testify that everything that was done at their hands was done out of the necessity of the bitter reality and was inevitable.

I blame them only for one thing – for their criminally committee trust in the Germans. Seeing how they wiped out community after community, without leaving a trace behind,

[Page 93]

still believing the Germans that promised them that Mizocz would stay standing if German orders were fulfilled to the letter…

Moshe Rudman served as secretary of the Judenrat. His moral standards were always dubious, and he fit the role quite nicely. Over time, he wanted to be the Judenrat's final adjudicator, and when they denied him, he went to the Gestapo and informed on the Judenrat that they had betrayed the trust of the authorities; he informed the Gestapo that he had proof that the Judenrat had exempted the Rabbi from the requirement of handing over of his cloak to the Germans and that they themselves not only did not hand over their jackets but took for themselves those that were intended for the German army…

For its part, the Judenrat blamed Rudman for the disturbance in order and for the incitement of the population against the Judenrat. The two charges were of course baseless and fundamentally lies, but they constituted a big danger to all of us. In the end, Rudman was incarcerated, and two days after, his wife and two children were also incarcerated. They were shot in the basement of the Ukrainian police, but the rumor went that they were transferred to the Zdolbuniv jail.

A testament of the extent of the helplessness and blindness of the Judenrat was the fact that: we knew that all the towns in our area were purified of Jews. In Dubno, Rąwne, Radzibilov, Rokovich, Ozerna, and other towns, not one Jew remained there. The Germans, however, managed to convince the Judenrat members of the fabrication that those Jews were wiped out because they had not followed the instructions of the authorities and had incited rebellion. The murderers wanted until the end to exploit the blood of the Jews, their strength, and their assets.

During the German occupation, I worked in the sugar factory as a roustabout. About a week before the day of the extermination, the boss of the sugar factory called me into his office (he was a Pole and had been a good acquaintance of mine for a long time) and told me that during his visit to the brick factory, which was administratively linked to the sugar factory, he noticed a motorcycle. While he stood and wondered about the motorcycle rider, he saw Otto the German gendarme inspecting the brick factory's pits. To his question as to what he could do for him, the gendarme replied that he received a command to determine whether one hundred thousand bricks, much needed for German construction, could be obtained here. The manager, suspicious of something, called the *gebietkommissar* [area commissioner], and the *gebietkommissar* answered that they did not at all have a need for bricks. He therefore, risking his life, informed me that the end was near and that what could still be saved should be saved.

I of course immediately relayed what the manager had said to the Judenrat. Without delay, they sent Hersch Goldbrenner from Biłgoraj, who represented the refugees in the Judenrat, to the Germans. He, who by the way was a good friend of mine, knew how to

[Page 94]

behave with the Germans and was well received by them. Loaded with precious gifts and with lots of gold coins, he presented himself before the Germans.

He returned without the gifts but not quite calm. He of course did not mention the manager's name to the Germans; he only told them that the Ukrainians were bragging that the end was near and that it was even known to them that the brick factory's pits were chosen to serve as the mass graves for the community. The Germans answered him that this idea was born out of the Ukranians' own desires, and since they wanted our extinction, they fabricated it. In the end it was advised not to listen to the lies and to continue to work. Just in case, one of the Germans solemnly reiterated his promise that if matters were to be worsening, he would notify Goldbrenner a few weeks beforehand. Eventually, Goldbrenner became emboldened and said that the Ukrainians were even saying that he, the very same Otto who made the promise, was himself seen by the pits. Regarding this, the Germans did not reply with a single word.

This fact indeed saddened some of Judenrat, but they wanted to believe in the Germans' lies, and so they dismissed every warning. And so the day of extermination came about.

I have sat down a few times already to write something for the book, but I have failed. I hope you understand my state of mind and forgive me. I will always help you in other matters.

Always yours,
Yehuda Braunstein

The train station in Mizocz

[Page 95]

Bits of Memories from the Holocaust Period

by Miriam Kashuk-Szprync

Translated from Hebrew by Corey Feuer

In the first days of Nazi control in Mizocz, life carried on as usual, and the Jews were hardly harmed. I remember that the mothers whose sons had fled with the retreating Soviet army cried and mourned, jealous of the mothers whose sons had stayed in Mizocz, as it seemed that things were not as bad as expected. My mother was one of these mourners. Her only son – my brother Yitzhak – wandered far away, to suffering and hardship, while others were living in Mizocz with their families safe and sound.

The quiet days, however, did not last. Already on the fourth day of German control of the town, we all realized how miserable we were. And it was just my luck that I happened to be among the first harmed. As ordered by the Ukrainian police, about two dozen of us girls, the prettiest and most educated of the town – including the sisters Bella and Tzvia Trochlier, Eva Finkel, Mnucha Miller, Adla Fidelman, and two of the refugee girls whose names I forgot – presented ourselves at the government offices. Our parents and loved ones of course parted from us with cries, prayers, and beating hearts.

When all of us were gathered, we were stood up in lines, and we marched in procession through the town streets. On the way, the police harassed us, abused us with the rudeness characteristic of the Ukrainian rioters, and tried to make love with us. We did not respond. We concluded amongst ourselves not to cry and not to plead with the rioters no matter what. We therefore marched in silence and sorrow without muttering a word. After going around the town three times, we were led to the hospital, which was at the time installed in the count Karwitzky's palace and was full of wounded Germans from the battlefront. They brought us into the laundry room and gave us piles of undergarments and clothes stained with smelly blood to be washed immediately. It was terrible and awful. But we worked and did not break. Only when Anton the policeman took with him one of our friends, a refugee girl, did we break. We did not see anything –we only heard her terrifying screams from the adjacent room. When half an hour had passed, she returned, and he followed. She was as pale as whitewash and did not look at us. An oppressive silence prevailed in the laundry room. Anton walked out and she asked: "Why aren't you asking anything?" We continued to be quiet. There was no need to ask; everything was clear. Suddenly, she began to wail in an inhuman voice. She dropped face-first onto the floor and banged her head against the bricks. We all broke out into bitter crying and mourned our bitter fate.

At the memorial service, I was asked to tell of our lives in the ghetto, in the forest, and in hiding places, and to tell of the miracle of our rescue. But I have no more tears left in me and do not have strength to return to those terrible days.

[Page 96]

I am no longer that cheerful girl that you, my fellow townsmen, knew and were acquainted with. I am already a mother to two daughters, a broken and destroyed person who has the period of the Holocaust imprinted in their flesh and blood. I cannot, however, refuse you and will tell you only a little about my life from the day of the ghetto's destruction in our town. I cannot recall everything, and there are many things I also do not want to remember. Before my eyes stands my old elderly 80-year-old grandmother, with her white hair unkempt, her face fiery, her skinny hands spread out to the sky, and she is praying to God: "Master of the universe! I want to come to you. But please not by the hands of the murderers." I remember my parents and their parents, all of our loved ones, surrounded by the murderers, rushing and hurrying and seeking refuge. Screams and gunshots were heard. On the Ghetto's fence were already lying the corpses of those who had tried to flee. We resembled at that time mice looking for a hole to escape from the claws of a predatory cat. I hear my mother's voice, unforgettable: "Manitchka, you are young, save yourself. My death will be made pleasant when I know that you are saved, I will go dancing to the pit if I do not see you there." And from that point on, I decided to live. I turn to my father to show me the path to Meizlitch's flour depot, where I worked all the time, and which was three houses away from ours', and where I was used to going month after month, every day. He does not know how to answer me, and I am confused. We all looked insane. Terror ran rampant and wives fought with their husbands, parents with their children, young people and old people. I was pushed as if by an unknown force to the fence and I jumped to the other side, not that far from the police officers that kept anyone from crossing over. But they did not notice me and that to me was a good sign. From a distance, I noticed Yakov Grossblatt and his relative from a nearby village. I approached them, and together we broke a board off from the wall of the flour depot and went inside. And there immediately arose the problem: and what next? Through the cracks of the walls, we saw death moving about in the form of the Gestapo men with big dogs. They all wore steel helmets with the symbol of death on them. Shooting machines are in their hands and everyone is dragging and beating Jews. We saw how they were dragging a mother with her baby who was found hiding between a pile of wood in the yard of the depot. We saw blood marks all over. We heard screams and gunshots, looked at each other, and were silent. Eventually, following Yakov's instruction, we all started to break off a floorboard, and the three of us crawled into the hole that was created. For three days and two nights, we lay motionless in that grave of a hole. I felt all my strength leaving me. I was suffocating. I begged the others in the pit to let me leave, but they refused, saying it would be better for us to be burned alive in the big fire that spread at that time through the town – because the living Jews had lit their houses on fire before they were taken out to be executed–than fall at the hands of the Germans. However, the Germans succeeded in controlling the burning and the fire did not reach

[Page 97]

the mill. The Gestapo dogs wandered through the spacious yard of the mill, sniffing and sniffing but never finding us. And then the others acquiesced to my leaving the pit on the condition that if I were caught, I would not reveal the hideout. Stunned and shattered, barely able to stand up, I left the hole and managed to call the manager without anyone noticing. I had trust in him and revealed to him our secret. Under the pretext of closing the floor on which we were hiding, he came to take my companions out from the hole and gave us something to eat and drink. We were a terrible sight, and our situation was hopeless. He advised us to separate for our own good.

He directed the guys to Horvy village and decided to take me to a different village. On the way, he told me that he was bringing me to his sister under the condition that if I was found by the Germans, I would not reveal to them that I was helped by him. He walked a few meters ahead of me and led the way with a lit cigarette. That is how we reached his sister. I was there [with the sister] for two days, until the Germans announced heavy punishments for those who were hiding Jews. In the darkness of night, I was expelled from the house and reached the forest. To describe my life in the forest in hiding, my many encounters with death – I will not be capable. Chills grip me even now to remember those days. I will tell only a few tragic/comic incidents that, with all their horror, put a bit of a smile on our faces. We once hid 11 Jews in a pit dug in a stable, below the living space of a large workhorse. The pit was covered in manure and its entrance was through a small, narrow lid which was always covered with manure and on top of that the horse. We breathed in the air from a few narrow cracks. During one of our sleepless nights, the ceiling suddenly collapsed, and the horse fell right on us. Its feet were in the pit and its body in the space above. We stayed without air and without the option to move. We were certain that this time the end of our suffering had come, and they would find us. In the pit were nine men and two women –me and Senka, a cute teenager from nearby Varkovychi. However, this time as well the matter ended in fear. They rescued the horse and also removed us from the pit, and we were only forced to move to a different pit. We migrated to a new place and to a new pit. On the way, some among us met their merciful death, and among them was my companion in suffering and sorrow – Senka. She was incredibly beautiful. Everyone who saw her was fond of her. She had two long braids, deep eyes full of sadness, a gorgeous figure, and a delicate face. Once, during our time in the pit that had collapsed, she fell gravely ill. She was always suffering from a headache and complaining of strong pains. Us "doctors" started to check her head and discovered the disease; her head was covered in wounds and in the wounds swarmed hundreds of lice … We cut her braids, cleaned her, and she recovered. Later, after she had regained her strength, she was murdered. And she was only 17. Here I wish to mention the good and righteous man Yonah Firer, may God avenge his blood, who saved some Jews with his money and gave a slice of his bread to those who were hungry. I too made it this far

[Page 98]

thanks to his helping me. May his memory be blessed, and his soul bound in the bundle of life.

The day of joy arrived. The Red Army expelled the Germans, and we went out into the light of day. How much did we hope for this day? How much did we wait and pray for it? And here it had come and we, how miserable we were, I – of all of my extended family was left by myself and alone. Sick, broken, and penniless. I could not really walk. My friends carried me out from the pit, and with their help I practiced the art of walking. I made it to Mizocz. More accurately, the place where Mizocz once stood – my beautiful and dear town. I came to say goodbye to the grave of the brothers of our martyrdom, to those youthful days of happiness that I once had there. I stood by the grave and saw a plot of land covered with fresh grass. But when I kept looking, it seemed to me like the ground was rising and I heard a voice crying softly, similar to the sound of my mother's cries. I tearfully choked up; my eyes cried on their own. Broken and exhausted, with a curse in my mouth, I ran away from the place forever.

The Horrible Days

by Ida Eisengart-Fliter

Translated from Hebrew by Eiden Harel Brewer, Noa Etzyon and Ofir Horovitz

"Hey, you! Where are you? Do you hear me? The dawn is breaking and you need to scram!" I heard- and oh how I heard. I hadn't slept, and it was so warm in the pile of hay. It was so nice and safe until…

"You must escape!" Escape where? Where would I go? Is there a place for me under the sun?

The voice continues and increases in agitation! "Come on, where are you? I can't have them see you here. Take some bread for the road and get out of here right now."

I left my hiding spot, wrapping myself with the scarf that I got from a woman farmer in exchange for my "Jewish" sweater, I took the bread and left the silo. Darkness still ruled the universe, and I took off without being seen. To try my luck with another farmer, that might let me hide at his place for a day or two–I couldn't. Everyone was sleeping deeply. If I try to wake someone from their sleep, I'm prone to wake their anger and frustration and then… and the moments crawled on like forever.

I entered the yard next door and tried to dig myself into a pile of hay that stood and seemingly waited for me. The dog burst out and barked so loud that it woke his owners.

[Page 99]

A light turned on inside the house and two farmers came out with axes in their hands. "Who's there?" they called angrily.

"I'm begging you," I answered, throat saturated with tears–"don't you also have children"----

"Don't come any closer," one of them yelled at me. "Don't come any closer! I'll cut you into pieces!" he added as a response to my begging. I noticed the other disappeared in darkness and I realized that he went to alert the police against a dangerous criminal like me. Every precious second, every little delay was bound to be fateful. Hidden by the darkness, I ran for my life from Kunyn Village. I just couldn't understand why the murderer yelled "don't come closer". Was he really so afraid I would kill him?

I ran with all my might and tried to get as far away from the dangerous zone as I could at maximum speed. At dawn I arrived at a new place and hid in the first hut I saw on my way. I will never forget the owner of that hut for as long as I live and will always remember her with warmth. She was a lonely old woman with a heart of gold and a sensitive soul. She made room for me in the compartment above her stove, fed me and was ready to help me. She spoke to me in almost a whisper because the wall of her hut bordered that of her greedy and swindling son, and it's a miracle she survived his murderous hands. While she was away from her home, he tended to enter through a covered passageway to the hut and steal all that he could. She tried not to leave me alone - for, if the son discovered me, we were both doomed. It was good for me to stay with her. It was warm above the stove, quiet and safe.

A few days later, the old woman was forced to leave me alone for a few hours. Her son was aware of her absence, and he entered the hut through the covered passageway. Obviously, he immediately saw me and was no less startled than I was. Once he recovered, he asked me to not tell his mother about his intrusion into the cabin, and promised me help whenever I may need it in return.

Once the old woman returned, I told her everything and she agreed to let me stay one more day. The night passed by full of mental torture and negative thoughts, and only once the sun rose, the old woman headed to the city. That's when I got off the stove to stretch my body and take a peek outside the window. The worrying thoughts of tomorrow continued to intrude. I got back onto the stove and started to think. At noon I got off the stove and looked outside once again, and immediately felt a weird movement. And then – oh no, what a sight! Three German Gendarmes are walking towards the hut. I froze and was scared out of my wits.

[Page 100]

Public meeting in front of "Dom Strzelecki" (Shooting House) in Mizocz

[Page 101]

A hand touched the door and I could already feel death creeping upon me. But then I hear a voice saying: "not here. Not here. His mother is here. The entrance to his hut is on the other side". Immediately I heard noise and conversation from the other side of the wall. Then followed the weeping of a woman and children but it quickly turned to silence. The noise stopped, the screams stopped and a threatening silence lurked. It was hard for me to believe that they hadn't meant me and that I had been forgotten.

By nightfall, the old woman came back and she explained it all; her son belonged to the Banderites[1] and believed that the Germans would grant independence to Ukraine. When his hopes proved to be in vain, he began to hate the Germans. He once said what was in his heart in front of a large audience in Mizocz when he was drunk and later forgot about it. And in time, he got his punishment from the German police.

I remained at the old woman's house. Indeed, I never forgot that her son was likely going to reveal to the Germans that I was at his mother's house, but the woman's resilience and her good spirits kept me in place.

One day, I saw what I didn't hope to see. It was in the early morning, I was sleeping deeply when I was awoken by the old woman yelling, "Run for your life. We're all burning!"

I ran outside and from fragmented, nervous sentences I started to understand. In response to the murder of three German soldiers, the Germans invaded the village, ordered all the men into one of the big cowsheds, and burnt it together with all the people. In the meantime, I mingled with the crowd and turned into one of them. I managed to see the Ukrainian murderers, who were thirsty for Jewish blood and who were happy when the Germans abused and killed Jews, now being chased and burned by their German friends. All of a sudden, a decision was made in my head: Ida does not exist anymore. From now on, I am a young Ukrainian woman named Lida. I am from a Polish-Ukrainian village whose inhabitants were punished by the Germans in the same way as the people from the village Kunyn, just to live and I will still have days of vengeance on all the people who hate Israel and in order to curse the Germans with Hitler in command. Just to live!

* * *

I arrived at a Czech town in the area of Zdolbuniv. They were in need of working hands, and I was gladly accepted. After a couple days of work, I felt like they were paying too much attention to me... I also heard the man of the house saying to his wife, "She speaks Ukrainian like a Ukrainian from birth, but that face... who knows?" I didn't wait to see what would happen and I ran away to a different place. Here, the first farmer I turned to for work asked me why I lit a match like a Jew.

[Page 102]

Another said there is no way I am who I say I am, and nonetheless they want to help me, but surely, I know the current situation they are in now. And I knew very well in what situation we were in!

Only when the harvest time came and they lacked helping hands was I able to get a job from a Czech man and played my part there for a while.

* * *

Then came a cold wintry day. I worked in a potato picking field. The two little girls of the Czech man I worked for ran towards me in excitement.

"Lida," they yelled. "Two nice men, with guns on their shoulders, came and asked for you." My heart felt like it stopped beating. I felt like giving up and thought: maybe now I really should end my dog-like life? Winter is approaching. Running away from here to another place will not be easy. I won't be able to get a job. And even so… the girls are urging me to come to the guys.

Once I recovered, I told the girls: "these guys are good acquaintances of mine. Go fast because I'm coming right away. I'll just gather my belongings and brush my hair.

The girls left and I faced towards my "home." I didn't take the main route but rather went by way of the fields with the intention of reaching the forest that bordered the house. Running away to a different place hadn't even crossed my mind then. I thought that I'd get to the forest that borders the house and there decide what to say and how to act towards the murderers. I arrived at the garden that bordered the forest and saw my "friends" that came to visit me. They sat beneath a nut tree and snacked on some fresh nuts. They sat, ate and enjoyed themselves, waiting for their victim. I entered the forest. For a long time, I'd been known as "Lida," the hardworking Ukrainian laborer. However, having to run across the fields after the harvest while the hay was prickling my feet was still not something I could do. This time I made my way to the forest, across the post-harvest fields, like an experienced expert. Interestingly, I didn't feel any pain in my feet. Could this be because I was so preoccupied with the fear of dying? Maybe. However, I think it actually happened because of my will to live. This will to live is what pushed me towards these daring adventures. To live! Every hour of breathing freely was worthwhile for any suffering. To live! Even without tomorrow, without hope, without family and living the life of a beaten and wandering dog, with constant danger hovering your head. But to live! Just live! To live and hope! To fight and to outwit but live!

I sat in the forest until sundown. I then got up and headed towards my landlord's daughter who lived in the far corner of the village.

[Page 103]

"Ah, Lida," I was greeted with reluctance. "You may not be *Zhidovka*, but you also may not enter our house. It's enough that you're suspicious." Then the landlord continued with a stinging remark: "you may not be *Zhidovka*, but *Ibraika*[2] for sure."

"I believe you," said the woman, "but, it's only for your own good if you escape here as fast as you can". The "men" said they have no interest in killing you. They want to capture you alive. They told my dad that he will need to dig a grave in his yard. What should we do? They want to capture you alive, it seems, so they can torture you a little. They even offered a reward to anyone who would bring you alive."

That night, I slept in the silo. At night, I returned to my landlord, and was faced with a prolonged silence as he looked at me as if he was seeing me for the first time. It was hard for him to believe I was Jewish. I remembered then, how in one of the evenings when Jews knocked on the window and asked for just a little bit of food, he answered that he would willingly give them food but was afraid to do so in front of the Ukrainian woman that worked there.

Despite the honest doubts of the Czech, I distanced myself from the village. The reward for my head enticed many of the farmers in the village…

Later I came to know that one of the policemen that put the reward on my head had been an "acquaintance" of mine for a long time. This guy wanted to be near me and made advances. Once, when he went too far, I decisively rejected him. And then he told me for the first time: "Lida, you are not Ukrainian. You are a rude Jew! A Ukrainian woman would never act the way you do. I managed to remove the disguise from your face."

The next day I left the village and went on to graze cows at a different pasture. And here they discovered me yet again.

* * *

I walked at daylight towards an unknown direction. Police, soldiers and German officers passed by me. I walked with confidence and enjoyed the beauty of the world. In my head I started rewriting the history of my life and made-up explanations for the reason for the absence of my identity documents. Once the connections in my head were completed, I entered the village not far from the city of Dubno. My confidence in my abilities grew, the will to live beat with all its might, and I was "Lida," the authentic, typical Ukrainian cowherd once again. Lida Romanchenko was hired for work.

* * *

The days pass and I am disconnected from the newspaper and society. I pass my days with the cows or the sheep, in the pasture or in the field. The village in which I work in is not far from the bustling road of Rivne-Dubno.

[Page 104]

On one of the days, I discovered that the traffic on the road is different than any other day. At night, I saw a German army driving panicked towards Dubno. Sometimes, German units spend the night at my village. I listen to the officer's conversations and discover that the defeat of the Germans is near, and redemption is coming. It was hard for me to believe this miracle and I was living on high alert. The echoes of the Soviet raid can be heard. The village is full of retreating German soldiers. Lida, among other girls, was recruited to peel potatoes. I'm peeling the potatoes on high alert and listening to the German soldier's conversations. One of the officers offers to take Lida with the retreating army. I run and hide with a family that's leaving the village due to the fear of the retreating soldiers. The Czechs are perplexed. They're scared of the Germans' strength and trembling with fear from the Russians. Meanwhile, the Red Army enters the village. Four months have passed, and I am still playing the role of a cowherd. Why? It's hard to explain. I was scared. I was scared of the new reality and I was scared of the loneliness, until fate brought me back to life with the surviving Jews.

Translator's Footnotes:

1. Banderivtsi – Banderities, members of a right-wing Ukrainian nationalist organization
2. *Zhidovka*, a borrowed word from the Polish, Ukrainian and Russian languages for a Jewish woman. From the spelling, this reference was probably derived from Russian and in the 1930's had a derogatory connotation in that language. (It is since considered derogatory in the Ukrainian language, but not in Polish.) *Ibraika* is a feminine word borrowed from Russian/Ukrainian for a Jewish woman. It is a phonetic variation of 'Hebrew,' a transitional form to a modern Russian/Ukrainian word yevrey- 'a Jew.'

The Struggle for Life

by Yona Oliker

Translated from Hebrew by Nida Kiali

The last of the Soviets had left Mizocz. The situation was yet unclear. A threatening calm before the storm had spread throughout the town. The German army had yet to enter the town and the Ukrainian thugs roamed the streets, looking for an excuse to begin attacking Jews and plundering. They threw rocks at the Jews' windows and shouted profanities at us. However, no one responded. We swallowed the insults, condoned the minor damages and kept to our houses.

All of the residents felt great astonishment as they saw that the leaders of the provocateurs who were openly calling for attacks on the hated Jews were none other than Ivan Pickoretz and his friend Yarmaliuk. Both were known veteran communists, who were arrested at times for communist activity in the days of the Polish regime.

These two rounded up the bloodthirsty peasants nearby, agitated them and led them to wreak havoc. If it wasn't for the quick intervention of the German army, this day would have led to the town's demise and only a few might have escaped death. But, as it happened, after the first few victims were killed, the German army marched into town before the aggressors

[Page 105]

could manifest their lowly desires. Then, their commander announced that they were the ones who would order when and how the hated Jews would be attacked and that they were ordering everyone to back down for now and disperse. But still, during their rampage, the Ukrainians had managed to murder Hannah Trochler, Chaya Bicks and a small refugee girl. They had mutilated many bodies and looted a lot of property. Elie Schindelhaus was especially severely injured at the hands of some of his good Ukrainian acquaintances.

The "organized" german regime was then established. They founded the Ukrainian police and placed that scoundrel (*shaygitz*)[1] Winogradsky from the village of Mizoczik as its captain. The primary duties of the police were to oppress and scorn Jews. By their command, Jews were forbidden to leave their houses from sunset till sunrise, or from 7 p.m. to 7 a.m. Shopping in the marketplace was allowed only after 10 a.m. and after the Christians had finished shopping.

On the first days of this new ruling, the memorial day (*Yahrzeit*) for the Schindelhaus's father was supposed to be held. Having a *Yahrzeit* in the synagogue like in years past was impossible; houses of prayer were desolate come evening and no Jewish foot walked the streets. But the Schindelhaus brothers wanted to say *Kaddish* for their dead father on his memorial day and decided to secretly arrange a "*minyan*"[2] in their house in with their neighbors.

Since our house included several males, we were also asked to join the "*minyan*." I did tell my father and brother they should not risk themselves at this hour and go to the "*minyan*." However, as a very religious Jew accustomed to praying in a "*minyan*," father said that we must not refuse such an important *mitzvah*[3] and urged his sons and the rest of the neighbors to join the "*minyan*." We had only begun praying when the Ukrainian officers barged in, drove us out while beating us senseless, and led everyone to the police building located at that time at Meir Rosenblatt's house on the other side of Mizocz.

They started investigating us with cruelty while abusing, humiliating and brutally beating us. At midnight we were released. The next morning, all of the participant in the *"minyan"* were gathered according to a list. Accompanied by two German officers, we were marched across town several times and finally were brought to the police station.

They rounded up any Jew who happened to cross our path, guilty or not. Everyone was savagely and relentlessly beaten by the time we reached the police station. Then Abba Shtivel, who served as a Soltis[4] while the Poles ruled and later as the chairman of the Judenrat,

[Page 106]

explained to them the meaning behind the custom of the *"minyan."* He then clarified that many were arrested who did not participate in the *"minyan."*

The Germans then exempted those who did not partake in the *"minyan"* and drove them away with lashes – to their homes. We, the participants in the "minyan" were led to the Gemeine[5] and were tortured to exhaustion. We were later carried – because we couldn't walk – to a prison cell near the Gemeine that could barely hold three men and crammed all ten of us inside. We were there for four whole days, narrowly escaping death only thanks to the post office employee Broinowski's wife. She was of German descent and during the Polish regime had a close friendship with the Jews.

Mrs. Broinowski was appointed as an official translator when the Germans captured Mizocz. She helped many Jews, but the Ukrainians informed on her to the authorities and she was moved to Ostroh as a result.

One of the punishments for our participation in the *"minyan"* was doing chores for the gendarmes. Once, after completing my day's work at the commander's house, he called me aside, gave me a pack of margarine, and said, "You fools, why didn't you retreat with the Russians? Did you not know that the Germans are exterminating the Jews?" Weeks and months passed. The Jews managed to bribe the local German government, befriend the authorities, and outsmart rulings and aggressions. Besides two or three tragic cases of killing or the disappearance of some Jews, we hardly felt the aggressor's hand. Some Jews worked, some traded, and nothing was lacking. When the Ukrainians saw the German's tolerance towards Jews, they too stopped harassing us, and many of them even renewed commerce with their Jewish acquaintances.

However, to our great detriment and misfortune, it was not the local officials who decided our fate. When the order came to exterminate us all, they followed it with great conviction and belief.

One dark night, on a Tuesday in October of 1942, we found ourselves surrounded by armed officers and large German shepherds. Only a few managed to escape the encirclement. Some hid in pre-made hiding places, some managed to hide at the last moment, but most of the ghetto's inhabitants were forced to gather at the town square, in front of the stores, and were sent on the death march into the pits.

Before leaving their homes, a few Jews managed to light them on fire, which spread out and engulfed the whole town. The Christian population and the authorities began

[Page 107]

extinguishing the flames, but it took a while to get the fire under control. In the meantime, several Jews took advantage of the mayhem, broke through the encirclement and fled.

The town square became crowded. We were horrified by the screams and shouts of those found hiding and forcibly brought to the square. When the officers canvassing the ghetto houses finally announced that there were no others in hiding, the death march began to the pre-made pits in the vicinity of the Sosinsky woods by the sugar factory.

We followed suit, trudging almost in silence as the Gentile neighbors gazed upon us. There were no emotional outbreaks, no crying or defiance. Everyone had humbly accepted their fate.

When we got on the bridge on the river Stoblke, I snuck out of line, quickly got down under the bridge unnoticed and hid in a corner. The officers did not notice me and the march moved on.

Much to my surprise, I immediately felt that I was not alone under the bridge; a woman hid not far from me, a refugee from Brisk who resided in Mizocz in the last days of its existence. She already had experience, surviving the exterminations in Rivne, Dubno, and nearby Borkovich and now she had succeeded also in surviving Mizocz. She told me she had a daughter married to a Christian in a village near Dubno and that she was trying to reach her now. At night, we both came out of hiding. I showed her the way to Dubno and headed back to Mizocz. I went into our home and found my father dead. All of our belongings and furniture were missing. All had been stolen. I entered my brother-in-law David's house, to face the same horrendous sights. My uncle lay dead and the place was stripped bare. A dog started barking in the distance and I ran into Isaac Schindelhaus's house. Like the ones before, this house was completely empty, with only the murdered lying naked inside. The killers stripped them of their clothes before or after murdering them. I left the house and the sound of a child's weeping had reached my ears.

I followed the sound and came across a horrifying scene: Miriam Koppelman, my cousin, sat dead with her son between her arms. I tried to pry the child from his mother's frozen arms but couldn't do so. I tried over and over, but the child kept weeping even more and I couldn't remove him from his mother's embrace. The child's weeping and the gunshot sounds nearby alarmed me and I ran for my life. Later I found out that the child agonized in his mother's arms for two more days, until his pure soul perished. I was told that one of the Ukrainian wives wanted to save and adopt him, for she was barren, but she was not allowed.

I traveled from one acquaintance to the other, seeking a place to rest for a day or two, but was lucky to even find a place where they would look the other way for one night as I slept at the granary.

[Page 108]

For the most part, I was chased out with threats and sometimes even beatings. Finally, the situation became unbearable and I returned to Mizocz to surrender to the Gestapo. A few dozen meters from the Gestapo building, I came across an unknown Gentile. He berated me, comforted me, and said, "My dear one, it's too soon to die. Run and fight for your life." I took his words to heart and headed to Ozirky Village. Peasant Gerasimchuk's wife let me into her house and introduced me to Perel Mizocz, Lyssa Melamed, and her son Yasha.

Lyssa told me that on the day of the extermination, she was hidden in a bunker with many other Jews. Jacob Mizocz (Yankel Crisis) and his wife Raizel and their children were among them. Raizel was forced to strangle her little daughter with her own hands because she wouldn't stop crying and they could have been discovered…

We stayed up all night, sharing more and more stories of the miracle of our survival. At the break of dawn, I continued my travels. During these travels, I met at least fifty surviving Jews like myself. We were always thrilled during these meetings. We would sit and exchange stories and notes, and part ways hoping to meet again someday. I once entered the house of a Ukrainian acquaintance named Krupniok. I sensed his son promptly sneaking out of the house and I suspected he went to call the police. I immediately left the house; the officers that came by could only shoot at me from afar. I once again managed to escape unharmed.

With the lack of a better option, I returned to Ozirky Village, to the house of the Czech where Lyssa Melamed hid. However, he was poor and could not support us all. So, I was again forced to leave.

Hungry and thirsty, afraid and suffering from the cold, I wandered about. I looked into houses through the windows and when I saw food served on the table, I barged in, took whatever I could and ran like hell[6]. I quenched my thirst with snow.

When I've once again returned to Mizocz, some people gave me food, but in no way would they provide me with shelter.

I was able to get in touch with the *Soltis* (Magistrate)[7] of the Ukrainian Mizocz, Madas Pochbula, my long-time acquaintance, and he agreed to help me. I arrived at his house, bathed and shaved, and when I wanted to take my shoes off, I couldn't. My legs had swollen, and the shoes stuck to them. Pochbula carefully cut the shoes with a knife and carefully removed them. He comforted me and promised to accommodate me until my feet healed. From him, I went to his brother-in-law Milter and back again at night. In the evening, I slept in the granary, and at dawn, returned to the woods and fields. I stayed with them for a while in that manner. Once I was late to exit the granary,

[Page 109]

A "HaShomer HaLeumi" group in Mizocz

[Page 110]

and I saw that Milter came and closed the hole I used to come and go from. I immediately made a second hole, and since then came and went unnoticed. However, since it was made clear that I was not wanted, I had to seek another place to hide. I found a granary that fit my needs with another farmer and made it my sanctuary without its owners knowing about it.

At this granary, I met with Isaiah Braunstein. He had undergone such a transformation that I didn't recognize him until he identified himself to me. The poor man perished after a while, along with Gittel Braunstein and Rachel Mendyuk. Some say they literally starved to death.

In Mizocz, someone informed on me and the police came looking for me at my hideout. I happened to be away at that time and was saved. After that, I decided to relocate permanently to the woods with Nahum Kopit. I couldn't find his hiding place and got lost, ran into some officers and survived only through unimaginable miracles.

At that time, respect for us had risen somewhat among the Gentiles, thanks to the partisan company of Isaac Wasserman. Everyone dreaded him and many feared his vengeance. In this forest where Nahum Kopit lived, there gathered many of the survivors of the Mizocz ghetto. We used to meet every so often and provide each other with advice and any needed assistance. We came across the Banderovites every once in a while, and each of those encounters would result in many a sacrifice.

Once, I saw Arye Firer talking to someone. After inquiring about him, I've offered to eliminate him, for I sensed him to be an agent of the Banderovites. Many resisted my proposal, saying that he was Polish and also a refugee like us. I then suggested we flee and see what would come to be. However, while we were debating and thinking, that man came accompanied by a company of Banderovites and opened fire on us. I was once again successful in escaping. It is interesting to note that the Banderovites, as they came across small groups of Jews, would present themselves as Soviet partisans, offer food, and suggest that all those in hiding should go with them. They managed to cunningly trap the naïve every now and then. After gathering a large group of Jews, they mercilessly eliminated them.

Once, Neona Langer and her daughter found themselves in their midst. They fed her and told her to bring all the other Jews hiding with her under their protection. She promised and went to get them. But unlike the other naïve victims, she saw through their deception, ran far away, and was saved.

I was then forced to again ask for the favors of that Czech peasant where Lyssa Melamed hid. To my surprise, he happily accepted me, for his conscience bothered him for having sent me away before. He was sure I had perished, and when he saw me alive and well, he was delighted and immediately provided me with shelter.

[Page 111]

After that, the Czechs protected me until the arrival of the Red Army. When the survivors from Mizocz met after the war, we numbered only nineteen, out of the many hundreds who managed to escape on the day of the Mizocz Ghetto extermination and who perished while stubbornly fighting for their lives.

Translator's Footnotes:

1. שגץ shaygitz , in Yiddish the masculine counterpart to "shiksa" – a disparaging term for a non-Jew
2. A religious quorum; ten adult Jews
3. A commandment, a religious duty
4. Soltis = magistrate or mayor (Polish)
5. City Hall
6. The Hebrew expression כשד משחת meaning a daemon from hell to culturally refer to someone who is energetic.
7. Title used to refer to the head of a community.

Dovid Fliter Tells His Story

Translated from Yiddish by Clair Padgett

From faraway Brazil he came to the land of Israel. He came with his brother Barukh, with whom he had lived through the horrific age of Hitler. He came so that he could get together with friends and relatives, introduce his wife, and meet new incoming family members. He had already long dreamed of a visit to the country. The various businesses of his had, however, not made this possible.

And here he sits at my work table. Slim, elegant, and well-dressed. He smOchs without pausing and tells. His dark, penetrating eyes run around restlessly in their sockets. His hands and feet, all of his facial features work together to help him express clearly and distinctly what his speech alone is not capable of rendering.

[Page 112]

For a while, I close my eyes and carry myself away with the memories of the remote past, to our beloved little shtetl, Mizocz. I picture him now: Dovid, he stands before my eyes a barefoot little boy: emaciated, but so lively. A slightly soot-blackened, clever little nose, sharp eyes, and always ready to "earn" a piece of candy. Before my closed eyes quickly pass countless images of daily life in Mizocz. The years run by, and Dovid stands before me as a fully grown young man. He works under his father in the photography business, immortalizing with the Leica apparatus countless peasants from the surrounding countryside. He yells orders at them, drills them, showers them with little Ukrainian jOchs so that they laugh and the photo turns out to be a happy one.

I open my eyes again and the same Dovid sits before me. The same, yet so different; a skinny young man has become an enterprising adult. From a shtetl boy he grew into a man with an acute understanding of the world and its many disappointments. From a backward provincial to an interesting conversationalist. Only the eyes are the same. They are, however, much more restless than they used to be. This becomes especially apparent when he talks about the horrors he lived through in the ghetto and the forest. At these moments he relives that time, and it is as though I too am dragged into reliving it.

"I remained at home when everyone was already concealed in the hideout." He takes another drag from his cigarette, thinks a little, and sits there a while. "You remember Mamtsye Srolik's wife. In the ghetto she gave birth to another child and they lived together with us at my grandfather's house. The child was abandoned in that house during the chaos. I remained with the child until I saw the Ukrainian police coming. The child was sobbing and I barely managed to make it to uncle Shmuel's hideout. I couldn't even get in the hideout. It was disguised from the outside and if I tried to move everything out of the way I would endanger everyone inside. Before I got into the hideout in the attic I heard the police shoot the child. It became painfully quiet after the child's crying was silenced.

[Page 113]

From the hideout we heard the Ukranians discovered my grandfather's hideout. My grandfather was already a very old man. Living in the ghetto had aged him even more and he had become blind. With glasses he could still see a little, but without them he was as helpless as a child. When the murderers found him and my grandmother, they began beating the old couple and broke grandfather's glasses. We heard how he pitifully begged them to give back his glasses and how the murderers beat and mocked him. He then asked my grandmother to give him a hand and lead him, since he couldn't see well enough to take a step. In powerless rage, Shmuel ripped his clothes and bit his fingers until they bled. Through his clenched teeth came a desperate cry and we were all pained with inconceivable sorrow until we heard my grandparents driven out of the house. The house that they had built and cared for, in which they had nursed children and grandchildren and hosted the parties, which had always been so bright, happy, and good.

That night, we crawled out of the hideout and approached the ghetto's fence. Two Ukrainian policemen were standing there armed with two rusty guns. We started begging them to let us through, but it was futile. They drove us away with ridicule and threats. Now, looking back, I see how senseless and stupid it was how we, around 30 young people, stood there and begged two murderers armed with two rusty guns. We could have easily run them off and been free. Instead of doing that, we ran back to our hideouts.

From an attic window, I saw how the murderers dragged Jewish infants from every corner and flung them into peasant wagons which stood ready by Finkel's drug store. The infants cried and screamed and the murderers laughed. It reminded me of the times we used to ship geese to the slaughterer. If anything, the geese were handled better. We were careful not to hurt them. These small Jewish children were thrown in wagons as geese right after slaughter…

[Page 114]

I quietly knocked on the door of my father's hideout and gave the sign that I was one of us. My father came out and told me that my mother had lost her mind and was laughing uncontrollably. We cried good and hard together and parted ways.

At dawn the Ukrainians returned again with the Germans to rummage through the house. They looked into every hole, checked every corner. I heard the German policeman, a "good friend" of ours, shout angrily that he didn't see a single one of the Fliters at the collection point… We readied ourselves deeper in our holes and held our breath waiting for nightfall.

Together my brother Barukh and I knew all the paths and routes in our big house. We knew about every hidden passageway and cavity and that our photo-studio opened out into Rakovtchekhe's orchard.

As soon as I took my first step outside the ghetto, I felt freer. I became a completely different person. Something became lighter on my soul and I desired to live. Even more, I felt in myself a force to fight for my life."

* * *

With one sip he finished drinking his glass. He lit a fresh cigarette and became lost in thought. With half-closed eyes he sat and looked out at the distant past. You could see him relive every dramatic day. He stood up and began walking across the room . He finished smoking his cigarette, lit a fresh one, sat down and continued.

"We were both very hungry. We had eaten next to nothing for several days. Soon we were in the Czech village Zalisie. We set out to find a Czech we knew to beg for a little bread.

[Page 115]

Barukh stood outside while I went into the courtyard to beg for food. The Czech told me to wait in the barn while he went to get food. I did what he said. Then he dashed over and slammed the barn door shut. He began shouting "Jew! I caught a Jew! Police!". His wife and neighbors begged him to let me free, but neither their begging or my desperate cries helped. The Czech only shouted louder and more vehemently: "Police! Quick! I caught a Jew!"

Barukh didn't skip a beat. He ran up and gave the Czech a good knock on the head. The Czech then struck at Barukh, and, fighting the Czech all the way, Barukh succeeded in reaching the barn, opening the door, and yelling "Dovid, it's open – run!"

In the middle of this the police arrived. Barukh saw them immediately and told me. I was able to go back in the barn and grab my coat and boots. When I came back out of the barn, the police were already coming close to us. We took off running like an arrow from a bow. The police shot after us, whistled, chased us, and we barely made it out of their hands.

Tired, hungry, but glad about our first victory in our fight to live, a Czech acquaintance of Barukh's who lived completely separated from the rest of the town. This Czech gave us food and drink and agreed to shelter us. However, we couldn't trust anyone anymore after the disaster with the other Czech we knew.

And so we set out on the road again. The road went back to Mizocz. Going to and from Mizocz we faced gangs of beaming peasants. They were content, weighed down with Jewish property. We boldly went on and pretended that we were with them."

* * *

[Page 116]

The ash-tray was already over-full. Dovid ordered a strong coffee, wiped the sweat from his face, lit a cigarette from a new pack, and continued.

He told me the details of everything he lived through, all of the miracles of survival from when his life hung by a thread- it wasn't possible. Entire books could be written about the things in his head. I will record only the particular events that have become engraved on my memory.

"One time we ran into a little old Jewish woman who must have been around 90 years old. When we asked her why she was running from the ghetto, she answered "at a hundred and one it's all still the same", meaning that even hundred-year-olds have a will to live.

The Fliter family – a picture from 1930

The old woman was in hiding at a safehouse somewhere and came out now due to some danger or dire circumstance. We decided then that it wouldn't be bad for us to have a hideout somewhere, too. We took this seriously and with the help of a Czech we knew we made a hideout.

[Page 117]

At night we would sneak around in search of food and during the day we would lay hidden. When we went in or out of the hideout, we would always wipe our footprints out of the snow so that nobody would find us.

The hideout wasn't even suitable for an animal, but we were happy to have a place to hide. After a few weeks of living in the hideout, in darkness, moisture, cold, and desperation, Barukh caught a terrible cold. He was so far gone that he couldn't speak. He wrote down that he was very ill. A heavy rain poured and we felt it in our hideout. The rain came in, flooding the floor and bed with water. We quickly fled the hideout and searched for shelter under thick trees.

We walked a few dozen meters and heard a thunderclap like a cannon. We went back in the direction of the sound and came to the hideout, which we had left minutes earlier. It was in shambles. If we had not abandoned it then, we would have been buried alive… another miracle. We then went to the Czech who had helped us build the hideout and told him everything. He took us into his house and began healing Borekh with warm compresses. We put warm compresses on him the entire night and he became better by morning.

From time to time we would run into Soviet partisans. All of our arguments and requests to join them were of no help. They demanded we give them weapons as a stipulation for joining. One time they ordered all the inhabitants of the village we were staying in to go inside their homes and not show their faces. Through the window we saw the Ukrainian police being disarmed by the partisans. The partisans sat down and ate with the police and they spent an entire day together. At night they got up and left at once and in the morning they came back with all of the weapons.

[Page 118]

One evening when we were eating with a Czech we knew, the door opened and a group of Banderites came in. The leader demanded a room for himself. He shook everyone's hand and ours too. I soon recognized him as an old school friend. He, however, didn't recognize me. Afraid that he would, I left the room claiming I had something to take care of outside. In the yard there were plenty of Banderites, some of whom I recognized. They had also survived and lived to see the day when the Red Army arrived in the region. That was in January 1944."

"Jan-u-ar-y nine-teen four-ty-four." For some long moments he sat there and was silent. It was clear that the memories from that time were causing him anxiety. I poured him another glass. He lit and began smoking a fresh cigarette. The sadness disappeared from his face and he continued with a smile.

"You have to understand, my dear. No! You can't understand and feel what it means when I say 'we were free'. But we were also out of strength and exhausted, naked and barefoot, without relatives and without friends. Alone without a home and without a future. We both chose to enlist in the Red Army. There we would take revenge for everything and everyone. For the youth that was stolen from us, for the blood of our parents and all of our relatives, for our destroyed home and for all the suffering and tears. Secondly, we could bathe and have clean water, eat until we were full and rest soundly.

We presented ourselves to the recruitment officer to enlist . The major asked us multiple questions and eventually said that they were searching for the people who wanted to evade service. However, those that came voluntarily to the military would go into civilian service. Given that we were photographers by trade, he would find a way for us to use our profession for our benefit and theirs.

[Page 119]

I got a suit instead of the usual clothes and put them on. However, when I went out in the street with the black, elegant suit, people laughed at me- and rightly so. I had to go back and change. At least in my dirty, torn up clothes I wasn't a laughingstock.

Our former partner, the Czech named Savulke, assisted us as much as he could.

* * *

In Mizocz we were quickly convinced that the world was only for the goyish thugs. All of the German accomplices, all of the Ukrainian lowlifes and antisemites held all of the important positions and offices under the new regime.

I went right away to the NKVD and spoke plainly. I pointed out all of the Banderites and Jew murderers to them and demanded that they be punished.

Matsiuk, the baker's wife, was known as a Jew hater by everybody. She was a big shot among the Jew killers during Hitler's occupation. The greatest thieves and bandits used to stand by while she instructed them who to rob. I discovered huge quantities of stolen Jewish goods in her cellar. Unfortunately, I was forced to let her have them, due to the antisemitism that ran rampant even after the Germans were defeated.

Such events quickly made me realise that it was impossible to get rid of all the antisemites. Even worse, I was convinced that my life was in danger. The Soviet security agency plainly and clearly informed me of that. The earth was truly burning under my feet. I became consumed by animosity and grief seeing how the world treated Jews. I went to Rovne and with luck began working as a photographer. Little by little, I cooled down.

Once, as I was walking in the neighborhood of the market in Rovne, I ran into one of the most relentless Jew murderers who had headed the Banderites in Mizocz. This model citizen was armed and accompanied by a group of Soviet officers and wore the badges of a Soviet partisan officer.

[Page 120]

I walked right up to him and began yelling- how dare a Banderite like him desecrate a Soviet uniform. He didn't panic, but instead came at me with a stream of verbal abuse. His friends, the Soviet officers, quickly came to his side and began berating me, arguing that while he was fighting with them in the partisan ranks, I was hiding in Tashkent. The mob with him burst out laughing and voices were heard, in Hitler's own style, saying that no one should dare dishonor Ukrainian heroes.

The tallest officer in the group, a major, forcefully pushed me aside and with an admonishing voice told me that I should be more careful accusing partisans who he personally knew to be heroic fighters."

"And you didn't have any other choice than to go along with it?" I asked, throwing in a question. My Dovid became upset. It was apparent that my question had irritated him. He answered me with clenched fists:

"Do you really think I was the same little Dovid that you once knew? I fell flat on the ground and screamed so loud that the partisans were frightened. I told the major that he was taking a great responsibility upon himself by sheltering a German spy who had handed over Soviet partisans to the Gestapo. I demanded he take us both to the police so that they could question both me and Orlov, the head of the NKVD in Mizocz.

Meanwhile, a large crowd was gathering. They were all eager to see how this would end. The partisans couldn't belittle my accusations on the spot to save the murderer. The Major then began arguing with me that perhaps I had made a mistake. It had been years, how could I recognize someone with such certainty? Secondly, it was a fact that the young man had been a Soviet partisan and he would testify himself that the young man used to fight among the partisans.

[Page 121]

However, I was certain about his identity and I was determined that the murderer would not escape this time. He had too many Jewish lives on his conscience to go free. I then questioned the major and asked: comrade major, when did you meet the miscreant? When did he join your partisan regiment? Did you investigate his background before you took him into your detachment? Do you mean to say, comrade commander, that you took a dangerous liability when you defended such a criminal? I am convinced and responsible for everything I have said. I demand that we both be arrested until the hearing for my accusations.

Although the antisemitism was strong enough and everyone wanted to save the murderer from justice, it was, after all, very hard to ignore my accusation that he had handed Soviet partisans over to the Gestapo.

The military police arrived with the investigator. They soon called for me and put together an official report. The major temporarily let the murderer go free and said he would be responsible for him appearing in court and that I was obligated to appear as a witness and testify against him.

A few days later the major came to me in my studio, apologizing to me and asking that I not involve him in the matter. He asked me to say that the individual had changed sides after his career as a Banderite, and that I had of course recognized him. I began talking with the major, speaking very plainly. I told the major that I had no problem with him personally, and that if he didn't do everything in his power in order to save the miscreant, I would in turn make an effort to help him get out of the situation and would forget his conduct at the beginning. He then told me that the man had already been arrested and that he was sentenced to death. He thoroughly apologized for his conduct. He told me that he was a friend of the Jews and that he thought I had made a mistake, since the bandit had disguised himself well and was a brave partisan.

[Page 122]

From my talk with the major, I discovered that the lowlife had joined the partisans once everyone saw that the war was being lost. The major had believed all of his stories and took him in as a partisan. He had advanced himself, and would have become a big shot among the Soviets if it weren't for me.

The major left and feverish days ensued for me. I had to look for witnesses, particularly among the Ukrainians against the criminal. This was not easy, since Banderites made people tremble with fear.

I knew that his friends and fellow antisemites would do everything possible to save him. I also knew that the accusation of murdering Jews wouldn't be enough to bring him to the gallows. That is why I stressed that he handed over Soviet partisans to the Gestapo. I brought enough witnesses, even among the Ukranians, who confirmed my accusations. He only confessed to killing Jews. He claimed that it was Soviet paratroopers that he had turned over to the Germans.

His guilt, however, was clear and demonstrable. He was sentenced to death and I was there at the execution.

Shortly after, we left Rovne and escaped the land that had absorbed so much Jewish blood."

[Page 123]

Dreams are Not False Omens

by Baruch Fliter

Translated from Hebrew by Nida Kiali

As the wave of oppression in the ghetto intensified, all glimmers of hope for a better foreseeable future had vanished and the humiliated Jews had no choice but to escape into a world of delusions and dreams…

Everyone had dreams. Many had experienced revelations that held a special meaning. Many different rumors with a mystical timbre traveled about from mouth to ear. Everyone waited for an upcoming miracle. Every dream and delusion was interpreted as a prediction of imminent salvation. There was lots of talk in the ghetto about "salvation," so much so that even the word itself reached the Christians without them realizing its significance to the Jews.

Like in the good years, when the house of my aunt Leah, Asher Ben-Oni's mother, attracted the youths of town – whether because of its joyous atmosphere or because of all the heated talk about important topics that took place there – so too, now, during the somber days of Hitler's regime, the house served as a hub and a meeting place for all those who were thirsty for reliable news, rumors, interpretations and also actions.

In the basement of this house, a powerful radio was hidden. The spouse of Sonya, the daughter of my uncle Samuel Horowitz, also known as Puntik, was a regular listener to London, Moscow, Switzerland and other radio stations. He shared all that he heard and understood, along with proper interpretation, to those worthy of knowing.

Later, the house was used as headquarters to plan a mass escape to the forest. Of course, all rumors concerning a new hallucination or dream of upcoming salvation had soon reached this house.

Among the permanent household members was the mute Yisheyahu Melgalter. Thanks to his exceptional cleverness, he was always on top of things. He was always eager to learn what was reported on London Radio and what the world had to say about our situation. He was one of those who had insisted on escaping to the forest and fighting the Germans. Too bad I never followed up on what had happened to this wonderful young man. In April 1942, I too had a dream about the date of October 13th. I rushed to this house and talked about my dream and this date, October 13th.

Buzi Berman, one of the regular guests who used to attend the house meetings, was jotting down every date, hoping to disperse any illusions and ridicule any dreams and hallucinations.

[Page 124]

When the expected date of an omen expired, Buzi used to ironically declare that Baruch's date, October 13th, surely wouldn't disappoint and would bring about salvation.

On October 12th, just as I entered Aunt Leah's house as usual, Buzi approached me with a sarcastic question:

"Well, Baruch, what about your October 13th?"

I answered in the same manner, "just wait, Buzi, there are 24 hours until the 13th." I prophesied and did not know what I had prophesied.

The ghetto was surrounded by armed soldiers and trained dogs a day later, and the liquidation had begun.

All the occupants of our large and roomy house hid in a shelter prepared in advance. For some reason, I lacked the desire to hide in the shelter and remained in the house. I closed the doors and the windows, crawled beneath the pantry, and covered myself with carpets that were there, awaiting the forthcomings.

I did not need to wait long; a crowd charged toward our house. They stormed into it and started looting whatever they could find. I saw them all. They were good neighbors and acquaintances. I couldn't believe they were capable of such viciousness. Once the rioters had left, I came out of hiding, closed the doors and the windows once again, and went back into hiding. I had heard how the Koppelman family, who used to live in our house, were kicked out, and after this, no one visited the house anymore till evening.

Before everyone dispersed to their hiding places, mother took out a bag filled with gold coins. She divided them among us and said that it's better to have something in hand. Because of the lack of time, we separated, and every family member sought shelter in a different place. I had no clue as to where my siblings and parents were hiding.

After nightfall, I left my spot and headed to the attic where I met with my brother David and my uncle Samuel who were in the midst of planning their upcoming steps. Upon noticing me, they hurried to break the news to my mother that I was alive. This brought great joy to everyone's heart. However, I could not meet my mother. It was too dangerous to open their shelter. We could only talk through the door for a little while, and I received her last blessing for the unknown road ahead of me.

While carrying on a disjointed conversation in the attic, we fell asleep. I do not know how long I slept, and when I woke up, only I and my brother David were left in the attic. Uncle Samuel went missing.

I woke David up. We went down from the attic. I was able to get out of the ghetto and headed toward the village of Kunyn[1].

We did not have far to go when we came across a familiar Gentile –

[Page 125]

Mikolay. He was on his way to Mizocz, not to save Jews… He started to justify himself, saying that he was going to find his son and then he directed us toward the village and went on his way. We walked for a few hours and met Mikolay again at the break of dawn… It seemed that we were walking around in circles. This time, with his help, we arrived at the village and entered the house of Havra, an old acquaintance. We gave her a few gold coins, and promised many other valuables in exchange for shelter. She agreed. The next day, Uncle Samuel, his sister, Riva, accompanied by Bebe Stifer, my cousin, joined us. In order to gain Havra's favor, we told her the location of the hiding place for our clothes and valuables in our house in Mizocz. Then we sent her to bring it to us. She returned and told us that she had found the hiding place, but it was empty because others got to it before her. We didn't believe her and suspected that not all of the story was true. Nevertheless, we remained silent and said nothing.

Two days later, we were forced to leave the house alongside our cousin, Bebe Stifer. Havra refused to host us all. We headed toward the town of Klopit[2]. While there, we heard a rumor that our friend, Yehiel Greenberg, a man with numerous local connections, resided in Zalissya[3]. It wasn't difficult to get to the woods of Zalissya from Klopit. Indeed, we met with Yehiel and a girl named Hava, from the village of Holchi[4] who was in the same ghetto with us. Yehiel broke us some happy news. He informed us that his Czech acquaintance promised to help us. We decided to take refuge in the woods where we could live and hide.

We hid in rock crevices in the woods, while planning our future. We were able to get hold of tools and started preparing a shelter. With Yehiel's limp and Bebe's swollen feet, it was decided that my brother and I would go and bring a few days' worth of food for everyone. Just as we came down the hill toward the valley, we heard loud footsteps. We looked up and saw German soldiers running. We were able to hide in a pile of leaves the autumn wind had stacked, and listened.

We heard gunfire, followed by shouts of soldiers and then more gunfire. Then silence filled the air. We didn't leave the shelter during the day. Experience had educated us about the dangers of doing so. At night, we left the pile of leaves and went back to our shelter in the rocks.

We found Yehiel and Bebe, murdered. Bebe was lying down barefoot. The killers stole his brand-new boots. His socks weren't that far from his body. I picked them up and put them in my pocket.

Depressed, we returned to Havra's. To answer Samuel's question "where is Bebe?" I showed him the socks. He understood and burst into tears.

[Page 126]

Despite what we had gone through, we could not afford any more delay at Havra's. That same night, we went back to Zalissya.

Hungry, weary, and depressed, we decided to approach Savalka Vorozhnilik's uncle to ask for bread. I stood by as David asked him for food. He told him to enter the granary and wait over there, for he feared being seen while feeding a Jew. Once David stepped into the granary, that Czech started shouting out loud, "a Jew! I caught a Jew! Police!" I was able to hear how his wife and the neighbors were begging him to leave my brother alone and to let him go. He did not stop and kept shouting, "I caught a Zhid[5]! Police, hurry up!" My brother's scream had also reached my ears: "Mr. Voroznshnilik! What have I done to you? I want to live. Open the door for me." I got a bit closer. I saw my brother getting undressed, attempting to break the window lattices of the granary to escape.

The Czech then grabbed a thick rod and started hitting my brother's arms, trying to push him back into the granary.

My heart was pounding and tears of helplessness and anger poured out of my eyes. I approached the Czech. He was surprised to see me, and without thinking, he hit my head with the rod. I fell to the ground and he continued beating me. The blows caused me to regain consciousness. I started getting closer to the granary while wrestling with this bastard. We were lucky that the granary was closed by a latch and not a lock. I was able to unlock the latch and open the door with my head. Right before my strength gave out, I screamed: "Get out, David, the door is open."

Half-naked, David ran out of the granary. The Czech tried to assault him, but David was quicker, hit him in the head with a rock or a piece of metal, and knocked him out. Before the police arrived, David managed to make it back to the granary and took his clothes. Upon leaving the Czech's backyard, the police appeared. We ran to the nearby forest as fast as we could, escaping the officers who chased and fired upon us.

We rested and relaxed, and arrived at the village of Zhovkva[6]. We were provided with shelter for some time by an acquaintance of ours. We were uncomfortable eating his bread for free. We had little money to spare, and nonetheless, he refused to get paid. Therefore, we decided to come to Mizocz to try and find another hiding place, retrieve our belongings and valuables and use them to compensate that acquaintance.

We arrived at Mizocz. The hiding place was completely empty. Empty-handed, we went back to Zhovkva and broke the news about our failure to our acquaintance. We thanked him for all he has done and parted ways with him.

While wandering, we arrived at a remote town and knocked on the door of an isolated house. They opened and welcomed us, and a strange thing happened. The owner of the house started kissing

[Page 127]

us, hugging us, and crying with joy. As we wondered about her manner, she revealed to us that she was Henya Bronka, our housekeeper who worked for us when we were children. Then, we recognized and remembered her. It was at her place that we had a hot meal for the first time in many weeks. We learned about other Jews hiding in the vicinity. And most importantly, her husband accompanied us to the woods, found us a spot for a shelter, and even helped build it.

I became gravely ill at that shelter and only through sheer miracle did not perish. I was too sick to speak. The shelter collapsed during the rainy days, moments before we left it. While roaming, we came across many survivors from the Mizocz Ghetto and other towns. We met good people, whose kindness and good deeds restored our faith in humanity, but we also met some who were worse than wild beasts and more dangerous than any four-legged predators.

As a result of the action of Yitzhak Wasserman's partisans, who took righteous revenge on those who killed his parents, respect for us with the local population had risen for a long time. Every town and village spoke of the heroic deeds of our fellow town resident, who incited fear in all haters of Jews.

One time, we came across Max Weltfreint of Sosnivka[7], who lived in the ghetto of Mizocz. He was seriously injured, and his hands and legs were tied. He told us that he was caught by two youngsters, almost lads, who tied him up with a rope and tried to slaughter him. They couldn't do it since they didn't have a sharp knife, only a dull blade. One of them went to grab an appropriate knife, and then he gained consciousness, hitting his guard in the stomach with his tied legs. He undid the rope until he could move, and here he was. We got all the ropes off him, washed him, and bandaged his wounds. Since then, he stayed nearby and we met a few more times.

We were aided by the Evangelicals[8] multiple times, who did it for moral and religious reasons. In return, we were required to participate in their prayers and rituals more than once and pretend to be believers of their faith.

One woman from the Evangelical families greatly desired my neckerchief. I handed it to her without any hesitation, and I won her heart as of that moment. Over there, we learned that my father was alive and wandering about in Mizocz. The Germans permitted him to live there in relative freedom. By allowing that, the Germans wanted to concentrate all the survivors in Mizocz, leading them to believe that there was an option to live if only they served the German masters. And indeed, the rumor had reached some naïve people who came out of hiding. They were discovered and killed without delay. They did not kill my father. They implied to him that he should run away, but he had had enough with life and didn't care one way or the other.

We wrote a letter to him and asked him to join us. The letter was to be delivered to Svolka by our acquaintance Bonchkovsky, and Svolka had to deliver the letter to Dad. Bonchkovsky could not set off on the appointed night, because of the heavy snow that covered the roads, and he came with the letter to Mizocz one day after Dad was executed…

Svolka helped us by sending clothes and food. He never turned us down. Over time we got to know people and learned how to get along. We would help the evangelists with the housework, and we especially specialized in grinding flour on a millstone.

While we were hidden in an attic at the Czech's home, the Germans unexpectedly stormed the village. They gathered all the people outside, including women and children, and placed them facing the wall. Then they started setting all the houses on fire. The people were about to be killed immediately afterward for real or imagined support of the Banderovites[9] or partisans, I do not remember anymore. We decided to burn alive and not come down from the attic, because if we were discovered, the whole village would be destroyed without mercy. We covered ourselves, confessed, and waited for the fire to come. We only asked God that death come without too much torture. When the fire lingered, I peeked from under the lid. Through the cracks, I saw that the Czechs were rushing about with packages and that the Germans were gone. We came down from the attic and learned that at the last minute, the residents were pardoned and were only ordered to change their place of residence. They marveled at our courage, that we would rather burn alive than harm them. In return, they promised to take us to the village of Borshchivka[10], to which they had to move.

In that vicinity, we met with Bronia Weinzweig of Zdolbuniv[11], who spent every summer at Mizocz with her relatives, with Velvel, the barber, and with the children of Asher Schapira. We built a new shelter nearby and lived in it. Bronia was then apprehended by the Banderovites when she was on her way to look for food. However, she was released and lived to see the day of triumph over the Germans.

Both of us – my brother David and I – went through many more adventures and miracles. More than once, we were separated during a sudden onslaught on us, but we always found each other after a while. On the verge of liberation, of all times, when we knew that the days of German rule were numbered and victory was at hand, we were particularly harassed by the Banderovites, and there was a great danger of being killed just before redemption.

We were very careful for our lives, and with the help of the One Above, we lived to see our liberation by the Red Army.

David immediately joined the ranks of the Soviet security forces. Svolka then came to us

[Page 128]

and asked for his sake to pardon his uncle Vorozhnilik, who at the time locked David in the granary and wanted to hand him over to the Gestapo. I did not give him a clear answer, but David said he was willing to pay Svolka for everything he did for him, even with his life. However, the uncle who wanted to kill him unjustly he would not forgive. David did not say he would hand him over to the authorities, and I promised Svolka to influence David to forgive his uncle, for that was Svolka's wish. In the end, When David approached the village with the Soviets, without any intention of hurting him, the uncle quickly ran and hung himself in the granary, where he had wanted to detain David…

After quite a few wanderings, we settled in Rivne[12] and helped a lot of surviving Jews, thanks to our connections with the authorities. I rescued Michael Kornik by chance, from a group of Banderovite criminals who had been exiled and were on their way to Siberia, and he happened to come across them. We supported the others materially or helped arrange certificates. That's how, for example, I reinstated Asia Baraz to Judaism, etc.

A high-ranking Russian commander once implied that we should leave Russia. We felt the anti-Semitism around us and decided to do as he advised. I managed to meet my future wife, Ida Eisengart, take her out of her gentile environment and restore her safety. After wandering across many countries, we finally reached a safe haven in our country, in the middle of the War of Independence and managed to contribute our humble powers to the establishment of the Hebrew state.

Translator's Footnotes:

1. Kunyn (Кунин), small village 1 km north of Mizocz (Кунин)
2. Klopit (Клопіт), a small village 1 km east of Mizocz (Клопіт)
3. Zalissya (Залісся), an area between Kunyn and Klopit, about 4 km northeast of Mizocz
4. Holchi – Believed to be village associated with modern map reference for Hil'cha Persha (Гільча Перша) about 9 km east of Zalissya.
5. Derogatory term for a Jew- זשיד
6. Zhovkva, this location not identified.
7. Sosnivka (Соснівка), a village approximately 20 km southwest of Mizocz.
8. Evangelicals: Reference to minority Protestant denominations in the region, likely including communities of Czech origin.
9. Banderovites: or Banderites, followers of Stepan Bandera, leader of the militant wing of the ultra-nationalist Organization of Ukrainian Nationalists (OUN) that aligned with Nazi Germany during the war.
10. Borshchivka (Борщівка), an area about 7 km southeast of Mizocz
11. Zdolbuniv (Здолбунів), a small city 18 km northeast of Mizocz, about halfway to Rivne.
12. Rivne (Рівне), the regional capital, 30 km north-northeast of Mizocz.

[Page 129]

Father Saved My Mother from Death with a Speech

by Asiya Braz

Translated from Hebrew by Gabrielle Cooper

When the German occupation forces based themselves in Mizocz and started to restore and resume economic enterprises and factories in the region, my father was sent to the village Buderazh to establish a dairy there.

I was a girl of eleven years then, coddled and cared for by my parents as the apple of their eyes. My only brother – Izya–studied at university in Lviv and we supposed he had succeeded in escaping to Russia with the Red Army.

The decrees and spiteful proceedings against the Jews became more frequent and more numerous, and for my father, the illusion that the Jews could still find days of respect and calm faded; he befriended a Polish couple without children and they agreed between them that the Poles would adopt me as a daughter. Father explained our situation to me, and he appealed to my heart to leave home and go willingly to the Polish couple in Buderazh. Of course, he promised that when the times changed, I would return home and we would live a happy life as before.

[Page 130]

One bright day the couple turned up at our house and wanted to take me to the village with them. I did not agree. I cried, and I shouted, and I said that I did not want to be separated from my beloved parents. Since the whole deal needed to take place secretly, for obvious reasons, they were not able to force me to leave the ghetto without everyone knowing. With no other choice, it was agreed that I would stay with my parents but that Father would come to the Poles when the danger arrived. Father even took me to the house of the Poles once, so that I knew exactly where the place was and I could find them when needed. On that fateful night, when we were awoken and informed that the ghetto was surrounded and the destruction had started, all the occupants began to flee from the house.

I clung to my parents and did not want to separate from them. Only when my mother said to me that I was bothering them and was getting in the way, did I say goodbye to them and run away to Motia, a Christian acquaintance who served in good times as a maid at the home of our friends, the Vigoda's, who then lived at the nearby Hartstein house.

Motia's husband was a baker and he shut me in the closet immediately after I entered their home. While I was in the closet a police officer entered the house and I heard that he came to inform them that finally the end had come for the Jews of Mizocz. Just after the police officer left, the closet was opened and the baker said to me: "My child, we cannot keep you."

I did not understand the situation: I was dressed as a *shiksa*[1] and in my hand were the identity documents of a Christian girl and I thought that the danger had passed from me. The baker did not stop talking and listening to my explanations, he only took me in his arms, took me to a warehouse and put me into a big box full of bones which had been in the warehouse since the Soviet days.

I lay with the bones for a long time. There was night, day, and night again. I heard shots, shouts, dogs barking. I was sad, very sad, lying helpless and numb.

The Ukrainians looted at will from Jewish houses, and they turned the Hartstein's warehouse into their base. They would come with stolen objects, leave them in the warehouse and return to continue looting. They even reached the box where I was hidden among the bones and filled it with things from Jewish homes. To this day it is hard for me to understand how they did not find me there.

On the third night, Motia's husband came, took me out from the pile of things and bones, and he gave me a bag with bread and said: "My arm is too short to save you. The city is now burning in a great fire. Everyone is busy putting out the fire and now is the time to escape." I stood there powerless, not yet fully understanding the situation. Bayer (the name of the baker was Bayer) then took me by the hand and forcefully dragged me

[Page 131]

The drama club of the public school

[Page 132]

to the Polish cemetery. Here he parted from me. He wished me luck and told me to run away from Mizocz. He also advised me not to go the usual way through the paths in the fields. He expressed his confidence that good people would help me.

I didn't know the way to Buderazh, it was a dark night, dogs were barking, and I was scared to go. I knocked at one house and asked permission to stay with them. Through the locked door they answered: they did not want to hurt me but they also could not help me. I started to appeal to the mercy in their hearts and they answered me with threats. I left the house and continued into the unknown. I walked all night and as it turned to morning I came to the village Holchi, the opposite direction from the village Buderazh, which I aspired to reach. Here I was attacked by a large dog. I gave him a big piece of my bread and he left me. I continued to walk and I came across a *goy*[2] with a sack. I presented myself as a Christian, and to his question of where I came from and where I was going I answered that I was returning home from a visit. He understood who I was, gave me a tasty pierogi with beans, and showed me the way to Buderazh. The *goy* himself said that he was going to Mizocz to take for himself what was the property of the Jews.

Broken, tired to death, hungry and desperate for rest, I arrived in Buderazh at the house of the Poles who once wanted to adopt me. They told me that from now on my name was Marussia and that I was a relative of theirs whose parents had been deported by the Soviets. I pretended and did not tell them what I had been through. The woman invited me to cut firewood before I could rest or catch my breath. Despite my great tiredness, and although I had never done it before, I started to saw the trees with the woman. While working I told her about everything that had happened to me and I asked her if I could rest. The woman brought me home immediately, fed me a proper meal and laid me down to sleep. I slept a lot, and slowly, slowly regained my strength. Only the landlady knew my true identity; all the rest of the family members, including the parents of the woman, knew no more than the rest of the residents.

A few days after I arrived in Buderazh, an order was issued by the Germans to hang at the entrance of every house a list, approved by the police, of all inhabitants of that house. My documents were accepted by the police. On the tenth night of my stay in Buderazh I dreamed a dream: my parents were walking on a narrow path ridden with obstacles. They marched and approached me. In my dream I felt that someone touched my head and gently awakened me. I opened my eyes and standing before me were Father and Mother. I almost did not recognize Father. He was dressed like a typical rural Ukrainian and it was hard to recognize him as Jewish. Our happiness was great and each of us was yearning to take advantage of the moment. I told my parents what had happened to me and my mother told me that she had succeeded in entering the Finkel's hideout. There was no space for Father in this hideout, so he hid on the roof. Of course they searched for them thoroughly, because they were well known and their absences were noticed. But the hiding place was good and they were not discovered. All of the Finkel family had Aryan documents, and they remained in hiding until spirits in town calmed. Then they came out of hiding and my father instructed everyone on how to escape from Mizocz. My parents were with me for a few days, until Gabrova, the landlady, told them to go. She added that she would honor her word and save me, but that my parents were endangering her and me as well by staying. There was no choice. I said goodbye to my parents and have not seen them since then. I was cared for in a farming community of Polish children near Rivne[3], and I was out of danger.

Father had rescue plans and also appropriate documents, and was certain that they could go to a safe place. Unfortunately, on their way to Buderazh they encountered a group of young Ukrainian men who were merrily returning from a party. These men were well acquainted with my Father. My parents' pleas did not help, nor did the bribes and promises they offered to the Ukrainians. The merry men led my parents to Mizocz to deliver them into German hands.

The Germans assembled a crowd to witness the killing, and father was ordered to dig a pit for the two of them. Father dug the pit and told Mother that he was going to save her and that she must endure, because her children were still alive and she should remain to care for them. The pit was prepared and they were commanded to stand at the edge of their grave. Then, Father turned to the Ukrainian police and asked them to fulfill a last humble request before his death. They were puzzled when they heard him ask to be allowed to speak to the community, in order to say goodbye, and they agreed. Father then turned and said: Dear citizens! I receive this punishment from heaven inflicted on us Jews and I go to death without anger or complaint. However, at death's door I want to reveal to you a secret that we have guarded for years, and ask that my wife Rosa be buried in the Christian cemetery after her death, because she was a member of the Pravoslav[4] religion… I could not reveal this, because my parents and relatives would have prevented me from marrying her.

But now that I am about to take leave of you forever, I hope you will not deny my last request to you. For many years we lived in friendship, I have done no injustice to any one of you, nor insulted anyone. I am afraid to face the Creator of the world with this injustice I did in my life, when I deceived a Pravoslav girl and joined her to a people not her own. We are both about to receive the punishment we deserve and we will die without complaint. But I will be pleased to die when I know I have righted what I wronged and my wife can complete her eternal years among members of her religion and community.

[Page 134]

A murmur passed through the big crowd. Women sobbed and cried out: A pure Pravoslav soul to save! Don't you dare harm her!

The commotion grew and my father's words were swallowed in the crowd's voice. No one

The "Beitar" group on a hike in Sosenki forest

[Page 135]

doubted my father's "confession." On the contrary, many of those gathered started to remember many "signs" and "proof" that my mother was not a Jew. The best proof by far was that she did not resemble a Jew at all and in her mastery of the Russian language she surpassed even the holy Pravoslav vessels.

In the end Father was executed on the spot and Mother was handed off to a Pravoslav priest. From there she moved to the village of Derman and worked as a nurse. The priest's son Vasya, an old acquaintance of ours, helped her a lot and taught her the ways of the Pravoslav religion so that she would not reveal herself.

I received two letters from her. In them she told me that she was working as a nurse in the Banderovites' battalion but told me nothing about my father's fate and how she had gotten to where she was.

When the Soviets were about to conquer the region, my mother was summoned once at night into the woods, to provide medical assistance to the wounded. The Banderovites murdered her in the forest because she knew too much about what they were doing and they were scared to leave her alive under the Soviet regime. And that is how I remained, on the verge of liberation, orphaned from my father and mother.

The Gordonists of the Mizocz branch

Translator's Footnotes:

1. *Shiksa* is a Yiddish term for a non-Jewish woman or girl
2. *Goy* is a Yiddish term for a non-Jew
3. Rivne, historically Rovno, a city in modern day western Ukraine
4. Russian Orthodox Church

[Page 136]

The Partisan Izya Wasserman

by A. Ben-Oni

Translated from Hebrew by Isaac Makovsky, Joshua Metzel and Samuel Rotenberg

The winter stood with all its might. After the snow fell heavily for three consecutive days and entirely covered the land, a bitter chill prevailed accompanied by a raging wind. The streets of the village of Elirania[1] were devoid of footprints, and the desolate trails glistened in the white. The peasants secluded themselves in their huts and kept warm.

Thick, dark-gray smoke billowed from within chimneys, and the smells of rendered-fat or fresh pastry permeated through doors and windows. At the same time, the Wasserman family hid in the basement at the mercy of the Polish farmer, Omanski; in exchange for a small sum, Omanski gave them hot tea, food, and news to raise their spirits. They remembered their home as spacious, convenient, bright and warm, and they thanked God for providing a roof over their heads in those troubled times when the regions of Rivne, Dubno, Zdolbuniv and Ostroh were declared "Judenrein," or completely exterminated of Jews. By the fading lantern light, they reminisced about "the good old days" when they spent the winter evenings in their home, surrounded by friends and acquaintances, around tables filled with delicacies, and we calculated that their gold and the jewels could last at least ten years and then …

Only one thing disrupted the Wassermans' relative contentment: their only son,

[Page 137]

Izya, did not want to hide and patiently wait for the wrath to pass. When the Germans invaded and commanded the Jews to wear the patch of disgrace, he immediately acquired a weapon and fled to the forest. Until the extermination of the Dubno Ghetto, almost nobody heard from him, and only when they were rescued and fled to the forest did they learn their son was alive and the leader of a small and brave group of partisans. They met him in the forest, and convened regularly from that point forward.

Each time they met, he never mentioned the raids of the partisans, his wars with the Germans, or the help he gave the Jews in the forest. They only heard about their son from the mouths of the Jews and non-Jews of Mizocz and Dubno whom they met in the forest; they heard of the courage of their Izya, of the deadly acts he and his company committed against German positions that were scattered and isolated in the area, and of the severe punishments inflicted upon the German collaborators, and those unwilling to aid the hidden Jewish population.

When his parents tried to dissuade him from endangering his life by fighting for the partisans, he would stand up and leave.

Three days ago, he arranged to visit them, but never arrived. They assumed that he did not come because of the heavy snow and bitter cold. However, in the morning, the owner of the basement told them that, after a hard and bloody battle with the German Gendarmerie in a nearby village, in which all the Germans and their weapons were destroyed and captured, Izya's company ran away to the forests of Shumsk[2] and Kremenets[3]. Mrs. Beila Wasserman, Izya's mother, suspected that something happened to her beloved son, and asked Izya's brother-in-law, Moshe Meislitsch, who married her daughter Malia, Izya's sister, to leave the hideout at night to hear about Izya'' fate. The final knock on the entrance to the basement terrified its occupants. They quickly hid their jewelry and gold rings, and the father, Yosef Wasserman, opened the door.

The owner of the home brought hot tea, bread, meat, tallow and even vodka. Every time they served their victuals through a concealed hole. They only opened the door for the owner of the house when he had something important to tell them. With any preparations he told them that the Germans conducted extensive house-to-house searches throughout the nearby villages, looking for Iyza's partisans. In Elirania, they prepared to arrive sometime in the evening, or the next morning. They did not doubt the possibility of an extremely meticulous search of his home because, rightly, one of the residents might have told the Germans, in secret, about his connection with Jews. For the sake of everybody else, the owner of the house wanted the family to leave the basement for a few days, until the search concluded. He already found an appropriate place for them in the forest, and he will bring them there after dark. Yosef Wasserman sent a farmer another decent gift,

[Page 138]

and the arrangement between them was, when the Germans close in on the village, the farmer will bring the refugees to the hideout inside the forest. They will return to the basement by the farmer's son, an hour after the search.

The farmer left the basement and the Wasserman family sat to eat. A malaise prevailed through the basement, gnawing grief in their hearts; Still unmoved, they lived under the sky once again; left to the kindness of the winds and the snow with fear constantly looming above their heads…

Moshe, who needed to leave the basement to be informed of Izya's fate, and, to prepare for the road, he gathered camouflage clothing, a little money, matches and candles and waited patiently for the village to fall asleep. Suddenly, a fearful scream from the neighbor Krashinsky pierced the walls of the basement, they cupped their ears and listened clearly to the words coming from the mouth of Krashinsky: "The Germans have already reached the village. They are robbing and assaulting, extorting and burning. Escape and save yourself!"

They still did not understand the situation, as they heard the final knock on the door. The farmer entered in a saddened hysteria, and said to follow him, because the Germans reached the third house down.

Half-naked, frightened and confused – the Wassermans went out of the house with the farmer, and set their faces toward the forest. The farmer ran, they were after him. They breathed heavily, falling from the weight of their belongings and from their exertion, then they stood back up and continued to run.

They passed through the thickness of the forest, and were close to their hiding area as Moshe and his family became separated. Moshe headed in the direction of the village of Hurby[4] to try to explain why Izya never showed up. His watch showed that it was still early, 8 p.m., and at that hour, the level of danger heightened when the Germans surrounded them. He slowed down, examined his surroundings and sat down in a comfortable place to do his business. He paused and continued on his way.

There, before he stopped to breathe and relax from the exertion, he heard terrifying cries from the depth of the frozen forest. Moshe contemplated the familiarity of the voices to him. He stood up alert and listened closely, but the shouts did not change. Maybe, he thought, he heard screams? Maybe his exhilarated imagination misled him? But that's not possible! Did he not hear the horrible cries of his wife from his own ears? He accelerated his pace towards the sound of the shouting. A few dozen meters away from him, four silhouettes slinked past him. Moshe stood behind a thick tree watching the figures drift away. He recognized a tall figure as the Uzbek, the former Russian prisoner who worked for the farmer with whom they lived in the basement.

[Page 139]

Moshe covered much ground while running and found an observation point where he could see without being seen. He immediately identified all of the remaining silhouettes. The man with the staff in hand was the owner of the house that led the family to the so-called new hideout. The eldest son, Wladik, ran from the left side of his father with an ax on his shoulder and the brother-in-law of the landlord from the nearby village. He retraced his steps and made his way toward the hideout in the woods. A few meters from the place, he was separated from his loved ones, and he found everyone with broken skulls. Everything was clear and understandable…

* * *

The killers returned to the house, smiling and happy. They killed the hated Jews without any resistance or difficulty. Only one or two of them managed to yell before they died. Omanski still hadn't washed the drops of blood from his face and hands, when he ran to the basement where the murdered family had been hiding. Like a hungry predator attacking its prey, he pounced on the suitcases he had taken out from under the beds. He turned on them and his head spun with joy; there were gold coins and tons of platinum, more than he had ever seen. He could not even imagine jewelry like this and he had never worn clothing as good as this. He closed the basement with a lock and a latch, went up to his house, showered and changed his clothes. Right after, he called out to his Uzbek servant and the rest of his family and sat to sip a glass of vodka to commemorate the expulsion of Jews from his house. Everyone was happy about the riches that had fallen into their hands and even more happy because only them and their neighbor, Krashinsky, knew about the murder. Everyone in their family, the neighbor Krashinsky, and the Uzbek servant all received gifts from the property of the Wassermans and a promise of a portion of the clothes. Only the old father did not take part in the happiness, and sat sadly in the corner. Even though he agreed that it was good to get rid of the Jews because of the danger in it, he said it's enough to take their property and expel them. He believed that there was no justification for killing and also that the Germans wouldn't be forgiven by God. This is what he told his son, but his son stood his ground and argued, because if he took the Jew's property and left them alive, he would not know peace, because they may return when times change, and demand their fortune and disgrace back. Now he can relax and be safe and enjoy his wealth without disruption and live his life.

* * *

Sleepy and exhausted, but extremely content, the members of Izya's company arrived at their base on the cliff in the Shumsk forest. The raid was very successful. The German unit surrendered in the village with barely any fights. They eliminated the guard without making a sound. When they infiltrated the building,

[Page 140]

they surprised the rest of the unit who laid in their beds without weapons. After some verbal resistance, they bound the hands of the Germans and captured all their weapons, money, documents and property before disappearing into the thick of the forest. The Germans stood trial: interrogated about their deeds and sentenced to death for their participation in the atrocities of the ghettos, theft of the population's property, and occupation of foreign lands. The Germans were miserable prisoners. They begged for their lives. They cursed Hitler, appealed to the partisans' consciences, promised they did not touch their Jewish friends, but their sins were known and they were all shot.

The partisans prepared a tasty and filling meal with the supplies they looted, finished with aromatic cigarettes found on the desk of the commander of the German unit. Just this once, they slept with their guards down. They closed the door and secured it with three sandbags then fell into deep sleep. Izya, alone, suffered from insomnia despite his exhaustion. Strange nightmares tormented him and he longed for family like never before – they attacked him. The snores of those sleeping bothered him, so he got up, got dressed, and went out. He felt a bitter taste in his mouth and had a slight dizziness from heavy drinking and physical exertion. All around, a threatening silence prevailed. The thick trees concealed not only the Partisan base, but also the sky and the white expanse.

Izya stepped out from under the trees into the field. The fresh air and the cold dispelled the dizziness like a magic wand; it seemed to disappear. He stood up. He removed the gun from the holster, pressed the cold, metal handle to his forehead and cheeks, then he checked the mechanism, they loaded the bullets and set off on the road. A large gray rabbit flew by, disappearing in the forest behind. The sky stood bright, flooded with the light of the full moon, which floated between the clouds and looked over his sad face at the universe. "The nights are really nice in Canaan, cool and bright." He suddenly started to hum. What a wonderful night! The fugitive by himself. Usually, on nights like this he would harness a pair of galloping horses with a cushioned sled, and sit with his girlfriend for fun. And now... "The nights are really nice in Canaan, cool and bright." Without a doubt, he pondered for his enjoyment, when we succeed and arrive in the land of Israel, I will often miss this sky, the white snow and the thick forests. And when the land of Israel came into view, he forgot about his situation, his status, his roles and even his longing for his parents that was usually in his heart, but their figures appeared before him in every event or vision he imagined.

[Page 141]

Izya decided that tomorrow he will visit. He will visit and demand they move to a secret location on his street, but Izya did not know that he will never see his parents again, nor be able to visit their graves.

* * *

The word spread before Moshe had time to tell anyone about the treacherous murder, and everyone already knew that the Wassermans were murdered by the owner of the basement who coveted all their belongings and money. Two Polish people from his company immediately informed Izya about the crime and told him about the heinous acts of their fellow brothers.

He already decided the form of revenge and punishment, and asked for three volunteers from the company to carry out the death sentence of the murderers of his parents and accomplices. The entire company volunteered despite the inherent difficulties and dangers of the mission. From the volunteers, Izya chose the best of the company, including good friends, the brothers of Jurgilewicz, Polish people from Dubno, and his girlfriend, Ms. Anda. In his last words to the company, he made them swear an oath that they will not let down their rifle until they annihilate Hitler and restore freedom to the subjugated nations. He appointed a replacement for himself and inspired confidence as he sat with his friends, to part with them in peace. The four partisans left their forest hideout at 6 p.m. to go to a village in Elirania to perform retaliatory action.

* * *

After a two-and-a-half-hour walk, they stopped half a kilometer from the target. Anda was sent to patrol the village and to report back. Most of the villagers were sleeping already, so she never found anything special about the village and never found a trace of any Gendarmerie officers. After a short meeting, they decided to enter the village without delay and start the action. They proceed cautiously. Izya had the machine gun, the elder Jurgilewicz had a pistol and grenade, the youngest brother had a submachine gun with bullets, and Anda was carrying a small gun, which had a beautiful silver grip that was stolen from the German officer in one of the operations. The house of the murderer stood at the edge of the village, slightly isolated and well protected. The young Jurgilewicz knocked on the window and ordered in German to open the door. When asked why they were bothered at night, he replied that he was informed by a qualified source, because in this house they were hiding Jews, and therefore they had come to conduct a search. The owner of the house answered that if there were Jews here, he would have been the only one to kill them, and he opened the door. When he saw Izya, he fainted. All the people of the house went out from their beds, and they stood in a line by the wall, and were forced to answer all the questions. The farmer, who recovered from fainting, denied everything, and began to beg for his life. The investigation was cruel, yet short. Izya

[Page 142]

got a message from the killer, describing the murder and explaining the motives of the despicable act. The Uzbek servant was shot first, followed by everyone else. Only the elderly father of the killer survived. Oil and gasoline were then spilled on the house and lit on fire, along with all the corpses and their belongings.

The next day, the whole community was anxious. The Jews who hid in the nearby villages fled to forests or villages further away. The fear of Izya and his company fell on all those whose hands were filthy with the blood of Jews and whose consciences were not clean of informing. The Germans also awoke and sent a large, powerful force of Lithuanians.

In the meantime, legends and stories have spread on the deeds and heroism of Izya and word of the mouth recounted and delivered the miracles and the successful wars of the partisans against the Germans. This was not very pleasant for the Germans, who decided to capture Izya at all costs. And when they didn't succeed, they decided to set a trap and have a meeting between him and a Gestapo officer in Dubno: a discussion of the conditions in which Izya would be ready to dismantle his unit. I couldn't succeed in finding authorized and verified facts about the meeting. However, according to multiple prevailing legends, between the remaining survivors of Mizocz and the Germans, while Izya met with the Gestapo commander in Dubno, Izya informed the commander that he would not lay down his arms until he had fairly avenged the blood of his people and seen the defeat of the shattered Hitlerite Germany. How he got free of the trap is unknown; it was said that there was an important ally in his company, the Germans spoke about their commander, his heart was not content with the murder of the Jews and in his heart, he strongly disagreed with Hitler. I heard from the mouth of a Ukrainian from Mizocz, that it was as if the company of partisans were guarding the two throughout the entire conversation and therefore the Gendarmerie did not try to capture them … however, the story itself, is that on Izya's appearance in the offices of the Gestapo in the big district city of Dubno, proves without a shadow of doubt that before us is an unusually brave Partisan, intolerable by the Germans. These stories only made them hasten his elimination.

* * *

Izya Wasserman was born in Mizocz in 1919. Growing up, his parents became very wealthy and his father was considered to be very rich around his community. His parents procured them the landowner's home. The small palace's degree of splendor stood out. He became educated there and was also an active and dedicated member in the local Beitar branch. At the time of his Bar-Mitzvah, he joined the Polish Government School in Rivne. There he encountered his first manifestation of anti-Semitism. Since then, he has become extremely zealous and began to influence his father to settle business in Poland and to make Aliyah to the Holy Land.

[Page 143]

When World War II broke and the Soviets entered Mizocz, they nationalized all their assets and were known to be sent to Siberia. The father successfully secured a portion of his wealth, at the advice of a Soviet officer. The father has changed residences and moved with his family to Dubno. There, he managed a job, but no one had known about his past. The occupying Germans took the Wassermans in Dubno. When the German order came, forcing the Jews to wear the yellow patch, Izya rebelled and went to live with his Polish friends, the Jurgilewicz family. When the Germans began enslaving workers (this was before they liquidated the Ghetto in the city), he escaped to the forest with two sons from the Jurgilewicz family. They obtained weapons and lived by weapons. Slowly, they gathered until they selected some people, 15 people to be exact, but no more for their company.

When the Dubno Ghetto was liquidated, the company began militaristic action against Germans and their collaborators. The Soviets wanted to connect with them, and the first commandant of the underground requested to annex them to train, but they remained independent organizations. They readily relocated, where they were during the day was not where they were at night. Due to their connections, and the bravery of the population hostile to the Germans, their steps could not be traced, and they produced headaches for the Gestapo. When forced to leave the forests of Dubno, Mizocz and Hurby, they moved to the Shumsk forest and fortified there not far from Kamyana Hryada[5] on a cliff that shares a similar name.

Throughout the Volyn Territory, the search for Izya and his company began. Expensive rewards were promised for any information on their whereabouts; there were harsh sanctions to any village that allowed them access.

Even more so, Izya and the partisan retaliations hurt the Germans more and more. In one incident, they forced two German officers to march the streets condemning Hitler. After they dressed the two officers with the yellow star, they sent them to Shumsk. At midday, they used to attack German convoys parading goods stolen from villagers, and giving it back to the people the same day. Lately, they stopped killing the German they caught, only mutilated them and set them free. The German feared more from Izya's Partisans than fighting the front line, the German decided they had to be rid of at all cost.

At the end of the summer of 1944, accidentally, or due to betrayal, the Germans discovered the hiding place of Izya's boys; one farmer, who brought supplies to Izya's base, was captured

[Page 144]

The "Beitar" group in Mizocz. Fourth from left is Izya Wasserman

[Page 145]

when returning from the base and was forced to lead the Germans to the hiding place. There are those who say it was a matter of chance and there are those who say, it was due to betrayal. Anyway, the place was discovered. A big, strong German force came and a long, bloody battle broke out. Many dozens of Germans fell in the final battle against the brave partisans. They were only able to capture the point once they brought cannons. The partisans fought until the ends of their souls and fought until the last man. Until today the farmers and remnants of the Jews from Dubno, Mizocz and the surrounding areas, mention with a tremor of admiration and respect the name of the brave and proud partisans and Izya Wasserman. May he rest in peace.

Translator's Footnotes:

1. This village could not be located on available maps.
2. Shums'k (Шумськ) approx. 50 km south of Mizocz
3. Kremenets (Кременець) approx. 65 km southwest of Mizocz.
4. Hurby village no longer exists. The general location in 20 km south of Mizocz. The Hurby Protected Tract and a monastery of the same name can still be found. This area was also the site of massacres of the ethnic Polish population by the UPA, and subsequent massacre of UPA forces by the NKVD.

5. Kamyana Hryada can be a village of Hrada (Града) not far from the town of Kremenets, or can be just a name for one of the hilly ranges. 'Hryada' in Ukrainian means 'hill or mountain range'.

[Page 146]

The Zionist Organization

[Page 146]

Memories from *Hashomer Hale'umi* (Zionist Youth) in Mizocz

by Lisa Nemirover

Translated from Hebrew by Eiden Harel Brewer, Noa Etzyon **and** Ofir Horovitz

When I remember the first few days of *Hashomer Hale'umi*[1] in Mizocz, I am taken back to my childhood. The years at the Polish school, reading many books about the heroism and sacrifices of Polish kids on behalf of their nation and country. I can still remember the strong impression the book "the Ship from the Green Hill" left on me. This book described the lives and responsibilities of the Polish scouts. Oh, how jealous I was of the Polish people! All I wanted was for us Jews to also have a scout program, working on behalf of our nation and country. To my joyful surprise, I found out that there was an upcoming initiative to institute a Hebrew scouts group called *Hashomer Hale'umi*. It was 1928, and I remember how happy and proud I was standing in front of my parents asking their permission to sign up. A Hebrew *sabra*[2] will never understand how overjoyed we were. We were thrilled to be able to sing a Hebrew song, and to march with a Hebrew flag. We were elated knowing that we Jews also have heroes, and we were working together to build us a homeland in the remote, yet near Eretz Israel. However, our happiness was short lived: the Polish government required a special permit for a Jewish movement, and receiving one was very difficult.

Our first gathering was at the house of Bechan. We began working to furnish and decorate it, but the police shut it down before we were done. We did not give up and we rented a new room at Langer's. There we worked quietly for a longer time. However, eventually, the police found out about our new location. Thus, we decided to work underground using private homes and even going outside. We were young, we had no guidance, support, financial means, or experience. Of all the other parents, only my father (may he rest in peace) was supporting us financially and giving us advice.

[Page 147]

He worked hard helping us to get the official permit for our organization and took on the role of the Executive Chair. To this day, I can still feel the bursting excitement and exhilaration we felt when we got the permit. We were elated to display the big, beautiful sign at our club's door, with the Scouts' symbol. The sign declared the club Poland's "*Histadrut Hashomer Hale'umi*", Mizocz Branch" in Hebrew and Polish. From then on, the club became our regular place to meet. There, we had conversations, we danced and sang, and we also dreamt about our future in Israel.

Certificate of membership in "Hashomer Hale'umi" (Zionist Youth)

Maintaining the club was costly beyond our reach. Many of our members were poor, and some could not get the money from their parents to pay the membership fee. So, we began working various jobs – mainly woodchopping– and we used the profits to keep the club running and also to establish a nice library. We were represented in all the Zionist institutions in town, and we were considered one of the best organizations. We were in close contact with the official leadership in Warsaw, from which we received materials and guidance for work. The Galil Leadership in Rivne also helped us in our everyday work. In our work we emphasized teaching the Hebrew language to all our members – the *Shomrim*. Nearly every Sabbath, we hiked through the forest, and we marched through town with our national flag.

[Page 148]

The "Hashomer Haleumi" branch in Mizocz

[Page 149]

One summer, we had a big celebration when the Ostroh branch came to visit us. They built their tents in the Sosinski forest. Those days, we spent our whole days and nights working with them in the forest.

I remember one morning a rumor spread in town, according to which the Polish scouts had attacked and vandalized our camps. I ran to the forest with all my might. When I got there, the war was still going. Member S. was attacked by a Polish man with a big knife, while trying to defend himself with a small, thin stick. I did not have time to think, and I jumped and disarmed the attacker. Ever since that incident, we were highly respected among the non-Jews. Even the Polish man who attacked member S., later came to our house, and asked me to not testify against him in court. Thanks to this incident, we were now more respected among the Jewish people, and our organization attracted older members. My sister, Rachel was one of the active members in that new cohort. She worked hard and was one of first immigrants to the Land of Israel from our branch.

Translator's Footnotes:

1. Hashomer Hale'umi translates literally to National Guard and was a Zionist youth movement in Eastern Europe similar to other international scouting movements. Also see jewishvirtuallibrary.org/scouting.
2. Jewish person born in Israel.

Gordonia

by Reuven Melamed

Translated from Hebrew by Adam Lamb

In the early 1920s, after the establishment of Polish rule in western Ukraine, activity of the Zionist movement started in Mizocz. Our "Union" party was one of the first parties of this movement in Poland. Its founders were Shmuel Gantzberg, Yosef Kleinman, Shlomo Koppelman, and the writer of these columns. In 1928, with the expansion of the Zionist movement, the committee decided to establish a youth organization in order to teach the youth in the spirit of the movement of Aaron David Gordon.

In those days, there didn't yet exist in Poland a comprehensive center for the Gordonia organization or a unified youth movement. The movement then had several youth organizations in different names, under several different leaders. On the matter of a youth movement, we contacted the center in Warsaw. From there, they transferred us to the leadership of "Gordonia" in Galicia, and eventually the center in Galicia, under the leadership of Pinchas Lavon (then Lubjaniker), organized a national youth movement called "Gordonia" all over Poland. The branch in Mizocz was therefore one of the first for this movement in Poland.

In the beginning, we concentrated on bringing the Hebrew language to the youth, conducting "conversations" about historical Zionist topics, and about the lives of the leaders of the Zionist movement.

[Page 150]

Only with the activation of the National Center's operation in Warsaw did we started to evolve in the right direction: we then received training material, instructions, and help in day-to day organizational work. Our practical work was expressed in actions for the Jewish National Fund and in education for agricultural work. Since the beginning of our first step, we preached for a working life in agriculture, so we decided to rent land and to grow vegetables in it with our own hands. Responsibility for the implementation was placed on members Shlomo Koppelman and Reuven Melamed. We then rented 10 dunams of land from a Jew, and without any experience, without guidance, and with restricted means, we started to grow all kinds of vegetables with considerable success. In this field of work, members Sara Kestenbaum, Deborah Koppelman, Sara Teller and Blyoma Likwornik excelled. On market day, there were our girls sitting together with the peasant women from the surrounding area, selling their produce to the customers. The Jews of the town enjoyed this spectacle a lot, and this was the talk of the day. From the money we received in exchange for the vegetables, we bought books for our library, and we signed up for all the publications of the labor movement in Poland and also the newspaper "Davar".

When Reuven Melamed and Blyoma Likwornik left for training, a reorganization occurred in the branch management and the management accepted more, younger members, Yitzhak Port, Yacov Mulhalter, Yechiel Likwornik, Taibel Kornik, and Rachel Gantzberg. The new leaders took it upon themselves to expand the framework and to integrate developing youth into the ranks of the movement. The mission was successful and then in 1933 "Gordonia" in Mizocz peaked in its development and numbered over a hundred people. At that time, the talents and dedication of Yitzhak Port (of blessed memory) started to stand out, and a lot of the success of the movement should be attributed to him. In addition to our work for the Jewish National Fund, we also participated in the celebrations of Lag B'Omer, the 20th of Tammuz, etc. Particularly memorable is our parade on Lag B'Omer, which was also attended by "Gordonia" from Dubno and the movement's training squad, which was organized on our initiative in Mizocz. The beginning of the training squad was disappointing. However, over time 40 members were accepted into the organization, from all parts of the country. We received work on the railroad and in Kaput's sawmill and also temporary work in the town' Among the members of the training squad there were several with education and teaching experience and with their help the squad organized different cultural enterprises. For example, Seder night in the squad was always unforgettable and attracted a large inquisitive crowd. Also, members of other organizations would come to participate in the squad's Seder celebration.

In 1933, Yacov Fishfeider immigrated to Israel. A year later Alter Gurewitz and in 1935, Deborah Koppelman, Haya Reznik, and Tova Likwornik. Before them, during the time of the Maccabiah in Israel, Reuven Melamed and Lioma Likwornik immigrated. As the graduates of the "Union" party and a large part of the leadership also made aliya,

[Page 151]

"Gordonia" at a farewell party for Comrade Gurewitz's aliya

[Page 152]

the young people of the movement who were educated in it from childhood took the helm: Gantzberg David, Moshe Feldman, Kornik Yosef, Gelman Yacov, Likwornik Yosef, Schwarzgorn, Eliezer, Brinstein Meir, and Abrach Aharon. Then, a difficult time began for us. The authorities put obstacles in the way of our development, the experienced ones among us immigrated to Israel, some split away from all activities, and many became indifferent. However, the activity did not stop and continued without a break. In 1936, Fleisch Sara, Abrach Aharon, and later Moshe Likwornik, who is now a lieutenant colonel in the IDF, immigrated with Youth Aliya.

Shortly before the outbreak of the war, Avraham Sternberg also had managed to immigrate. With the outbreak of war and the division of Poland by the Germans and Soviets, Mizocz fell to Russia, and then the summer came to an end. The youth and all Zionist activities. The "Gordonia" archive was in Yacov Gelman's possession at the time, and he destroyed it with a hardened heart and great pain. The flag was cut into pieces and all the activists received a piece as a souvenir. Some of the members did not want to and could not come to terms with reality and were looking for ways to get to Israel. Gelman, Schwarzgorn, and Kornik got as far as Lida, which was then a smuggling station into Lithuania, but failed in their mission. At the end of the war, the survivors began to immigrate to Israel and almost all the survivors now reside in the country and some of them occupy important places and respectable positions in the country and in society.

The "Gordonia" in Mizocz

by Yosef Ben Yosef ben Gedalyahu

Translated from Hebrew by Adam Lamb

In our town of Mizocz, almost all the young people were organized and affiliated with a Zionist youth organization. We had the "Union" party with its "Gordonia" youth movement. The Tzahar Alliance with its Betar youth movement, Meir Grosman's Hebrew State Party and "The National Guard" (Zionist Youth). Relations between the various parties and the youth unions were quite strained and only in certain areas such as fundraising and distribution of monies etc., was there any cooperation.

I joined "Gordonia" in 1929, when I was a ten-year-old boy; due to the lack of a government permit, the work was conducted in hiding and only on Shabbats and holidays. Serving as lecturers and instructors were Shmuel Gantzberg, Shlomo Koppelman, Yosef Kleinman, the late Avraham Gantzberg, and Reuven Melamed, who is very much alive and now a member of the Mishmar Hasharon Group. My group instructor was Jacob Likwornik.

[Page 153]

"Gordonia" in Mizocz at the center for counselors from the "Union" party

[Page 154]

The latter devoted all his time, energy, and knowledge to us. I especially remember the excursions we would make every Saturday at dawn; we would get up at 5:00 in the morning and hike until 8:30. At 9:00 we went out with our parents to the synagogue, for Shabbat prayer. We kept to this arrangement strictly, in order not to provoke the parents' objections to our actions in the movement. The success of our group raised morale, and despite the lack of a permit the number of members in "Gordonia" then reached close to one hundred. In the early 1930s, a training program of about 35 members was also organized with us. Among the members of the training program was Comrade Israel Zeltzer from Zdolbuniv, who had a lot of education and knowledge and also served as an emissary on behalf of the main leadership. Thanks to him the training program was on a high cultural level and the branch enjoyed him quite a bit. According to reliable information, he perished in the Warsaw ghetto during the uprising, participating and acting on behalf of the movement. Blessed be his memory.

As for inter-party tension, I remember the case when we invited the "Gordonia" branch in Dubna to come to us and celebrate Lag B'Omer together. The local leadership placed the responsibility for performing these celebrations on my group, called "Awakening". We worked out an entire plan and we determined that the next morning we would go out to the forest and clear our camp on the hill in the middle of the forest, which had beautiful stairs and a suitable grass surface, easy access, etc. We would arrange a field kitchen and welcome the guests with a hot meal made by us.

However, Betar became aware of this decision. When we arrived at the place, the hill was already enclosed by ropes and on it was the camp of the Betar platoon... We immediately gathered for an urgent meeting and decided not to get into a fight with Betar, and instead we immediately went to work strenuously to prepare another place for our camp. Our whole group worked then at night and so did Israel Zeltzer, arriving on foot from Rivne, who joined the work despite his fatigue. At the dawn of Lag B'Omer, our camp was standing. We were able to build it at the entrance to the forest, we built a beautiful and large gate on which the national flags were hoisted. Out of pinecones we strung together the symbol of the movement that hung in the middle of the camp, and we were filled with joy. We came out ahead, because, since our camp was set up at the entrance to the forest, all those who came to celebrate the holiday in the forest visited us.

The activity of the parties always intensified in preparation for the distribution of fund' and reached a peak as election time approached the Zionist Congress. Although the main work was placed on the shoulders of the adult members of the parties, the members of the youth movement also worked hard. Members of the "Union" party, who had close ties with the residents of the city, took advantage of every opportunity to distribute funds. Moshe Mendyuk, who is currently

[Page 155]

The "Awakening" group in the "Gordonia" branch

[Page 156]

in Uruguay and who was a member of the municipal charity fund committee, distributed money to all those in need of the fund, without exception. The late David Gantzberg and I, who were among the worshippers in the Kloyz[1] of the Trisk Hasidim, were assigned to distribute funds in those circles. With the help of Michael Nemirover, a member of the Zionist Youth but a good friend of ours, we succeeded in the task.

As election time approached, all parties sought to bring to town the best of their leaders, well-known names, good speakers, to influence voters.

In 1938, sometime before the 24th of the month of Shevat, the day of the death of A. D. Gordon, we learned from the main leadership circular that Comrade Pinchas Lubjaniker would attend a convention of training groups from the "Nativ" organization in the nearby city of Dubno. We immediately went to Warsaw and asked that Comrade Lubjaniker also come to Mizocz. Based on a courteous, authorized but non-binding answer, we issued a permit for Lubjaniker's lecture, but two days before the day of the lecture, a telegram arrived, which read: "Lubjaniker in Romania – Lev will come". On the advice of one of our comrades, we did not reveal the matter to anyone. First, the permit for the lecture was in the name of Lubjaniker, and as for his replacement with another speaker, it would be enough for the police to revoke the permit. Second, we did not want to jeopardize the promised success for Lubjaniker. And this is how it became known to many, only when the chairman of the assembly gave the floor permission not to Pinchas Lubjaniker, only to Attorney Lev… The assembly itself was successful on all counts, but of course we failed tactically. However, after many efforts, we succeeded in bringing Lubjaniker to lecture a few days before the election for the Congress, and he was a huge success.

The night before election day, young people had a night of guard duty. We painted all the fences, walls, sidewalks and roads with different slogans and posters. We made sure to keep an eye on anyone considering leaving the city at dawn to bring outsiders to the polls, and we did not stop the publicity until the last minute. The police forced the Jews to wash the slogans from the sidewalks and the road, but since we put a special glue in the whitewash, they could not wash the text, but rather the water added luster to the posters, and the cops came to terms with our work.

Gordonia's impact on the city was very notable. Apart from our training squad, we also had influence in the drama club under Mr. Fidelman's management, in the charity fund, in the bank, and in all the municipal institutions. The branch and especially the training squad enjoyed the support and help of several well-known families; among them I will especially remember the help of Shmuel Bonis and his wife, Shmuel Fliter and his wife, the Nemirover's, the Gantzberg's, the Breizman's, Shpanover, and others.

[Page 157]

The branch saying goodbye to Reuven Melamed and Lioma Likwornik, who are making aliya

[Page 158]

The soccer team called ZKS (Zhidovsky Club Sportovi) was along party lines and was at a high level. Among its outstanding players that should be mentioned are Asher Kantor, B. Langer, J. Mizocz, and Yishayahu Melgalter, the son of ritual slaughterer [kosher butcher] Yosef David, who was deaf and mute from birth. This guy, despite his disability, was accepted in society, because apart from being a tall and handsome guy, he knew how to dance beautifully, play chess and in almost all sports took a top place… Shortly before the war, our team overcame the team of the Polish cavalry, which camped in our town, causing a savage attack on our players by the Polish mob. The approach of the war and the antisemitism that grew in Poland put an end to the party quarrels and caused a mutual rapprochement and sincere friendship between the members of Gordonia, Betar, and the National Guard. With the occupation of Mizocz by the Red Army, several attempts were made to reach the state of Israel via Lithuania, Romania, or Russia, but all failed. Yacov Gelman, Eliezer Schwarzgorn, and I secretly left Mizocz and reached the city of Lida, because we were aware that in this city there were members of the movement from the center, who smuggled people to Lithuania. Even the people closest to us did not know about our departure.

A newspaper wall in the "Gordonia" club

[Page 159]

Gordonia's training squad in Mizocz

[Page 160]

We arrived at Lida in one piece and rented a room in a Jewish hotel. We spoke Hebrew to each other, so that the Gentiles living in the hotel would not understand our words.

When the maid, who worked cleaning the rooms, heard our Hebrew conversation, she turned to us in the same language and asked where we were headed. Later in the conversation with her, it became clear that she was placed in this job on behalf of the movement, to direct members to the headquarters of the operation.

Half an hour later we met David Klonitzky – now living in Ma'aleh Hahamishah – and we were scheduled to cross the border in a few days through the town of Ashmyany. Unluckily for us, the Red Army conquered Lithuania and it became Soviet the day before we were about to cross into Lithuania…

Disappointed, we returned home and tried to leave the country via Romania, but we failed here too. In the meantime, many of us were drafted into the Soviet army, war broke out between Russia and Germany, and Mizocz was defeated. Out of the thousands from that cheerful village full of life, 19 survivors remain. Most of them are now in Israel and are rebuilding their lives in our free country.

Translator's Footnote:

1.   The Study House

The Gordonia Movement in Mizocz

by Moshe Feldman

Translated from Hebrew by Shira Zur

The Gordonia chapter in Mizocz was organized in the year 1928 at the initiative of leaders from Hitachdut: the members S. Gantzberg, I. Kleinman, S. Koppelman, and R. Melamed. There were fitting circumstances that allowed for the creation of the movement, because the majority of the young adults weren't connected to any other organizations and sought to organize a Zionist cultural and educational movement.

[Page 161]

From its beginning, the movement pronounced itself a pioneering movement in the spirit of A.D. Gordon, and the chapter gathered 120 members filled with Zionist spirit and ambition to act and implement their goals.

The first activists in the chapter were members of the Magshimim group made up of older teens and high school graduates. These members were the heavy lifters of theoretical ideas, conceptual thinking, and training of educational forces in line with the movement. A majority of the group went out to training locations and immigrated to Israel. The others stayed because of all sorts of reasons – mostly because of their families – and continued to work in the chapter.

The members of the group that immigrated to Israel were: R. Melamed, B. Likwornik, T. Scheinfeld, M. Scheinfeld, T. Likwornik, A. Sternberg, Y. Fishfeider, C. Reznik, S. Teller, D. Koppelman (z"l)[1], Gurewitz Alter. Later on, Y. Malgalter, Giebel Riesel.

The vibrant energy of the chapter came from the Mitorerim group, which consisted of teens ages 12-16 years old, including me. They were young boys and girls who all spoke fluent Hebrew, and whose teachers were Y. Gelberg, Y. Schochet, M. Gorntzel, L. Dayan., L. This group was well-known for its exemplary behavior, and its members acted as role models for other Mizocz youth movements that were active at the time, such as Hashomer Haleumi and Beitar. In addition to the pioneering education, we were given instruction related to sport and physical education. The clubhouse of the chapter flourished and gained traction, attracting all of the teens in town, mostly due to comrade Yakov Gelman's hard work.

Our expenses were funded through work we did during our free time from studies, such as cutting down trees, digging holes, and all sorts of different jobs that were necessary for the residents in the town. Education came through lectures and conversations that were conducted by the knowledgeable members from "HaMagshimim"; they helped expand the knowledge of the younger members. We put emphasis on scouting; we strived to take the members out to outdoor events in the fields and forest to build their relationship with nature. In the summer we'd go early every Saturday morning to the nearby forest to practice scouting skills, and during our breaks we would hold conversations and classes taught by the following members: I. Port, Y. Likwornik, Y. Likwornik, B. Kantor.

Lag B'Omer became a big event; during the holiday, all the youth groups from the area would meet at the nearby forest. We would walk through the town and towards the forest in a beautiful procession, portraying discipline and exemplary order; it made a strong impression on not only the Jews, but also on the Polish and Ukrainian communities in the area.

[Page 162]

In the forest we would spend all day singing and dancing, and participating in various sports activities. Our group would participate in every Zionist activity in town, such as donating to the Jewish National Fund, organizing Purim and Hanukkah dances whose profits were given to the Jewish National Fund, and fundraising for the Zionist congresses.

We were very active during the Zionist congress election days. Thanks to that activity, we also connected the parents to the Zionist movement, and the Zionist ideas also filled their ranks.

During this time, we moved from the Giebel House to a bigger meeting space in the center of town in the Bernstein House. The chapter continued to grow and more young members continued to join, fitting well socially into our group. Our academics and our parties for the 24th of Shevat in remembrance of A.D. Gordon developed a reputation for having a rich artistic component that we ourselves produced, under the direction of Y. Malgalter, Tova and Isaac Port, Eisengart Gittel, and Reznik Haya. During the parties, we would invite the members from the Hitachdut party, the Hachshara[2] group, and our parents. Attention was given also to handing out the movement's newsletter, *Slovo Mlodych*, which came out in Polish and was sent to us from Warsaw. We had a strong bond with the Hachshara group of the movement that was formed in Mizocz by the main leadership at the Batzan House. The party had 30 members who lived as a collective and trained to immigrate to Israel. They worked at the Kaput sawmill, at a sugarcane processing plant, and at the train station loading apples and grains onto export train cars. Party members worked hard to gear the public's attention towards our local branch's fundraising efforts.

From an organizational point of view, we were in contact with the main leadership in Lodz and Warsaw, and we spoke directly with the regional leadership in Rivne.[3] We participated in regional ceremonies that mostly took place in partnership with *shlichim* from the Land of Israel, and one of the chapter's significant experiences was the visit of member Pinhas Lubjaniker (Pinhas Lavon) in Mizocz from the main leadership of the movement. Moving the chapter to a new location in Gelman House strengthened the chapter in an organizational way; the clubhouse was decorated in good taste, and a lot of thought and work went into decorating the Jewish National Fund corner. During the same time, Yisrael Zeltzer (z"l)), from the main instruction organization, was sent over; he contributed a lot to the strengthening of the chapter through his instruction, and his lectures drew the club members closer to the movement and its ideas. Through the chapter's initiative, members from the younger grade, A. Abrach, Sarah Fleisch Shoham, M. Likwornik-Gat, moved to Israel.

In 1939, as the Soviet army entered the town, it became necessary to discontinue the Zionist movement. The chapter's archives and flag were hidden, and the town's Zionist movement was uprooted.

[Page 163]

Some of the members left in secret in the direction of the Lithuanian border to Grodno with the intention of getting to the Land of Israel, but they weren't able to and they came back. Some of them went to the Russian steppes and from there, through many twists and turns, were able to achieve their mission.

The teen members who stayed in Mizocz, and among them the members of Gordonia, were captured by the murderers and were murdered with the rest of the Jews in the town. Those that remained alive from the group are: A. Abrach, Yakov Gelman, M. Feldman, E. Schwarzgorn, Y. Kornik, Y. Likwornik, M. Likwornik-Gat, Sarah Fleisch Shoham, Y. Brezner, M. Bernstein, B. Tentzer-Schwartzman, Y. Feldman, Latochin (Mulman) Haya, T. Gantzberg, Shtivel Anita.

Translator's Footnotes:

1. Of Blessed Memory (Rest in Peace)
2. Agricultural training in preparation for aliyah.
3. Community representatives

The Beitar Movement and the Youth in Mizocz

by Moshe Perliuk

Translated from Hebrew by Hadar Khazzam-Horovitz

Taking a pen in hand and reminiscing about the times before the Holocaust, it's like taking a sharp chisel and poking a deep wound that has never healed ...

Memories always have a sequel, because they tell of life and events that were and which formed the background to the present and the future. A person who reminisces about his personality or a period of time deals with past events. But at the same time, they keep flooding him without cessation. Each section of the "memories" constitutes a link to an ongoing action and a basis for additional steps.

The memories that will be raised here are different, for this memorial book is a lamentation in which we must revive events and talk about lives and actions that ceased even as they emerged. And this is especially painful when it is about youth – a gentle seed, cut short at the time of its growth and development. I must talk about a wonderful plant, which grew in a cold and harsh climate, yet despite the difficulties it rose and flourished. This was possible because its roots fed on the spring of hope and its growth was influenced by dreams of the future.

And a terrible conflagration burst out, and the plant burned and perished.

Reviving that past, and talking about the Mizocz youth in general and the Beitar youth movement in particular, involves an enormous emotional effort. To evoke these memories, I must resurrect that time with all its heroes; exhume from their graves all the pure souls, and with them relive that happy and wonderful period.

[Page 164]

* * *

Nature had been gracious to Mizocz and surrounded it by forests, groves and hills whose beauty is indescribable.

The Jewish residents loved nature, and the youth took every opportunity to leave the city to spend time outdoors, climb the hills outside the city, and hike in the forest thickets.

The area within which the youth could travel was limited. Within a radius of tens of kilometers surrounding Mizocz – whose center was purely inhabited by Jews – there was a tangled network of villages, whose Ukrainian inhabitants stirred up anti-Semitic venom. Any trip outside of the city would have been accompanied by concern and calculation, to what extent it would entail danger from Gentiles, old and young.

I remember when the local Jews used to travel on their business to the big cities, they would organize large convoys just in case. If they were late to return, their relatives would be concerned lest a disaster had happened to their loved ones. Indeed, there was room for concerns, because there were times when the forests swarmed with bandit gangs and killers who harassed the Jews. Many of the residents often recited the "*Gomel*" blessing after their encounters with these gangs, grateful for returning "only" hurt and robbed. Every time my father returned from his long and distant travels, we saw him as if he was newly reborn, because it was very common at the time to throw Jews from the trains.

When I was brave and rode my bike to Rivne, Ostroh, Dubno, etc, I was seen as someone risking his own life. Even later, in more "quiet" times, when I left with my bike traveling around Poland to a Beitar convention in Warsaw, it was seen as a big operation. Not because of the athletic nature of this trip, but because of daring to take the risk of a Jew alone, passing through the villages and cities of the Gentiles.

Such was the climate and the atmosphere in which the youth of Mizocz grew and developed.

* * *

The First World War, which began in 1914, did not end for Mizocz and its surroundings in 1918. It continued with all its aftermath, conquests and retreats that occurred for several more years. These events left their mark and disrupted life in this town and its surroundings. The connection with the wider world was disrupted, and the echoes of what happened in the Jewish-Zionist sphere came late and in fragments. It is no wonder that because of the geographical situation of the city

[Page 165]

A group of "Beitar" members in Mizocz

[Page 166]

and the special status of its Jewish residents, the youth were far from any national aspirations.

I spent most of my youth in the well-known city of Ostroh, where my family lived for several years. When my parents returned to Mizocz, near the time of the Bolshevik invasion, I continued to study in Ostroh and I came to my parents' house in Mizocz during the holidays and summer vacation. With each visit, my heart ached over the condition of the Mizocz youth. Despite being inexperienced at that time, I decided to work on behalf of the young people My friend, Asher Gilberg (Ben Oni), shared my pain and my decision. We had many thoughts about how and in what ways to awaken the youth from their inactivity and motivate them to act. We both decided that at first, the youth should be organized in a scout movement, for fear that a Zionist youth movement (then "Hashomer Hatzair") might get a cold reception from their parents. To excite the youth, we both decided that in the upcoming vacation, upon my return to Mizocz, I must bring with me all the accessories used in the scout movement (sticks, buttons and shiny numbers for uniforms ribbons, etc). And that is how the scout movement was established in those days, which the best of the Mizocz youth joined.

The movement multiplied and in slow but sure, calculated steps, we instilled in it the ideology of Zionist work. The Zionist plowing done in this way was carried out in an open field. The heart of this youth had opened wide, absorbing knowledge of the glorious past of its people, and ignited within it was the fire of longing for return to Zion.

In this youth there arose contempt for the diaspora and the humiliation to which they had been subjected for generations. Also there arose longings for freedom, moral conviction, and great hopes for the future.

The Zionist fire expanded and gripped all the young people. Social life was buzzing and filled with faith. The youth were swept away under the influence this ferment and motivated to be part of the Zionist work.

The scout movement reached its goal and ended its role. And then came the turn of the Zionist youth movements.

* * *

In the second half of the 1920s, political and social life returned to normal. The invasions and wars ceased, and Mizocz opened its gates to the winds blowing in the Jewish and Zionist world. The Zionist youth movements also infiltrated this town, and the youth began to look for their way among the tangled and winding paths.

[Page 167]

* * *

When I visited Mizocz on one of my days off, I brought the idea of the Beitar movement.

The name Jabotinsky and its teachings provoked a wave of enthusiasm among many of the youth, who saw in political Zionism the rapid and only way to fulfill the messianic dream – the establishment of the Hebrew state. The youth responded to the call of the great teacher and leader Ze'ev Jabotinsky. And by joining the Beitar movement, the youth felt that they were on the right path leading them through the great Herzlian Zionism to their country.

The "Yardenia" group takes leave of Syoma Oliker on his departure for Israel

Beitar was established. Then began the cultural work, drilling exercises, camps, and trainings. The youth worked with great dedication and devotion, along with military discipline and the love for their destiny. Everything was done thoroughly and at the same time hastily, as if they foresaw the future – operating with the feeling that they should hurry so they would not be late...

* * *

In my mind's eye I can see the long gallery of boys and girls, the youth and the young men and women, appear and pass. And I see again the same dear youth of Beitar, at work, full of energy, dedication, self-confidence

[Page 168]

A group of "Beitar" leaders in Mizocz

First row from right to left: Asher Gelberg, Sarah Pogorilitzer, Asher Bat and the teacher Yitzchak Schochet

[Page 169]

and happy with the task they have undertaken.

From the conversations that took place in the Beitar branch, I realized that the youth felt they were living in an historical period during which the fate of our people would be determined. And that there was no escape from fighting on a real battlefield to achieve this goal.

More than once during conversations, I heard promises that amazed me with their determination to follow this difficult path, and to proudly carry as a banner the vision of Hebrew independence.

I remember that, with the establishment of Beitar, I had concerns about its fate and its future. I was afraid that its noble ideas would not be accepted into the hearts of these youth, who did not grow up nor were educated in a Zionist environment. But how proud and happy I was to see the vast reservoir of intense love that arose within their gentle hearts for the people of Israel and their land. More than once I was amazed at the youth's readiness for heroic deeds, and their proud self-sacrifice.

Given such loyalty to the movement, it was only natural that quarrels, bitter arguments, and tensions between Beitar and other youth movements began to form. Each of the movements tried to prove that only its ideology was correct and true. However, even when the fury was escalating, the entire Mizocz youth fought – not for the petty hegemony of our movement, but for the way in which they should hurry and build their country. Deep in their soul within, somewhere hidden, everyone believed that one day the limbs of the nation would once again be united to form a whole body, with one shared purpose and destiny.

At the same time as the Beitar movement, the other branches of the Revisionist movement: "Hatzahar", and "Brit Hachayal", operated and developed in Mizocz. The whole Revisionist family, the Jabotinsky disciples, carried within their soul the same grand ideal, the same great hope, uplifting self-belief, and longings for redemption. Altogether, the adults and the young had a collective aspiration and a wonderful spirit beating in their hearts.

* * *

I am approaching the end of my description of these collective aspirations, along with the illusion that these longings have been fulfilled. The illusion that all these dear souls – all the people of Mizocz – are alive and live in the land to which they aspired.

And how great is the pain that I must break away from the glorious past, and face once again the bitter and disappointing reality: the reality that the youth and Zionist camp of Mizocz did not arrive at their shared goal, but rather a mass grave.

[Page 170]

Among the first to respond to my call to form the Beitar movement was Shamai Oliker of blessed memory, who saw the purpose of his life in this movement and worked for it tirelessly, with dedication and love. He was fascinated by the idea of the Hebrew state, left a rich and spacious home,

**The first "Beitar" command post in Mizocz
under the leadership of Moshe Perliuk
(in the middle with glasses)**

[Page 171]

a carefree life, a society immersed in the delusions of a comfortable diaspora life, and immigrated to Israel in 1934. However, while working at the Dead Sea his health deteriorated, and he died prematurely in Jerusalem in 1958. Among the first members of the Beitar movement in Mizocz were Avraham Rosenblatt, Faivel Meislitsch, Bozi Berman, Dov Fliter, and many others, who all perished in the Holocaust.

I am sure they gave back their pure souls to their Creator, with the slogan "Tel Hai" on their lips. In their minds they were seeing, for the last time, the land in which they wanted to live and for which they were willing to die.

Their memory will be kept in our hearts forever.

The Mute Beitar Member
(From the Cycle, "The Wonders of Our Movement")

by Asher Ben-Oni

Translated from Hebrew by Jonah Silverstein

Here he is at seventeen; handsome, healthy, smart, and devoted to Beitar like few others in the movement. But G-d punished him and he was born deaf

Yeshayahu the deaf-mute

and mute. When the Beitar organization was founded in Mizocz, one day "Yeshayahu the Mute" (as he was known in the town) entered and submitted an application, signed in his own hand, to join the cell and they accepted him to fulfill all of the obligations of the cell. Afterward, his father, the ritual slaughterer, entered and informed us of his son's hardships and suffering since no one would accept him into any organization. But, without even waiting to answer they informed him himself that he was accepted. His eyes full of silent sorrow lit up, and suddenly tears– tears of joy and happiness– were seen in them. He stood for another moment, stared into space, and uttered a few strange syllables– then left. Who knows what those syllables meant.

[Page 172]

The next day, Yeshayahu appeared in the cell in full Beitar uniform. Weeks passed and months; he lived in the cell, participated in the discussions and meetings, participated in trips, and became– another. The melancholy left him, he cast off the nervousness and the agony. Afterward, happiness and joy were always on his face.

I visited the town, and after my lecture in the cell hall, Yeshayahu approached me and showed me the picture of the head of Beitar and asked if I had met him…the commander who stood next to him indicated that he should explain the difference between Beitar and Gordonia. Yeshayahu made gestures to hint at *Aliyah* and work. He wanted to say that Gordonia wants to travel to Israel and labor there. He straightened up– and with piercing eyes, he surveyed me to determine if he had made an impression on me. He then gestured to the Beitarists who surrounded me and continued. He paused and took the stance of a shooter, by which he meant that we (Beitar) travel to Israel both to work and to defend it…when I saw him sitting during a conversation or a lecture I almost didn't believe that he was deaf and mute, he showed such great interest and attention when he listened.

Slowly, with extraordinary diligence and patience, he learned the Hebrew alphabet and how to write syllables, names, concepts, and more. In the Beitar cell, there were already people who understood him and who he understood. Because of this, he was familiar with all the internal affairs of the cell and the movement.

Then came the days of *Tammuz*, 1933. The cell stood at a dangerous front with plotters who brought proof of the Revisionist Zionists' guilt for the murder.[1] It was dangerous to be seen in the street in a Beitar uniform. It is not known from where, but the fact is that the mute Yeshayahu understood what had happened and what was going on. He was the first to wear his ceremonial uniform in the street. He would buy "Moment" newspaper[2] and ask us to explain to him what was written on it. The *hakhshara*[3] unit then lacked working hands. Yeshayahu joined the line as a volunteer and urged all his troop to do the same. His dedication and hard work served as and continue to serve as an exemplar to this day. Meanwhile, the cell was preparing for their trip to Rivne to attend the lecture of the head of Beitar. Yeshayahu decided to travel there to put before our leadership a request for himself to be allowed to make *Aliyah*.

Rivne was bustling with crowds of Beitarists. The leftists incited and attacked a few Beitarists. There was also a rumor in the city that the leftists and the reds would disrupt the speech of the head of Beitar.

[Page 173]

With his healthy instincts, Yeshayahu sensed the seriousness of the situation. His eyes were embittered, gloomy, and he finally disappeared. After many searches to find him, they found him standing guard in the hotel lobby where the head of Beitar was staying. He did not then appear before the head of Beitar. However, he returned home happy because he had seen the leader.

Now he is undergoing professional training, gaining both knowledge and voice training– who could compare to him? In the P.S.C. Battalion,[4] he was the most outstanding and completed each action without error and with vigorous precision; in the defensive exercises, there was no one like him in the cell. In his pocket, you would find a Beitar certificate, a Dinar, vouchers from the Tel Hai Foundation and the JNF, photos, and newspapers. Despite his young age, he lives by the sweat of his brow, through hard and tiring work, and hopes for the day when his dream will come true– to make *Aliyah* to his homeland.[5]

Translator's Footnotes:

1. Most likely referring to the murder of Haim Arlosoroff, who was murdered by Revisionist Zionists on the Tel Aviv beach in June of 1933. This high-profile assassination was a culmination of anger felt by Revisionists toward Labor Zionists, who they accused of collaborating with the Nazis.
2. "The Moment" was a Yiddish-language newspaper published in Warsaw in the early 20th century. It was one of the only Yiddish newspapers at the time to have been sympathetic to the Zionist cause.
3. "Training"; this word refers to preparations to make *Aliya* (immigration to Israel) and work on a kibbutz
4. The acronym פ.ש.צ. (P.S.C.) may be a specific unit label, or may be the initials for פלוגת שוטרים צבאיים (military police troop).
5. Published in "The State" No. 3 (25), dated the first of Adar, 1934 (2/15/1934)

Teaching and Education in Mizocz during Polish Rule

by Moshe Feldman

Translated from Hebrew by Caleb Bilodeau

An organized Jewish educational institution with a group of qualified teachers did not exist in Mizocz. Despite the relative wealth of the Jewish residents, the many attempts made by some parents and activists to establish a Tarbut school[1] were not successful. All Jewish youth received their elementary education in the Polish elementary school, which was of high standard and quality and did damage to the souls of the Jewish youth. The wealthy and the rich absorbed the values of Polish culture, spoke the language, read books in Polish and many also continued their studies in high schools in Rivne or Ostroh whose language of instruction was Polish. However, most of the youth, and especially the boys, received a traditional and Hebrew education with private teachers after their studies in the Polish school, The traditional cheder[2] had already disappeared from the horizon and was replaced by an institution more similar to a classroom in a modern school than to a cheder. The oldest among the Hebrew teachers in my time was the late Rabbi Yeshayahu Gilberg. As a member of a magnificent and wealthy family with many descendants rooted in Jewish tradition, he knew how to impart Torah to his pupils with reverence. He educated an entire generation of students, and in addition to teaching Hebrew and religious studies, he taught Russian, Polish, German and more. He used to hold his classes in his apartment and gave private lessons in the students' homes. He was a native of Mizocz,

[Page 174]

The first class of the Polish elementary school in Mizocz

Most of the graduates were Jews. Among the visible teachers were three Jews: Jania Schisel, Yitzhak Schochet, and Finkel the pharmacist.

[Page 175]

childless, respected and admired by all the residents. He acquired his extensive education on his own and died several years before the Holocaust.

Among the good teachers whose tuition was highest was teacher Yitzhak Schochet. He came to Mizocz in 1921 from Rivne at the invitation of some wealthy parents and immediately introduced the Sephardi pronunciation to the study of Hebrew. He also brought to the city textbooks, which until his arrival were not known in that place; his studies were at an appropriate level. Sometime later, another teacher like him, Leib Dayan.came to Mizocz. These two teachers greatly influenced the local youth, inspiring them and bringing them closer to the Zionist movement. They conducted study classes in their homes, would give lessons in private homes, and were also very active in public Zionist work; their influence was known in the town. After Teacher Dayan emigrated from Mizocz, Teacher Moshe Gorntzel took his place. This teacher followed in the footsteps of his predecessor. He was active in the Hitachdut party, and thanks to his good manners and knowledge, he acquired a large circle of students and many fans. His students spoke Hebrew to each other and were active in the Zionist youth movements.

For beginners and less able students, there were several more teachers, both locals and from outside. Such as Teacher Asher Zelig Krisik, Teacher Singer from Austria, Herschel Reznik, and the brothers Herschel and Feivish Milhalter (sons of R. Reuven the butcher). They would go around from house-to-house teaching Torah to Jewish children for a very meager salary. All the teachers, including the "greats," always worked in difficult conditions and their livelihood was meager. Our town of Mizocz was and remained Zionist until the bitter end, and almost all its youth knew Hebrew. This must be credited to all those teachers who, with devotion and loyalty, instilled in the hearts of young people love and respect for their people and their country – a fondness and appreciation for the Hebrew language and ancestral tradition. May their memory be blessed forever.

Translator's Footnotes:

1. The Tarbut movement was a network of secular, Hebrew-language schools.
2. A cheder is a traditional elementary school teaching the basics of Judaism and the Hebrew language.

Toward the History of the Revisionist Movement in Mizocz

by Arbi

Translated from Hebrew by Caleb Bilodeau

The events of 1929 in Eretz Israel[1] greatly depressed the Jews of Mizocz. The news on Polish radio about what was happening in the country was fragmented, unclear and sometimes just totally lacking. The Jews' desire was to know about what was happening in the land of their hopes and so circulation of newspapers went up and up.

[Page 176]

At that time, there was one active youth labor union in Mizocz, Hashomer Haleumi. "The Gordonia Federation" included young people beyond the age of twenty and had only begun an attempt to organize school-age youth in its ranks.

The lively young people did not have the patience to wait until the newspaper arrived from far-off Warsaw with the return of Nahum Tzipak from the train station, as he would slowly distribute newspapers. They would go out every day to greet the next train – a walk of 2 kilometers – in order get ahead in reading the news in "Haint"[2] or in "Moment." And the news was gloomy and sad. The bloody riots continued, every day Jews were falling from bullets and Arab knives. Jewish property was looted or set on fire and the English were unable to restore order in Eretz Israel and ensure the continued building of the homeland. Consolation for their angry feelings would be found in increased action on behalf of the Jewish National Fund and in articles in the newspapers which promised to establish two new settlements in place of each destroyed settlement and to bring ten new Jews to Israel in place of each murdered Jew…

One Sunday of the month of Elul[3] 1929, when the "Hashomer Haleumi" branch returned from a scout operation in the forest, we were surprised by the visit of the nearby Markovich Betar. The Betar members arrived with a police permit, dressed in beautiful uniforms. They marched through the streets of the city with Hebrew song on their lips and demonstrated some military exercises. Since almost all the Betar members had relatives, acquaintances or friends in Mizocz, all parties enjoyed this surprising visit.

In the evening, when the businesses closed and the streets were filled with people out walking, the Betar members stood at the corners of the main streets and handed out leaflets called "Stop and Read" published by the main headquarters of Betar in Warsaw, in three languages: Hebrew, Yiddish and Polish.

In this leaflet we read for the first time about the establishment of a Hebrew army to fight Arab terrorism, about a Hebrew state in the entire territory of Eretz Israel, and that a land is not bought with money but truly with blood and a difficult war. The leaflet ended with a call for Hebrew youth to join the ranks of Betar in order to achieve these goals.

In those days, World War I was still well remembered: the people were imbued with a so-called humane spirit and believed in general disarmament, in the canceling of wars, the Brotherhood of Nations and the League of Nations. They dreamed then about "Pan-Europe." The Socialist movement was gaining momentum, sympathy for Moscow penetrated all strata and ideological currents, and no one believed that Hitler would rise

[Page 177]

on the throne of the German Chancellor. The pamphlet distributed by the Betar members therefore seemed foreign and somewhat strange.

I'm Hungry, Kostia Riabtsev's Diary, All Quiet on the Western Front, I Burn Paris,[4] and the like were the most read books back then. Every self-respecting young Jew who wanted to be considered "progressive" or intelligent read these books. They also read other Marxist literature and political-economy and delved into the teachings of Martin Buber. The Zionist goal was understood as an aspiration to concentrate in the Land of Israel the best and brightest of the Hebrew people – to be an example to the world proving how to build a land without war and bloodshed…

The Revisionist teaching "Jews should be like all the Gentiles"[5] was too bold for the Jews of the Pale of Settlement[6]. They called the first Betar chapters "wooden swords and straw rifles." However, along with the ridicule of the Revisionists' "castles in the air," the enthusiasm for the regal and stately etiquette of Betar also increased.

And then the bloody events broke out in Eretz Israel.[7] Revisionist propaganda infiltrated its ideas into the hearts of the lost and searching youth and acquired followers in all places of the Jewish settlement.

The first branch of the Revisionist movement in Mizocz was established by Moshe Perliuk in 1930 when he returned to Mizocz during days off from the Gymnasium[8] in Rivne. Already in its early days, Betar was a great organizational success. It was joined by youth from the existing Histadrut, and most importantly, many unaffiliated youths were fascinated by Jabotinsky's idea of establishing a Hebrew army that would free them from the yoke of strangers who had plundered the Homeland. The joining of some young people, who were far from Jews and Zionism and immersed in a life of pleasures, made a great impression. These youth would never have come to Zionist activities without the Jabotinsky movement. At the head of this group stood Sioma Oliker. Immediately after joining Betar, he discarded all his usual habits, company, and activities and devoted himself entirely to the movement. When Perliuk immigrated to Eretz Israel, Sioma was appointed to command our chapter. Under his leadership, the Betar in Mizocz reached its peak success. The chapter's clubhouse was acquired in the largest and most beautiful building in town, the home of Wasserman. The chapter numbered about three hundred young people of all ages and strata, and it conducted very diverse cultural, sporting and organizational activity. Several of the locals were sent for military training, who successfully completed major courses and later served as certified guides in that place. Betar's orderly exercises and processions were arousing obvious envy in the Christian population, and more than once they also received praise from the commanders of the Polish army.

[Page 178]

The cultural work in the chapter was also of a high standard and was praised by the Betar Commissionary. The bulletin board founded by Asher Gilberg and the course for settlers run by him served as an example to other chapters. The Betar artistic club was very popular in the city and always attracted an audience of many hundreds for each of its performances. Betar in Mizocz was considered one of the best and most powerful branches of the movement in Poland. Over time, a branch of Hatzohar[9] and Brit Hachayal was also organized. After Sioma Oliker made Aliyah,[10] Abraham Rosenblatt served as chapter commander. At the time, a cell of the Irgun[11] was established in the chapter and many organized to make Aliyah. The war put an end to all hopes and dreams. Betar's commanders and managers dispersed and even those who remained could only meet from time to time and dream of the glorious past. In the ghetto, some of them tried again to organize and plan operations, but did not succeed. Only one of the members of Betar Mizocz fought the Germans and knocked down dozens of them. He would later fall in the war with the Germans with a weapon in his hands: this was Izya Wasserman (may G-d avenge his blood).

All the others met their death in the mass grave in the Sosenki Forest or in hiding places in the forest or in the villages.

Translator's Footnotes:

1. Eretz Israel is the Land of Israel, which is the traditional Jewish name for the land of the Southern Levant.
2. "Today"
3. Elul is the 6th month in the Biblical calendar between late summer/early fall.
4. *I am Hungry*, by Georg Fink (1920); *Kostia Riabtsev's Diary* by Nikolai Ognev (1924), *All Quiet on the Western Front* by Erich Maria Remarque (1929); *I Burn Paris* by Bruno Jasienski (1928).
5. In other words, the notion that Jews should fight like all the nations of the world.
6. Western region of the Russian empire between 1791-1917 that set the parameters for Jewish residency.
7. The riots of the 1920's.
8. Another term for high school.
9. Revisionist Zionist organization and political party in Palestine.
10. Immigration of Jews from the diaspora to the Land of Israel.
11. The Irgun Zvai Leumi (meaning "National Military Organization") or Etzel; a Zionist paramilitary organization active during the British Mandate of Palestine.

[Page 179]

Memories and Impressions

The 17ᵗʰ of September 1939
(From a book in progress)

by B. Asher

Translated from Hebrew by Hadar Khazzam-Horovitz

A gentle knock on the window woke me up from my sleep. I turned on the light and lifted the curtain. From the window I saw a young woman's face.

"Please open the window" she asked in Polish. "I wandered all night. I am soaked wet from the rain. Could I get a cup of tea, and something to eat? I will pay anything. My house has been destroyed, and we can't find refuge anywhere. That damn Hitler can get to me anywhere. We are all ruined. Ruined. My God, my God!"

My mom interrupted her speech by inviting her into the house. I quickly got out of my bed and got dressed. I was very tired. We listened to the news on the radio about the latest events in the front until very late, after midnight. I stepped outside. The night's shadows began spreading, and from the black clouds you began to see the light of dawn. Light rain was coming down. This vexing autumn rain perfectly matched the general mood. Our yard was full of soldiers, horses with carriages, canons, and refugees. The soldiers and the refugees walked around all wet or sat down taking a nap on the carriages. Many hid under the house's roof and shed. I was walking through the town's streets, and saw the same scene: soldiers, war gear and numerous refugees. Talking with the refugees and soldiers made me realize once again how serious the situation was. One sergeant told me that even in Mizocz, my hometown and its surroundings, they planned to form the new and final defense line. Wasn't Mizocz only 17 kilometers from the Soviet border? So how are you going to defend against the Germans?'He stated that the generals had the answers and left.

It was daylight. The rain had stopped. The town had woken up, and the typical daily routine had started. A few days prior to September 17ᵗʰ, several ministers came to town and set up their quarters at the palace of the Polish earl, Karwitzky. The town of Mizocz had never seen

Youth in Mizocz

[Page 181]

such esteemed men and elegant ladies. The high-ranking officials were strolling around the city, looking in vain for Christian stores. Despite openly expressing their contempt for the Jewish stores, these officials were buying their merchandise with the depreciated Polish currency.

That morning, along with the retreating army came the officers from the regions of Pozan and Shlonsk. Even though the streets were filled with people, starting early in morning there was no food shortage. This was because, before the war, Mizocz served as big storehouse for all of Poland. From Mizocz, daily trains full of produce, fruit, beef, poultry, sugar, wood, leather, and more were delivering supplies not only to Poland but to other countries as well.

At eight a.m., high-ranking army officers and ministry officials were in a frenzy. A rumor quickly spread claiming that the Russians had crossed the border marching toward the Polish army. Immediately, the stores were closed. The police were ready and banned any public gatherings. However, this ban was not followed. In every street, groups of people gathered, talking about the situation. It was unclear from Polish people's reaction,

Leadership of the National Guard in Mizocz

[Page 182]

whether the Red Army would help Poland or the Germans.

At nine thirty, as usual, we gathered in my house to listen to the radio news from Moscow. But before the broadcast had started, a young man from the nearby city, Hilcha, came in. He told us that he saw the Russian tanks approaching from Ostroh toward Rivne. He had spoken with a Jewish tank crewman who told him that, from now on, the Red Army had freed the Polish people from slavery, and in fact that the Poland of the corrupt landowners would not rise again.

Later we heard Mr. Molotov's presentation in which he declared that the Red Army had crossed the border to rescue and protect its brethren, Western Ukraine and Belarus, and so the situation was quite clear.

Nevertheless, the Polish government had not yet given up, and the chief of police – an irritable and stubborn man – was riding his bicycle, ordering people out of the streets. At the end, he courageously left the town to welcome the "rescuing" army. There he was told to surrender his weapon. He was instructed to return to the town and let the police and the Polish chief commander know that they ought to disarm and surrender their weapons to the Red Army. He was also instructed to have all the soldiers and the commanding officers assembled in the military base and stay put until further notice. With his orders in place and without his weapon, riding back to the city, the chief of police was no longer shouting orders. He rode the streets like a crazy person and was never seen again.

Those from among the army men who were aware of the dire situation changed out of their uniforms, mixed in with the refugees, and were ultimately saved. However, the vast majority assembled at the military base and awaited their destiny. Six hours later, a Soviet delegation appeared. They assembled the firearms and posted guards over the military base. At that time, many more were able to escape from the military base. The ones remaining were sent the following day to Siberia as war prisoners. One Polish officer with the rank of major made a big impression on the town when he committed suicide on Sormitch Street while shouting "Poland is not yet lost". In the meantime, the tension was escalating. On one hand, everyone was happy that the war had ended, but at the same time, they were anxious about the unknown future. In our city there were no communists, the city was a hundred percent Zionist. Even within the Christian population, there were no communists. Hence, there was no one to initiate official receptions for the newcomers. At the same time, since almost all knew Russian, all the townspeople came out to the edge of Sormitch Street to see the tanks and their crewmen.

The initial interaction with the Russian army was very friendly. The soldiers were communicating, answered questions, let the people approach them, and even let them touch the tank. Tanks at the time were an exciting new thing

[Page 183]

for the provincial people of Mizocz. However, in this first brief contact we could feel how the crewmen were impressed with our clothes, our houses, and estates, and even with the thin paper used to roll cigarettes.

At six p.m., the infantry arrived from the north. As opposed to the tank crewmen, these soldiers made a poor impression. They had wretched clothes and their marching was sloppy. Many of them were limping, carrying their shoes on their shoulders. They were mostly unshaved, walking heavily. It was clear that the infantry soldiers were drafted at the last minute and were sent straight into battle without proper training or preparations. Two hours later, the Russian army swarmed the town. The soldiers did not ask for anything, refusing to accept anything from the people, including drinking water. The townspeople were overly courteous, to the point of exaggeration. Only a small group of six, members of the "*Shetslitz*" (a government military youth group), resisted the Russian army with one shotgun. They were defeated within a half an hour. Beside that incident, there was no other defiance against the army. As the evening approached, the army declared a curfew, posting armed guards in every corner, prohibiting walking in the street. However, this curfew was not strict. Individuals were able to walk the streets, and even to talk with the guards. The first night under the purview of the Red Army was sleepless among the people of the town. There were family discussions, party meetings, conversations, and deliberations, and many concluded that "the devil[1] isn't as bad as they say."

A walk in the snowy streets of Mizocz

Translator's Footnote:

1.   The Red Army

[Page 184]

A Family in Mizocz

by Sara Shoham-Fleisch

Translated from Hebrew by Hadar Khazzam-Horovitz

I left Mizocz at a very young age. I only have very limited memories and recollections from the old days in the city. Nonetheless, I do remember well some of my childhood's experiences at my grandfather's house.

My mother's side of the family consisted of three patriarchal homes in Mizocz and a similar number outside of the country. They were the family of Baroch Fleisch, the family of Avi Mordechai – known as Mottel Fleisch, and the family of Avraham Abrach from Ostroh who married their sister Kayla. Beside them, there was one more brother in Russia and two additional sisters in America. The whole family lived in a big house divided into separate apartments for each family. Grandfather R. Moshele Fleisch was the head of the family. He was a Jew of average height, with a white beard, strict, and very religious. When I think of him, he always appears rapt in prayer, alone with his Creator, or angry over some religious transgression or violation of traditional rules. I was always afraid of him, and I did not like him that much. I was angry when he would not let me attend the youth group club. I also did not like the times he was upset when I wore a short-sleeved dress, nor his serious, somber running of the household. However, now when I look back, I often miss these old days filled with grace and beauty.

I remember the nights of *Yom Kippur*[1], when grandfather entered our house dressed all in white with his *tallit*,[2] and prayer book under his arm. He blessed us with the words *hatima tova*[3], before leaving to the synagogue for *Kol Nidre*[4]. The house was filled with purity and holiness, and at the same time with a special dread binding us all. Or the *Purim* nights when grandfather gathered the women and grandchildren, read the *Megillah*[5] in a version passed down for generations. And later the special dinner, *mishloach manot*[6], the Purim show, etc. To the Passover *seder* nights planned weeks in advanced, when the holiday began, and the gloominess disappeared while the rooms were filled with light and joy. The *seder* table was set with shiny tableware. Everyone was wearing formal attire, the house was clean and decorated, and I was excited to read the four questions of Passover as the eldest grandchild.

During the days of Simchat Torah, the congregation from the *kloyz*[7] along with the Trisk Hassidim – of whom grandfather was a crucial member – gathered at my grandfather's house. Along with *divrei Torah*[8] and joyful Hassidic songs, they drank a lot, ate a variety of pastries and *cholent*,[9] and rejoiced in the completion of the Torah's reading till their strength was spent.

[Page 185]

Today I see the patriarchal image of my grandfather differently. I understand his strictness and his determination to protect his ancestors' traditions, and it makes me like him more and more.

Of his two sons, my father was the most devoted to his religion. His eldest, Baruch, had spent years in America. There he shaved his beard and forgave simple breaches of religious rulings. My father – Mordechai – however, grew a long, black, thick beard, and followed all his father's rules. In their first marriages, the two brothers had lost their wives, and after a while remarried. My father was very quiet. He was a pious man and spent most of his time traveling to different villages for his trade. He had a special close relationship with the farmers of Derman village. For the Sabbath eve he would drop everything to bless the holiness of this day. Coming back from prayer in the *kloyz*, he almost always brought with him a guest for Shabbat. During Shabbat dinner, he used to sing soft and tender songs. My father did not like the fact that I joined the "Gordonia"[10], but at the same time he did not prevent me from going. And when I wanted to learn Hebrew, he hired the teacher Gorntzel, a well-known and expensive teacher, just to make me happy. He did object to my decision to make *aliya* to Eretz Yisrael. However, once he realized how determined I was about my decision, he came to terms with that, giving me his blessing. I was his only child from his first wife. With his second wife, he had two boys and one girl. I left the house when they were young. After leaving, I kept pleading with them to send me one of my siblings, but they always refused. Father was always withdrawn, worried and concerned, and thus naturally we hardly spoke with each other. Also, there was a strange alienation between us due to some previous circumstances. But now, his noble image, with his handsome face and his deep eyes, talks to me and tells me so much…

We were three cousins of the same age. Two boys and one girl. We all knew Hebrew and were involved in Gordonia. Aharon Abrach and I made *aliya* in 1936 to Ben Shemen, while Pessi Ben Baruch stayed in Mizocz. He was the talented one, with the promise of great achievements. But the war had begun, and he was killed before his time. My mom died when I was three years old, and I do not remember her at all. Up until the time my father had remarried, I was raised at my Aunt Chaya's. She was my mother's sister, a widow left with only one daughter. She was a good mother to me, and her daughter was like a devoted sister. From my mother's side, I also remember two of her brothers, Chone and Jacob, her sister Hannah Zisel and grandfather Velvel. I remember him vaguely with his tall figure, his white beard, and being constantly busy with his businesses. I clearly remember the day he died, as it was

[Page 186]

my tenth birthday. He left behind a fortune, causing frictions among his heirs. His talented son Chone inherited most of his fortune and moved to live in Rivne. In Rivne, he built a glorious house and ran significant businesses. His children received a national Hebrew education, and they all studied at the "*Tarbut*" gymnasium. His eldest son arrived in Israel after the Holocaust and adjusted nicely. Both my mother's sisters became widows. My Aunt Chaya's husband died a natural death, whereas Aunt Hannah Zisel's husband was murdered by rioters during the Petliura pogrom. My aunt, Zisel Langer, was a woman of valor. She raised her seven children with honor and with wealth. She had a big store for leather goods, and during the fairs I helped her, watching out for any potential thieves. I also loved my Aunt Zisel's house because there were always cheerful young people, meetings, and good parties. I never met her elder son, Hershel, as he died at a young age. But I really liked his daughter Marimka, who used to visit her grandmother and knew how to sing nice Czechoslovakian songs she learned in the village where she used to live. According to reliable sources, she now lives in Brazil.

I had a big and interesting family, and I find it very difficult to get used to the idea that it is all gone and never to be again.

Translator's Footnotes:

1. The Day of Atonement
2. Prayer Shawl
3. May you be inscribed in the book of life
4. the opening prayer of Yom Kippur
5. The Book of Esther
6. Exchange of food-gifts
7. The Study House
8. Discussions related to the weekly Torah portion
9. Sabbath stew
10. Zionist youth movement

Mizocz – the Place of My Happiness

by Soniya Polchik

Translated from Hebrew by Jonah Silverstein

When I think about Mizocz, I am reminded of the days of my youthful joys. I am submerged in memories of another world that was good and pure.

Experiences, impressions, and images from the dear days of my youth – standing lifelike before my eyes: here I see Hershka Rosenblatt's house engulfed in flames. There is not much running water in town. Thus, this precious liquid had to be pumped out of the deep wells by hand with much effort. Here is the living embodiment of a miracle of mutual aid. The whole town was aroused to extinguish the fire. They came with buckets, pails, and even bowls full of water to put it out. And so the house was saved with only minor damage.

Who from Mizocz does not remember the nights in which the *Halutzim*[1] songs were erupting from all the youth clubs and filling the city with joy? How is it possible to forget this? We were all like a big family – happy, joyful, and dedicated.

When a chapter of the "National Guardians"

[Page 187]

from Ostroh erected a tent in the Sosinski forest, youth flowed to it en masse. Beitarists, Gordonists, and Guardians spent time together in harmony. Like a long, unforgettable holiday also was the time the "Happy Town" circus stopped in our small town. In those days in Mizocz we didn't yet know about the cinema, and we would even chase a taxi with wonder. And such a thing sometimes came to us. The circus was situated on "Horses Square" behind the city council building, the "*Gemeine*." Both adults and children had a good time for days and nights on the field going to see the company of acrobats. Surely, more than one of us remembers the skirmish with the Polish Scouts – who came from afar and put up their camp in the Sosinski forest – provoking the Jewish youth. These were the first outbreaks of antisemitism that reached us from afar. Our youth were entirely Zionist and proud, they proved then to the antisemites that we were not dirty *Zhidikkim*[2], the Polish Scouts ended up in need of help from the police. As of then, our youth organizations grew and young people rarely visited the lovely Sosinski forest.

And the times when I visited the forest, it seemed to me that the trees were bowing to me and were begging for us to return and fill the forest with Hebrew song, and to dance the Hora excitedly. How would it be possible to forget the beautiful parades of our youth outside the town? And still today the dear song "*David melech yisrael chai chai v'kayam* [3]" echoes in my ears. This song embodied our yearning for independence in a Hebrew nation.

However, no one in their worst nightmare ever dreamed that the freedom we yearned for would cost us the blood of six million of our brothers, and among them our fathers and mothers, relatives and friends, and the destruction of cities and towns, among them Mizocz – the town that was my most dear and beloved. We who survived were a tiny remnant, an ember saved, lonely, and bereft of family and parents. Let us together embroider a free homeland with the thread of brotherhood and friendship, joy and goodwill, dedication and camaraderie that are so characteristic of the martyrs of Mizocz– never to be forgotten.

Translator's Footnotes:

1. Zionist pioneer
2. A derogatory term for Jews at the time
3. "David, King of Israel, Lives Forever."

Mizocz– A Town Where Guests Were Always Welcome

by Sarah Biber-Golick

Translated from Hebrew by Jonah Silverstein

From the day my older sister, Etty Levit Biber from Ostroh, married Levi Brizman from Mizocz, Mizocz became a second home for me. I would visit the town frequently and stay there for a long time. I liked its generous residents, its beautiful landscape, its way of life, and above all the familial atmosphere that surrounded the town.

The town of Mizocz was possibly the only town in Poland that did not know scarcity and poverty.

[Page 188]

Every Jew earned a living. To one Mizocz gave abundantly; to another, until satisfaction; scarcity was not known to anyone. Everyone worked and earned a living. One worked in trade, another in a factory, and another was a simple laborer in all types of work. In Mizocz they were not ashamed to do physical labor and the youth would work and toil, not sit around and do nothing. The reputation of the residents of the town reached far and wide as being hospitable and generous. In Mizocz they took care of the needy, fed the hungry, and supported everyone who turned to them for help.

To me, Mizocz looked like one big Zionist club. Everyone aspired to go to Zion, without exception. Some wanted to get there by way of the Left, others by way of the Right. However, for both the ultimate goal was Zion.

I especially remember among the businessmen and leaders the Gantzberg brothers, Joseph Kleinman, Shlomo Koppelman, Reuben Melamed, and Yehuda Braunstein. My sister Rivka and I spent time in their company when we were in the town. I also have many remaining fond memories of gatherings with the elders of the town. I would always relish and enjoy the enlightening conversations of Mr. Shmuel Eisengart, who lived in my brother-in-law's apartment. He was a smart and clever Jew that liked to speak to us in Hebrew. Joshua Dov Gantzberg, the father of the Gantzbergs, would often come to the house to play chess. During the game, they would sing Hasidic *nigunim*[1] and conduct interesting conversations about current affairs. And many others in the town were like them. Because of the special atmosphere of the town, the youth came from places near 'nd far to stay with relatives and acquaintances.

Together with all those native to Mizocz, I mourn the destruction of the town and the murder of her people by the wicked and the impure. Their memories will forever remain in my heart.

Translator's Footnote:

1. Melodies

———————

[Page 189]

Impressions, Memories and Evaluations

by Reuven Melamed

Translated from Hebrew by Nida Kiali

Nature had gifted Mizocz with unimaginable riches, evergreen forests, a most fertile land, rivers and lakes full of fish, and an astonishing good climate.

The Jews in town – like in all other places where Jews lived – engaged chiefly in commerce. A few earned a living from crafts and services and were an essential and substantial part of the economy.

The Jews had good neighborly relations with the Ukrainian, Polish, Russian and Czech residents. While their attitude towards the Ukrainians was rather dismissive because of their ignorance, their attitude towards the Czech was one of respect and sympathy. The Czechs' forefathers arrived in the vicinity of Mizocz about a hundred years ago, naked and impoverished, and were given barren soil from the government of the Russian czar, and neglected and forested land. They began uprooting the trees and preparing the land to be sown, and after years of intense labor, they turned their land into a luscious garden. The Czech villages excelled in their tidiness, beautiful houses, and blooming gardens, and they stood out due to their rich culture and high standard of living.

Almost all Czechs were rich and their villages stood in great contrast to the poverty-infested Ukrainian villages, where drunkenness prevailed and ignorance ruled. The Czech villages had model schools, drama troupes, bands, and various cultural and sports societies. They had given their youth education and knowledge and nurtured the values of their national culture and of the Czech language.

The Ukrainians were fiercely jealous of the Czechs but dared not lay a finger on them, for they knew the danger of provoking or harming a Czech person.

The Czechs were never patronizing toward their ignorant Ukrainian neighbors. On the contrary, they were always ready to share their experience and know-how about the farmland with their Ukrainian neighbors and teach them how to tend to the farming machines. They also knew how to raise sheep and cattle successfully and nurture fruit trees not indigenous to that location. They were never stagnant and were always interested in growing new species and plants. In this manner, they managed to pioneer and institute the growing of hops and clovers that were much needed for the developing industry, and these crops gave them great wealth. The bonds between the affluent Czechs and the Jews were tight and were beneficial to both sides.

The people of Mizocz were kind, caring, and always ready to lend a hand to those in need. With great generosity, they would give the needy help and aid – in a manner that would not cause disrespect.

[Page 190]

Sometimes it happened that an impoverished family refused a handout, and the experienced donors knew how to give their support in a way unknown to the receiver. Among those businessmen, I especially remember Rabbi Jonah Nemirover and among the women, Golda Chaim Yusis and Mirka, the rabbi's daughter. The number of those dealing with public affairs was great in Mizocz, but these were the ones that encouraged and urged those good deeds.

Many times, the Jews clashed with the law or the government and faced a heavy monetary penalty or incarceration. Here they were the beneficiary of the wisdom and prerogative of the experienced *shtadlan*[1] Rabbi Aaron Schenrik. He was like a member of the household of the *pristav* (the head of police) and knew how to bribe him and his officers and save Jews from all sorts of troubles and wrongdoings. Moreover, he managed to get the police to defend the Jews from all kinds of brutes and hooligans.

The danger was especially great for the Jews during times when local youth were recruited into the army; they would get inebriated, roam around the stores and take whatever they wanted without pay. They would also turn over shopping stands, and trample and beat Jews to their heart's desire. The police would turn a blind eye to these actions, and when the Jews complained, they would say that these boys were going to the front lines to die for their country and must be allowed to let off some steam. You Jews will lose some of your belongings, while they might lose their lives. Even if some kike gets beaten up, these follies should be ignored. Let the boys have their fun.

The new recruits always knew to pick on the weak Jews, and if they mistakenly came across young guys, they would get a beating and were thrown out of the store or tavern in disgrace.

Once a group of young recruits entered Fliter's kiosk, drank lemonade, and not only did they not pay, but they also started breaking the glasses and the furniture. Fliter had four young and strong sons, who subdued the hooligans and broke their bones. The hooligans called their friends for help, but they too were badly beaten and ran for their lives. A rumor spread among the recruits that the Jews were beating up the Pravoslavs. The police came and blamed the Jews for attacking the protectors of the Pravoslav homeland. All the evidence given was to no avail, and the whole thing could have ended in disaster, if it wasn't for Aaron Schenrik, who tipped the balance with the police in our favor with a decent bribe.

The police held the highest authority in the small towns, and the *pristav* who led it was an omnipotent ruler. Since Rabbi Aaron Schenrik could always bribe

[Page 191]

the *pristav*, the Jews in Mizocz were left to their own devices.

And then, in the year 1915, a new *pristav* came to our midst. He was a short man, with an imposing figure, wearing glasses and radiating pride. He invited the local dignitaries and told them he would not be prejudiced against any man and that it was his job to maintain law and order. All those who break the law will be punished to the full extent by him, and he is the last arbiter, for God resides in heaven, and the emperor lives afar in Moscow or Petrograd.

The Jews left in mourning, for they knew that even Rabbi Aaron could not help them this time, for this was a new *pristav*. A few brave ones tried to give the *pristav* expensive gifts the next day as a sign of goodwill, but they were expelled with disgrace and with a threat that if they ever attempted to bribe him again, they would stand trial.

The whole town was disheartened, and all were told of the bitter news that *"Er nemt nisht"*[2], meaning the new *pristav* does not accept bribes. How could they live when local youth were recruited into the army? They turned to Rabbi Aaron out of great desperation and begged him to save them and try to bribe the aggressor. Rabbi Aaron calmed them down and advised them to be extremely careful and try not to break any laws. He promised them that in due time he would crack that hard nut, but for now, they must have patience.

Rabbi Aaron began befriending the *pristav* and visited him using all sorts of reasons, and slowly became his friend and frequent visitor to his home. He would tell him about the *pristavs* who came to Mizocz penniless and left with great fortune. The *pristav's* wife would listen to these stories and utter a sigh. Once Rabbi Aaron took courage and asked the *pristav* why he didn't try to get rich and lived only on his small pay. The officer became angry with Rabbi Aaron and told him that he swore allegiance to the emperor to be loyal and do no foul. He wanted and would prefer to stay poor rather than break his solemn oath to the emperor and God. Rabbi Aaron explained himself and said bribing him didn't even come to mind, and he greatly appreciated his honesty and loyalty to the emperor. "But tell me, please," added Rabbi Aaron, "did your wife also swear allegiance to the emperor?" The *pristav* understood the hint, and his face brightened: "That's it," he said, "and I didn't even know there was a way out of this situation."

Ever since then, the Jews of Mizocz were once again at peace. The *pristav* kept his word, and his wife received the bribe. Before any request to cancel a decree, Rabbi Aaron gave the *pristav* warm regards from his wife, and his appeal was promptly taken care of. Eventually, the Jews benefited from this *pristav* more than from the former. He even protected

[Page 192]

deserters, and for a monthly payment to him and his officers, they could walk about without fear.

One time, the Cossacks and the military police came to town searching for deserters. The peasants turned the Cossacks against the Jews and told them that the Jews hid their wares from the peasants and refused to sell, just hoarding money and evading the front lines. The peasants especially complained about the iron store owners, who sold plows, sickles, and other tools and now claimed they were out of stock. The Jews avoided selling their goods for several reasons. First, they feared robberies and riots. Second, inflation was at its peak at that time, the value of money plummeted, and new merchandise was hard to come by. As the day unfolded, the peasants mentioned Feigele Melamed-Nemirover's cellar, which was loaded with goods, and asked the Cossacks to break into it. They immediately started to do so. The basement was heavily fortified, had an iron door, and could not be easily breached. Feigele's son rushed to the *pristav* and asked for his help. The *pristav* ordered his officers to go and round up the Cossacks and bring them to him. The officers weren't keen on following that order, as they were ordered to retrieve the Cossacks by force if necessary. However, they feared disobeying their master's orders even more. The officers arrived at the scene on time before the assailants could breach the basement. They quickly dispersed the peasants and ordered the Cossacks to follow them to the *pristav*. The Cossacks cursed the officers and blamed them for protecting the Jewish profiteers exploiting the Pravoslav people. The officers stood their ground and held the Cossacks at gunpoint. Two of them mounted their horses and fled. Due to his arrogance or lack of choice, the third one confronted the *pristav*. The *pristav* and the Cossack had a bitter argument, as the Cossack bluntly told the *pristav* that while he was fighting on the front lines, the *pristav* sat at the rear and was in cahoots with the Jews and was getting fat. However, the *pristav* was not alarmed and ordered the Cossack to surrender his weapon. The Cossack refused, and the *pristav* proceeded to take his arms by force. At that point, the Cossack fell at the *pristav*'s feet, begged for forgiveness and for his weapon to be returned. The *pristav* complied, and the Cossack rode away from Mizocz in disgrace.

The day of the revolution came. Rumors came to the town of the emperor's defeat and the rise of a new regime, but Mizocz still ran as usual. The *pristav* was the local lord with the police at his aid. Some tension filled the air, but it did not alter the regular course of life.

I remember a warm and nice Passover evening. The snow had thawed, the sun was shining,

[Page 193]

and the town was covered with mud. The *pristav* took a pleasant stroll on a sidewalk next to Rabbi Moses's house, and everyone tipped their hat at him as a sign of honor and cleared a path for him. Suddenly a young man of 17 came towards him, grabbed his suspenders, forcibly removed them, and shoved the *pristav* into a ditch. The young man left and the *pristav* was pulled from the ditch by Rabbi Moses and his wife. They took the *pristav* into their home, brought him water and soap, and cleaned the mud off him. The *pristav* was very depressed and kept mumbling about an upcoming holocaust. Since then, they all knew that the evil reign of the house of Romanoff was indeed defeated, and that the future was unclear and full of mystery.

Translator's Footnotes:

1. Yiddish for "intermediary" to "court Jew"
2. Yiddish: ער נעמט נישט

Derman, the Village

by W. Sudgalter

Translated from Hebrew by Nida Kiali

Derman was a large and peaceful village. Bathed in green and residing between the woods of Bochtza on one side and the forests that stretched till Ostroh on the other. Its location – in the vicinity of the town of Mizocz.

Jews inhabited this village for many years. By the beginning of the last war, 15 families resided in the village, numbering 80 men, women and children. Administratively, the village was part of the Zdolbuniv district and the Jews were part of the Zdolbuniv community, but spiritually speaking, Derman was connected to Ostroh and Mizocz. The older children were sent to study at Ostroh and the younger were sent to Mizocz. As a result, these places had a substantial spiritual influence on the village.

The village's Jews were all kind and hospitable. They were also considered earnest and loyal in trading. They were alert and showed warmth in every matter of charity and were very generous in giving to various public support funds.

All Jews in Derman were in the business of leasing the many fruit gardens that were the village's main attraction and source of recognition, and trading in fruit. They were occupied with their commerce and worked most of the year to make an honest living.

The village was closely connected to Mizocz by rail and the fruit commerce was conducted at their train stations. Similarly, the youth found a place in Mizocz because the Zionist youth movements resided there: Beitar, Gordonia, Hashomer Haleumi, as well as strong parties from all Zionist factions. The youth from the village was drawn to the lively town and enamored by it. The children used to frequent the Polish public school, and a teacher from nearby Mizocz came to give them Hebrew and religion lessons. After graduation,

[Page 194]

most of them remained in the village and worked in the fruit trade business along with their parents and only a few were sent to study outside the village. Young people found satisfaction reading books and newspapers in Yiddish – the only bridge connecting the small village to the outside world. By reading the newspapers, they were informed of the Zionist initiative, development in the Land of Israel, and Aliyah.

Under the shroud of darkness that followed diaspora life, the burden of Polish regime taxes, and the hate of the Ukrainian neighbors – hidden and open – the Jews' lives in the village marched on. However, the few young people residing there were tired of this life and aspired to find a new one in the ancestral homeland.

When the war broke out, the Red Army marched into Volhynia. The adults kept to their fruit gardens and the new Russian regime gave the few young people jobs and positions. According to the letters received by the writer of these columns while the Soviets governed the village, it seemed that the Jews were well and were not threatened by the calamities that were the fate of other groups of Jews. But the good days were numbered and it didn't take long for the Germans to find the Jews, even in remote Derman. The Jews in the village did not follow the Red Army, as they continued to believe in the honesty and decency of the great enemies of that generation(?) and thus fell into the trap laid at their feet. The Ukrainians, who were almost unanimously gathered under the banner of Bandera (who fought for the independence of Ukraine), colluded with the Germans and were the very ones to annihilate the Jews under the protection and approval of the Nazis. At the beginning of October 1942, they gathered all the Jews in the village and sent them to Mizocz. They were then led in mid-October along with the Jews of Mizocz into the killing pits.

This date[1] shall be written in blood – the day of the annihilation of the Jews in Mizocz, and its subsidiaries – along with the other dates of mass extermination of Jews by the Ukrainian and Nazi enemies. And my soul weeps over the innocent and naïve Jews of Derman who were slaughtered among millions of their Jewish brethren.

Translator's Footnote:

1.   the third of Marheshvan

[Page 195]

Life and Folklore

by **Mordechai** Scheinfeld

Translated from Hebrew by Gabrielle Cooper

Yosl Nassias takes a beating from Asher Zelig

When I was 11 years old, it became my fate to be the breadwinner of the family; this was during the first world war. My father was dead, my two brothers were in hiding far from home in order to avoid being drafted into the army, and I was forced to help my mother run the business.

We owned the Town Hall building that stood on the hill in the middle of the town, and housed within it were most of the shops of Mizocz. Misters Nemirover, Pogorilitzer and my uncle, Herzl Scheinfeld, began a partnership with us and merchandised everything they could lay their hands on.

As a young child, my job was to travel with the Ukrainian carters to the city of Slavuta[1], to buy and bring back oil for the public and the army. That work was considered easy enough and suitable for me. However, the truth was this was hard, exhausting, serious, and dangerous work. In addition to road trouble, frequent checks on behalf of police officers and the army, and the beatings I would take at every one of these checks, I had to watch the carters "with seven eyes"[2] so they would not drag me away from the precious liquid. On one of these trips I was able to bring brandy instead of petroleum. Our partners praised me greatly for this 'operation' and I successfully repeated it many times. The profit was large and considerable, and we all became very rich. Because I was the main cause of that success, I proved myself a knowledgeable and experienced trader, and I was given the trade in leather and in haberdashery.

The expert in these goods in our town was Yosl Nassias, and with him I arranged all of the purchasing. The goods were purchased in the nearby towns of Verkhiv[3] and Tuchyn[4]. We would travel there of course, but only in horse-drawn carts, on dirty, dilapidated roads, as was customary in those days. However, while it was possible to reach Verkhiv by direct roads, it was impossible to reach Tuchyn without crossing the Horyn River[5] on a floating bridge.

[Page 196]

To this day I remember the great impression crossing the river on the floating bridge made on me. I am always sorry that it lasted such little time. In almost every conversation I have, I mention the story of the floating bridge. I never tire of telling it; the horses standing harnessed to the carts, with their heads in their food sacks. They eat contentedly, and we sit on the cart, as we continue travelling…

On one of our visits to Tuchyn, we arrived at the hostel of Zlata, which we called Zlatopolska, to stay overnight. There we came across a young man and woman with their escorts who had arranged to meet there for an introductory matchmaking meeting. We invited them to our table and spun lively conversation with the other diners. The prospective groom sat silently, and hardly a single word left his mouth. I noticed his escort urging him to participate in the conversation and not sit like a dummy.

The first and almost the only speaker was of course Yosl. He didn't allow anyone else to lead the conversation. He spoke on and on, with and without a point, almost without stopping. The prospective groom, apparently wanting to seem like someone knowledgeable about matters of cities and towns, turned suddenly to Yosl and said it seemed to him that they had already met once in the city of Lvov[6]. It is possible that Yosl would have confirmed the words of the suitor, because he loved to seem in company like a worldly man. However, my presence interfered. He knew that if he confirmed that he had been in Lvov, I would immediately point out his mistake, because he had never been to Lvov before. Therefore, Yosl told that suitor that it was very possible they had already met in a different city, maybe in Odessa[7] or in another city, but that he was just getting ready to travel to Lvov for the first time in his life. I would have taken the opportunity of his admission to undermine him, but we were in fact travelling to Lvov in the coming days to make connections and trade with leather merchants in the city. After a few days we arrived at the train station in Ozerna. Yosl stood in line to purchase train tickets. He returned all radiant from happiness and told me that if it weren't for his ability to deal with the clerks, we wouldn't have obtained train tickets. I knew his weakness for boasting, so I added some praise and compliments on his great ability and knowledge…

Yosl also loved small and cheap pranks such as tying the tassels of prayer shawls together, so that they would slap the cheek or ear of a worshipper intentionally, and when they looked, he would make the face of 'one who does not know how to ask.'[8] Or he would tickle the head of another while he was engaged in complicated calculations or looking at a book, or praying the Amidah,[9]

[Page 197]

and enjoy how the other would hit himself in rage, trying unsuccessfully to kill or repel the seemingly bothersome fly…

Once we were inside the train traveling to Lvov, he walked down the corridor, peering into all the compartments, searching for acquaintances or just other Jews to spin idle conversation with. I sat in the compartment next to the window and perused the newspaper. I enjoyed the ride itself, in the swaying and upholstered compartment. Suddenly I heard the ringing of slaps on the cheek, and the voice of Yosl begging for forgiveness in Polish. I went out and saw a burly *goy*[10] beating Yosl and shouting, "ugly, miserable *Zhid*,[11] I will teach you a lesson!" And in contrast, Yosl's weeping voice claimed: "but I thought you were Asher Zelig". I barely got Yosl out of the hands of the angry Pole and brought him into our compartment. After calming down a little bit he told me that on his walk in the train corridor he noticed, much to his delight, that Asher Zelig from Mizocz was stretched out on one of the compartment benches, snoring. Yosl did not think much, entered the compartment, rolled up his right-hand sleeve, and with all his might landed a blow on the buttocks of Asher Zelig. To his astonishment – standing in front of him was not Asher Zelig, but rather an angry face with a large mustache … His explanations did not help. He shouted "but I thought that you were Asher Zelig" while enduring beatings.

The adventures of Lvov

We arrived in Lvov. It was early evening. The impression of the large city erased from our hearts the 'Asher Zelig' incident. We walked a little on the main streets of the city. When the shops closed, we started to look for a place to sleep. We did not know the city, and annoyingly, all of the hotels we wanted to stay in were full. At one hostel they promised us a place to sleep after 12 o'clock at night. Having no other choices, we agreed. Since there were four more hours until the appointed time, we again took to the streets of the city. By way of our walking, we arrived at the theater building. We bought tickets and went inside. Immediately at the entrance the usher stopped and said that he would take our coats to the coat-check. Yosl was wearing an expensive fur coat and was scared to leave it in unsafe hands. The ushers stood their ground, so Yosl handed the coats to coat-check, but he sat close to the door in the theater hall so he could keep an eye on his fur... the screen was raised and the show began. Here we realized we had fallen into a second trap; we thought that the show was in Yiddish (and how would it be possible otherwise?) but here everything was happening in Polish. Needless to say, we could not understand much from the show.

[Page 198]

And so, we had little interest in it. Yosl was obsessed with his fur which was in the coat-check, and every few moments he opened the door to glance at the fur in the coat-check. This annoyed the viewers, and as a result of their protests he was taken out of the hall. Yosl was pleased about this, because he received his precious fur in exactly the same condition that he had delivered it. We continued walking around the city until midnight, and then we returned to the hostel. We received for the both of us one wide bed in a single room. We undressed and went to sleep. Yosl did not let me fall asleep. He returned and said to me that without his knowledge of how to deal with the clerks, we would not be resting in bed now. When I asked him to let me sleep, he began to tickle me and fight with me. It only ended when the bed broke beneath us and we found ourselves on the floor... This scared both of us and we began to think about how to fix the appearance of the bed, at least enough for until we left the hostel. Yosl went down to the yard, found some bricks there, and brought them up into the room. We put the bricks in place of the broken legs, made the bed, lowered the cover to the floor, so the legs were not visible, and we lay on the floor... In the morning as soon as we heard the gate opening and the workers arriving, we paid and left the place quickly. After we ate breakfast, we went looking for acquaintances according to the addresses we had. At 10 o'clock we arrived at the apartment of a relative of Yosl's wife. On the main entrance was written: "the entrance is around the back." We walked around and the door was locked there too. We jiggled the lock this way and that and the door did not open. Then Yosl said, "Mottel, give me a hand." Together we pressed on the door and the door opened. A ladder used for painting was leaning against the door and fell. The ladder fell on a cupboard and broke the glassware inside it. There was a commotion. Women came out from the neighboring apartments, scared and shouting, and it was only by a miracle that we escaped from that place.

After we arrived safely to the street side our spirits changed, we decided from now on not to go anywhere alone. We had the address of one committee, where we needed to meet with a trusted person, who would guide us in our shopping. We decided from now on to only travel in the city with this person. We barely found the place. There we ate our hearts out, met with the man we wanted, and with his help we left Lvov in peace and with successful purchases.

The Mischief of R.[12] Yitzchak Baraz (Itzik Chukralnik)

My cousin Chone loved sleeping outside on hot summer nights, on a cart padded with fragrant hay. The cart would stand down by the town hall, with stones or bricks under the wheels so it would not roll downhill.

[Page 199]

R. Yitzchak once came to that place in the morning, took out the bricks from underneath the cart wheels, and it rolled downhill and came to stand in the middle of the market. After a short time, the market was filled with local farmers and city women who came to purchase their necessities from the farmers. The noise that arose in the market woke up Chone and he thought that he was by his home. He got up from the cart, rolled up his shirt, took off his underwear, and scratched himself with enjoyment... The women were surprised at this sight and became angry: It was so early and already the circus clowns had arrived...

* * *

R. Asher was rich in assets and almost all the Jews in the city made a living from him and were dependent on him. His son, Yishayahu Gilberg, studied and trained in Odessa, saw the big world, and also acquired education and manners. Every time he came to the house of R. Yitzchak, he would complain and complain about the boredom in town, the lack of cultured society, and his longing for the big city of Odessa. R. Yitzchak decided to teach the young man Yishayahu a lesson, and prove to him that Mizocz was in fact a nice and interesting town, and that he too might miss it and its people.

One day when Yishayahu came to his house and started, as usual, to complain of boredom in the town, R. Yitzchak invited him to travel with him to a nearby village, where he needed to make arrangements for a trivial matter, and meanwhile Yishayahu could alleviate his boredom. Since R. Yitzchak promised that the trip would not last longer than half an hour, Yishayahu agreed to his offer willingly.

Instead of half an hour, the trip lasted half a week. R. Yitzchak walked around villages and towns and did not respond to any of Yishayahu's complaints or objections. Only when Yishayahu said that he missed Mizocz, and that all he wanted to do was be back home already, did he order the carter to return to Mizocz. Since then, Yishayahu has not spoken in condemnation of his hometown, Mizocz.

* * *

Mottel the Stingy was very rich. His stinginess was as considerable as his wealth. He was sparing with his words and dressed like one of the poor. In the town they whispered that Mottel only had one pair of long pants to wear, for both the weekdays and the Sabbath. R. Yitzchak decided to check this and did so as usual with a clever prank.

In the morning of a cool autumn day he snuck into Mottel's house and took the pants that were lying on the chair and stuffed them into the chimney pipe. After he returned home, Mottel woke up from his sleep and told him that he needed to go immediately out of the town with him in order to buy a cartload of grain at a very cheap price.

[Page 200]

One of his acquaintances brought grain for his competitor Katz, but since in his heart he had resentment for Katz, he appealed to the farmer to sell his goods to Mottel from now on. He urged Mottel to get dressed as quickly as possible and in the meantime, he went out to ensure that the farmer would not reach Katz. R. Yitzchak came out and Mottel jumped out of bed as quickly as a snake bites to dress and run to arrange the purchase. He did not find his pants in their usual place. He started to run around the room searching in all the crannies, and when he did not find the pants he called his wife for help, but to no avail. In the meantime, R. Yitzchak returned to the house and Mottel had to go back to bed, because he was ashamed to walk around the room in his underwear. When asked why he wasn't dressed he began to stutter and said that he didn't feel well. He was attacked by stomach pain which he felt in his head. R. Yitzchak pretended to be worried and said that he was going to get the Polish doctor. Mottel was forced to reveal the truth, for fear that R. Yitzchak would really bring the Polish doctor, and that his 'cold' would cost him lots of money.

R. Yitzchak advised that he should wear his Shabbat pants for a little while, since the deal would be worthwhile. Mottel's wife intervened and admitted that the pants that disappeared were the only ones that Mottel had... R. Yitzchak 'found' the pants under a cupboard. Mottel dressed quickly and they both went to the place where they were supposed to meet the farmer. They both searched and called the farmer's name aloud, but it was all in vain. Many days passed and Mottel continued to regret that the bargain had fallen into his competitors' hands because of the pants.

* * *

A tale of two 'different things'

A home industry producing schnapps, called in Ukrainian 'samogon,' developed in our community during the time of the first world war. The whole population was very eager after alcohol became difficult to obtain, and started making it instead. Raw material was available, many jumped at the chance for an easy profit, and there were more than enough customers for endless products. We also became experts in making samogon.

The authorities of course prohibited making or selling samogon. First of all, they didn't want competition in this operation and second, they also feared for the health of the population. So, we produced samogon in hiding, far away and not seen by the community.

Our workshop for this illegal industry was located outside of town in the house of Rachel from the village Pivche (Rachel the Pivcher). We produced the schnapps at night and the waste liquid was stored in barrels.

[Page 201]

We could not spill the solution, because the smell would spread far and wide, and we would be discovered.

Once two pigs from a nearby village arrived and emptied a barrel filled with the solution. They got drunk from the solution and fell like the dead next to the house. We sensed this quickly and with the help of Zvi Trochler, we loaded up the drunk pigs into a sleigh, drove about 10 kilometers and threw them into the pit of the village Kunyn. Besides us, no one knew about this.

In the morning, a rumor spread in town that two 'other things' were found killed in the pit of Kunyn. The nickname 'other thing' in Mizocz was aimed at pigs and also at pigs that walk on two legs. Immediately the rumor said that it was two gentiles (goyim) found killed in the Kunyn pit. When the knowledge reached the police, a group of armed cops went to the place for investigation. Instead of dead people they found two fat pigs in a deep sleep… The policemen were very happy, brought the pigs to Lundowski the butcher and held a proper feast. In the morning the father of the police chief came and complained that two pigs had disappeared from his pen. However, no one saw the connection between the missing pigs and those found 10 kilometers from the pig pen of the complainant. Since then, the schnapps solution has been thoroughly guarded lest the pigs enjoy it.

* * *

Cancelled blessing

My Rabbi, the late R. Shlomo Finias, was a very devout Jew, hot-headed, and known for his obsessiveness. He customarily drank tea from the kettle that the Rabbi's wife prepared, at regular hours. He never departed from that custom. His favorite time to drink tea was the hour between the afternoon and evening prayer service. In that hour – while drinking tea – he would test our knowledge of what we learned in classes that day, and give us a proper beating for not knowing.

Among the students of Rabbi Shlomo, who rests in heaven, was the son of the town Rabbi, R. Hanoch – Mottel the Cat. Mottel was incredibly naughty. He would disrupt the life of the Rabbi and his wife, and each time the Rabbi put him back in his place he increased his naughtiness.

Once when R. Shlomo put the kettle on the table to drink tea during the hour of Mincha,[13] he was called outside by his wife. Mottel the Naughty grabbed the kettle and emptied his urine into it…

After a few minutes the Rabbi returned, and poured from the kettle into a hot cup,

[Page 202]

blessed aloud and sipped with pleasure. Immediately his face twisted and he started to spit. We burst into a huge laugh. After we had all received a decent beating, we told the Rabbi what Mottel had done. Then he grabbed Mottel's head and shouted: Woe is me! I have blessed in vain…

He got the final say

Chaim the Postman and Ashraka Oliker competed among themselves for a specific place in the cemetery "after 120." After a prolonged quarrel about this, they agreed between them that the person who would get the spot would be the first to go the way of all flesh. Fate wished that Chaim the Postman die first and a large crowd attended the funeral, among them the 'competitor' Ashraka Oliker. After the sealing of the grave, Mottel the Mild-mannered approached and said to him: "Oh, Ashraka! He got the final say, ha!"

How Lukacs went from an enemy to a friend

The policeman Lukacs fulfilled his role strictly and it was impossible to bribe him. In his position as deputy chief of police he also oversaw with seven eyes the rest of the policemen behaving harshly toward Jews. He demonstrated his disgust toward Jews and in almost all conversations he introduced himself as a hater of Jews. My mother suffered especially from him, because the tavern that was under her management could not be in compliance with all of Lukacs' increasingly tough laws… When she was not given an explanation that made sense, and pleas and attempts to bribe him did not work, she decided to change him in a very unique way. Knowing correctly that Lukacs would not agree to dine at her table, she requested that a Polish acquaintance arrange for Lukacs, on her account, a feast fit for a king. Lukacs no longer knew how to distinguish between the cursed Haman and the blessed Mordechai,[14] and he was brought to our tavern. Here he sipped a few more cups of drink, which worsened him, and he fell helplessly to the floor. Mother then called to us for help, and we moved the drunkard into a special room and laid him down on a white bed, after removing his dirty clothes.

That night he was guarded by my mother. She cleaned and ironed Lukacs's clothes. Every time she peeked into his room to see if he had awakened from his intoxication.

In the late hours of the morning Lukacs awoke. My mother wished him a good morning and served him tea with lemon. In response to his question of how he got there,

[Page 203]

my mother told him that she had found him rolling in the street, dirty and screaming. She apologized that she had allowed herself to do what she did, but added that seeing him in that condition, which was unusual, apparently, he had had a drink too many and had gotten drunk. Since that was not according to his status, people that would see him would find it disgraceful, so she decided and dared to take him home, with her son's help. She assured him that besides her family no one had seen him drunk.

When Mother handed him his clothes, cleaned and ironed, he could not restrain his feelings and said that he was wrong in his attitude toward the Jews, that he had thought they were crooks, greedy, and hated goyim.

Since then, he has become a friend of ours and changed his hostile attitude toward Jews.

Translator's Footnotes:

1. Slavuta, approx. 60 km east of Mizocz.
2. Seven is a recurring religious symbolic number, and 'seven eyes' appears multiple times in the Bible in reference to the Seven Spirits of God.
3. Verkhiv, approx. 15 km east of Mizocz
4. Tuchyn, approx. 60 km NE of Mizocz.
5. Horyn River is found about 1 km west of Tuchyn.
6. Lvov, now Lviv in Western Ukraine.
7. Odesa, major city in southern Ukraine, on the Black Sea
8. 'The one who does not know how to ask' refers to one of the four types of children present at the Passover seder, who is either too young or too uninterested to understand the religious significance of the seder.
9. The Amidah is also called "the 18" and is part of the daily prayer service
10. Gentile or non-Jew
11. Derogatory Slavic term for Jews
12. R., abbrev for Reb, a traditional Jewish title or form of address, corresponding to Mr.
13. Jewish afternoon prayer service.
14. Haman is the villain, and Mordechai the hero of the Purim story in the Book of Esther. However, this particular line makes reference to a verse from Megillah 7b:7 "Rava said: A person is obligated to become intoxicated with wine on Purim until he is so intoxicated that he does not know how to distinguish between cursed is Haman and blessed is Mordecai."

Pages from My Diary
From the series, "The Man and his Hobbies"[1]

by Isaac Braz

Translation from Hebrew by Corey Feuer and Nida Kiali

May 1941

I worked vigorously in order to sit my second-semester law exams. I am immersed first and foremost in my studies; I have no downtime to engage with my surroundings. I have not even been reading the newspaper. Things are happening in the world – but I do not know about them.

June 21, 1941

I successfully passed the last exam. I am ecstatic. As soon as I received the test results, I ran like crazy to Marisha's house, took her to a committee, and then took her on a trip.

That night was enchanted. The sky was studded with stars and the smell of flowers imbued the air with the intoxicating essence of summer. We returned home late. Her kiss lingered on my lips for a long time after.

June 22, 1941

I turn over in bed and ask to sleep for a little while longer; I returned home later than normal. Suddenly, the maid bursts into my room.

"Mr. Isaac, the war has broken out."

I try to dispel the rheum from my eyes.

"I just heard the news," she continues excitedly. "The Germans surprise-invaded Soviet Russia without declaring war first.

[Page 204]

"You can surely imagine what war would look like these days. These chemical weapons, all the new inventions, the giant airplanes – really more like flying fortresses! And my only son will be forced to go to the terrible battlefront… no, I will not be able to stand all these horrors!"

I comforted her as much as I could. I told her that it was not that terrible, that the war would pass very quickly, and everything would soon be calm once again. She calmed down, for she believed in what I said as though it was the word of God, and she returned to her room.

Only then did I begin to ponder what was going on in the world. My parents – how were they taking the news? Were they not worried about my fate in the same way the maid worried about the fate of her son?

No good will come from this war. It will destroy borders and raze the lands – and humanity will be forced to sow everything anew.

I walked in big strides around the room and a great flame burned in my head. War! War! A sort of masculine joy arose within me; I will also go to fight!

I hastily dressed myself and ran to Marisha. I did not find her in the house. "Where is she?" I ask the maid. "I do not know," she responds. "She went out an hour ago and did not say where."

I run to the university, running around floor after floor like a crazy person. I finally meet her at the administrative office, where she is arranging her papers before the journey to Rivne. We leave together in feverish discussion. After exchanging opinions about the situation, we begin making plans.

We came to a decision: we are traveling tomorrow. I part ways from her, as I also must arrange my papers before the journey. The city is buzzing like a beehive, it is impossible to escape the tumult. Crowding, congestion, excitement, an endless flow of cars. The whole town spilled onto the streets, and everyone is talking about the same topic: the war. There is already news from the battlefront: the Germans are approaching; the Russian defense is failing. What should be done, where to go, where to hide among the fascist surge about to engulf us?

I jump onto a meager buggy, harnessed to a lame horse, as it is the only vehicle I encounter on my path – and I travel to the law faculty's building. There is a long, twisting line in front of the door to the administrative office. Everyone is agitated, everyone is talking loudly. I wait until 5 p.m. and only then am I granted entrance into the administrative office.

Bad luck! At that exact moment, the sound of a siren erupts from the radio; German planes are approaching the city. Everyone stops their work and speeds downstairs,

[Page 205]

to the basement, as there are no anti-aircraft shelters yet. We crowd together there for close to two hours.

I breathe a sigh of relief as I exit into the fresh air – and return to the administrative office. This time they give me the papers without any more delays. I depart from there to go arrange personal matters, part from acquaintances, settle accounts, and prepare belongings for the journey. This went on until it was almost morning.

When I return home, I find on the table a hastily written note. I immediately recognize the handwriting and my fingers tremble as I bring the note closer to my eyes:

"I was at your place, I wanted to take you with me when I happened upon a car traveling straight to Rivne. Come by train immediately. I am waiting for you. Marisha".

On the one hand, I am happy that she has at least already left the city, and on the other hand, I am afraid for her life. The radio announces that Germans have gotten very close over the last few hours: my only hope is that the journey will go peacefully.

My train departs at 2:30 p.m. I emotionally part from the maid and her son and head to the station. There I am informed that the train to Rivne is no longer departing because the Germans have taken over part of the route. The information hits me like thunder on a bright day.

What am I going to do? I will not be able to see my parents. I will not be by Marisha's side. At that moment, a group of students surrounds me, my classmates, they too residents of Rivne. We discuss the tragedy that has befallen us and decide to go together to Russia; there we will certainly meet our relatives. There, we explain to each other, we will be able to enter the ranks of the army. Those Germans would soon witness our wrath!

This is how my dreams of Lviv ended. The magnificent dances, the theaters, the cinemas, and the rest of the youthful experiences. The wild waves of war were about to hit the sides of my meager boat. Yet I do not harbor resentment toward this city; I had so many beautiful moments there.

My precious parents! My Marisha! I would give so much in order to know what was happening with them now.

And in the meantime, we stand at a crossroads. Where to go? We eventually choose to head out in the direction of Kyiv; after that we will see what to do next.

Thanks only to youthful energy, we manage to squeeze our way into the train car. The train is so full that there is zero space left within it. There was not enough room even for a pin. And the roofs – it is hard to describe

[Page 206]

what is going on there. Despite police intervention, new travelers are constantly being added. The train is overloaded; the engine exhales heavily and we begin to move forward very slowly. We arrive the next day in Kyiv. At the train station, I encounter my best friend, Vladek, who is also a student in the Faculty of Law. "What in God's name are you doing here?" I ask, astonished. "When did you arrive?"

We decide we will stay together from here on out, and we head to town to book a hotel room. It soon becomes clear to us that we were daydreaming; every hotel in the city is full. We are willing to pay more, but to no avail. Each hour, the money was losing its value.

In the end, after long hours waiting in shelters, fearing the German planes, we successfully find lodging in a privately-owned house. But first we must promise that we will leave there the next day. In return for this kindness, I part with a wonderful suit sewn from England. It troubled me to do it, but I had no choice. The money we had no longer held any value; I paid an almost-unreal sum of money for a small bit of bread. After all, one must eat. And also sleep. We are only human.

In the morning, Vladek hurries to town and tells me when he returns that travel by water through the Dnieper River is open to us. The authorities had stationed boats for the purpose of immigration. We pack our belongings and set off again.

Another surprise! On our way, we encounter a resident of my city, Asher Gilberg. My happiness knows no bounds: our group has grown, and we proceed! We depart, after a short stay, from

Dnipropetrovsk[1] towards Kuybyshev[2]. Compared to other cities, life is still relatively quiet here. We decided to stay here a while.

Our first steps: to City Hall, in order to find out the residence options in the cities. The commissar politely explains to us that government officials are soon coming to the city and that all the empty rooms are already booked for them. On the other hand, he suggests that we go to the other adjacent villages, where suitable dwellings could certainly be found. "In a little while," he tells us, "Leave here with a load of wheat to Bezymyanka[3]. If you want, I will give you a note for the local City Hall and recommend your reception of it."

I did not believe that deep in the heart of Russia I would encounter people so kind. We received his suggestion with gratitude.

Several moments later, we are sitting in a truck. We thought that the driver would take us to a faraway place, but the vehicle stops after traveling only about 7 kilometers. Bezymyanka, it becomes apparent to us, is nothing but a kolkhoz. At the sight of the truck, a man holding a bundle of papers emerges from the kolkhoz's office.

[Page 207]

He hurls commands over his shoulder: the wheat must be unloaded at once, and do not delay the vehicle. It seemed he knew already we were coming given that he approached us without surprise and presented himself. After we gave him our documents, he sent us to our new place of residence.

It was a tiny, rickety hut. Inside was a table, two chairs, very old cooking utensils, and a bed with broken legs. It looked as though the family that previously lived in the house had hastily evacuated upon our coming. There were no windows, only two holes in the walls that reminded one of a prison from the Middle Ages.

The fact of the matter was that we were not all that surprised. We were ready for everything. We entered the hut happily.

Myronov – this was the name of the director of the kolkhoz – said that we would report to him the next day to receive jobs. He suggested that in the meantime we rest and gather strength for work. With intense physical labor, he informed us, we overcome the enemy and contribute to the victory of communism. It was clear that he had memorized these things many times. The propaganda speech continued for a long while, until I was gripped by nausea. Luckily, this speech was stopped by a not-ugly teenage girl. Of medium height, she entered the hut and brought us a basket of food – bread, eggs and other staples. We pounced on the contents of the basket as if they were treasure. In the last few days, we had not encountered any decent food.

The next day, we come to Myronov. "Good morning," he greets us, "how did you sleep?"

"Very well, thanks," I respond.

"Good. And now, guys, tell me something." That's how he opened a conversation that continued for almost half a day.

What did we do in Poland? What were our parents' occupations? Do we like the emergence of the Soviet regime? What are our political views?

We of course presented ourselves as the sons of poor workers. We spiced up our story with complaints of capitalism's treatment of us, and we declared very solemn-facedly that we had impatiently waited for the Soviets to come free us.

Myronov nodded his head in satisfaction. "Great," he said. "And now, you of course know that the Spring is approaching. Your first job will therefore be repairing the harvesting machinery." Since that day, I was busy dismantling machines, screwing screws, and shoeing horses.

At first, I thought I was going crazy, that I would not be able to hold on with the hard work, but I gradually adjusted to the physical exertion involved and even to the

[Page 208]

terrible food served to us, the sort of garbage dishes that we would feed the pigs in Poland.

Our kolkhoz was considered large, since it had 350 people. We therefore had our own doctor, or, more accurately, a female doctor. Her name was Lidya Iwanowa and she had only that same year finished her studies. She was a wonderful girl, with intoxicating blue eyes and a pair of beautifully sculpted legs and red hair – the only part of her appearance that did not appeal to me. Since we became aware of her, she had never left our side. We were, after all, the only people in the kolkhoz at her cultural level and with whom she could chat and banter with as students do.

At first, I did not notice that she gave me more attention than others, but one evening, I came to understand what was going on. It happened like this:

We took a trip for our enjoyment and to forget the problems of the kolkhoz, when Lidya gradually shifted the conversation over to personal matters. She suddenly asked me, "Yitzchak, tell me honestly, have you ever had a girl?"

"Yes," I replied succinctly.

"And where is she now?"

"I do not know."

"Do you still love her?"

"Yes."

Although it was the evening, I could see in the moonlight that the girl was pale as whitewash. If not for her holding on to my arm, she would certainly have fallen. After a moment, she recovered – and wrapped her arms around my neck.

"But you also love me!" she called out, "Me more!"

I did not know how to reply. I was silent, however in order to calm her down, I answered her kiss with a kiss.

From that point everything was made crystal clear. Lidya constantly begged me to make her a wife and asserted to me in a thousand ways that the bachelor life in kolkhoz is not very pleasant. I was in emotional distress: I did not want to hurt her feelings and become her enemy, as I stuck to the principle that we must live with everyone in peace, but on the other hand, I could not erase Marisha's memory from my heart. And I could not replace Marisha with any other woman.

I decided to leave the kolkhoz and travel to Stalingrad[4], where I had the possibility

[Page 209]

of continuing my studies. After discussing this with Vladek and arranging my papers with Myronov, I went to part ways with Lidya.

It was not a pleasant parting. When I announced to her that I was leaving the kolkhoz, her face began to change color like a spotlight on a stage. She didn't say a thing, just threw herself onto the couch crying. Eventually, she raised her face, drenched in tears, and asked, "Why are you doing this, Yitzchak? Is it bad for you here?"

I responded that I was going only because of my studies and that all the rest was of no importance to me. I comforted her and told her that at the first opportunity I had, I would come for a visit.

I managed to escape from the kolkhoz, in which I had been for close to two months. I unfortunately had to part from my friend Asher, who decided to stay, as he had no firm plans for the future.

* * *

Volga! The wonderful Volga! We observe the magnificent river from the deck and admire its beauty and size. The evening wind carries the yellow-sided boat across the water's surface like a gilded arrow. The lit red lantern on the bow illuminated everything in an enchanting shade. We feasted our eyes on the wonderful view and lay down for a little nap. We must get up early the next day.

Stalingrad. We arrived at night, earlier than we had thought. We lie down to sleep at the port and place our bags beneath our heads. Even though we were lying on the hard ground, we immediately sank into slumber. I did not have the time to ask Vladek if he felt comfortable on his bed, as I already heard him snoring loudly; I slept well.

In the morning, we took our first steps on the university grounds. The secretary immediately directed us to the academics building and there, based on the papers in our hands, we were accepted as students into the university's Course B.

Several days later, when I had to an extent acclimated, I set out to tour the city. I was deeply impressed. Perfect roads, big display windows, tall houses. In a word, a beautiful city.

The appearance of the students was monotonous to the point of sadness. All of them received from time-to-time monochrome clothing items, made from the same fabric and cut in the same way. The clothes did not suit the men and looked ridiculous on the girls, but they did not feel like it. On the contrary, I felt like an outcast myself, as I still wore a fancy suit sewn in Poland, during the good days.

[Page 210]

I eventually hung my clothes in the closet and started dressing like them. This broke barriers that had still been standing between us: I was now just an equal among equals, and I quickly forged friendships with many of the students. With practice, I learned to address everyone in the first person. The formal Polish way of addressing people was considered here to be one of the dangerous capitalist customs.

In the evenings, the students would congregate in my room or would invite me to theirs and ask me to tell them about Poland. Everything interested them: the government, the lifestyle, Polish culture. So as not to fall into the hands of the secret police and not to be incarcerated on charges of distributing anti-Soviet propaganda, I tried to portray life at home as gloomily as possible and even made-up different kinds of little stories with my best imagination.

I forgot the spectacular balls in which I once took part, I forgot the smell of cologne and the smell of the perfume wafting from the women. I did not again have to worry which suit I would wear in the morning and which in the evening. Life smiled upon me.

During the student parties thrown from time to time, the hall was always packed wall to wall. The air was thick and steamy like in a bathhouse, but this did not bother anyone. On the contrary, the tightness allowed for you to fondle your girl and pretend you didn't know what your hands were doing.

One night, the students brought a jug of homemade vodka and got properly drunk with the girls. Following that, everyone got horizontal with echoing revelry. They were drunk to the point of not knowing who was doing what with whom – and they did not care…

Life continued like this until December, when it was announced that due to the crushing German attack, the university would relocate to Tashkent. I received the announcement with great joy: I had heard that a Polish army was organizing in Russia, was parked for the moment in Tashkent[5], and would soon head to Persia. I had a strong desire to enlist in this army's ranks and make it this way to the land of Israel, the wish of every young Jew from Poland. I hoped that I would be able to move from the Polish army to the Jewish Brigade and fight the enemy shoulder to shoulder with Jewish soldiers.

Unfortunately for me, things played out differently. When I arrived in Tashkent, I was made aware that the army had set out on its way to Persia a while ago. Despite this, I did not lose hope, as I would still dawn a uniform in this war. From the newspapers and the radio, I learned of the events in Poland, of the horrors committed against the Jewish population, and the wrath suffocated me. I knew that I would never see my parents again; I knew that a couple of elderly people

[Page 211]

would not withstand these tortures. And thus, I decided to enlist in the Red Army and avenge my parents.

This plan also did not come to fruition. I was told that the Russians were not at all ready to accept into their ranks refugees from the West, although the authorities I had spoken to promised me that this would soon change. In the meantime, I had no choice but to grind my teeth and invest my youthful energy into my studies.

* * *

Tashkent. A big city, with 1.5 million residents, most of them Uzbeks and Russians, with a minority of them being Jewish, Armenian, Kyrgyz, and Azerbaijani.

The first thing that piqued my interest was the city's unique character. Tashkent was the first Eastern city I saw, both in the appearance of its homes and the appearance and behavior of its residents.

Most of Tashkent's residents make their livings from trade, here the flower on every branch. They take it upon themselves to outwit his friend, cheat him in matters of business, and to take the money from his pockets in ways both legal and illegal. Although the city was very big, its stores were devoid of goods and of people. The real commerce is concentrated in the market; there you can get all the things that were missing from the stores, buy ridiculous things at just as ridiculous prices, exchange money and meet friends. The place is also swarming with gangs of teenagers involved in stealing watches and wallets with so much agility that the local police failed in stopping them. It is my belief that the police sometimes purposely turn a blind eye because of bribes from the gangs. True or not, a visit to Tashkent's market is a multifaceted experience.

The Uzbeks are artists in all things relating to relentless haggling and deceiving. They can sell you anything, at a price much higher than the value of the object. Even if it is clear to you that they are squeezing money out of you for essentially nothing, you cannot resist the persuasive methods of these sneaky vendors. Despite their antics when it comes to commerce, the Uzbeks stand out in their knowledge of languages and the high level of culture in comparison to much of the rest of the population. Many of them obtain higher education, and their natural intelligence causes them to stand out in every area.

I had close ties to this stratum of the population, as my enrollment into the University of Tashkent obtained me many friends from among the Uzbeks. Here, they did not look at me like they would a stranger since I had learned in Stalingrad how to adjust to my classmates and already knew how to behave towards them.

[Page 212]

That being said, it was not easy for me to obtain residency authorization in Tashkent. The number of residents grew with the influx of refugees here, reaching up to 4.5 million. The crowdedness was awful, and the authorities requested to restrict as much as possible the number of new residents. Friends who came here before succeeded in getting the necessary license. I had no such luck. What will I do? I launch a campaign of badgering towards all the party and city authorities, starting in town and ending at the ministry, but all to no effect.

They send me from office to office. I spend half a day at the city registration office, standing patiently in line and waiting. Finally, I am let into the official in charge's room.

"I am very sorry," he says to me, "but I will not be able to fulfill your request. You yourself have certainly seen overwhelming crowdedness here. We do not have space for any new people…"

I erupt in despair. "All of my friends from university are here," I shout. "The professors with whom I studied were transferred here as well – and only for me there is no space? And this is the thanks I get for my partisan work and for being the secretary of my ward's Komosol?"

"If that is so," he says to me indifferently, "why have you not gone to the party and asked them to intervene on your behalf?"

I have again hit a dead end. Meanwhile, I am out of money, have no place to sleep, and am starting to get a taste of hunger.

With no choice, I become a porter. I am paid 30 rubles for carrying a package, while a kilogram of bread costs 120. On the other hand, I can purchase an abundance of grapes for just 1.50 rubles. I therefore feed on fruits, but I soon discover that I cannot survive without bread. I have no more energy. The money that I earn is not enough to rent a room; I thus spend my nights in the market stalls.

Only on Wednesday do I find out that there is a possibility I can make an appeal before the president of the Uzbek Republic. I inform him of my request in writing, and I receive in the mail in return a courteous letter from the president's office. Attached to the letter is an invitation: I am to present myself to the president in two days for a personal conversation.

I arrive at his office on the designated day at 1 p.m., as is written in the invitation. They move me to a spacious waiting room, in which many people are already sitting. The hall is furnished with great taste. Diverse reading materials are on the tables – newspapers, weeklies, and leaflets. The walls are decorated with Western-style sculptures.

[Page 213]

I have not yet stopped examining my surroundings when they call my name. My heart starts to pound; not ever had I been in the company of such high-level people.

I enter. It is a modest room. On the walls are pictures of Lenin and Stalin. Behind the desk sits a man in his fifties smoking a cigarette. When I enter, he stands up immediately and extends his hand to me.

"Please sit," he invites.

He then starts presenting me with questions that have nothing at all to do with my bothersome problem. He is interested in the lives of workers in Poland and asks that I tell him about them in detail. While we are talking, a pleasant girl in a white apron enters the room and asks if she can serve lunch?

"Of course," he answers, "and please, Lidya, bring another portion for my student friend. Dine with me, won't you?" he asks me. I was more than a little embarrassed, but I could not refuse. I thanked him for his great generosity.

Hence, I eat lunch in the company of the president. It has been a long time since I tasted such wonderful flavors. When I swallowed the premium champagne, it awakened in me memories of days past, and only with difficulty did I hold back the tears in my eyes. Fool, I said to myself, why are you going to cry? You will not be able to change your situation this way.

Only after we finished lunch did President Akhunbabaev[6] ask why I had come. I begin to tell him about my past, my dedication to the party, and the predicament I am in right now. He listens and writes something down on a piece of paper. Then he hands me the note and says, "Please, comrade student, everything is in order."

I thank him from the bottom of my heart and leave. Outside, I open the folded note and read:

"…Please immediately issue a residence permit within Tashkent and allocate a suitable place of residence…" Signed: President of the Uzbek Republic.

With the note in my hand, I swiftly ran to the city hall. I got there during their lunch break, and had to wait until 3 p.m. Eventually, the office opened – and I was again faced with the same clerk who had rudely rejected my request a few days ago.

"What did you come for?" he asks me, "If it's about the license, you can leave immediately. I have no time to argue with you, we don't have a residence, no…"

[Page 214]

"Fine," I tell him quietly. "But I have a letter addressed to you."

After reading the letter, the clerk became extremely accommodating. "Sit down, please," he said, offering me a chair.

"I will immediately resolve the issue, he continued. "Haven't I told you that I would gladly handle your request… I'll take care of it right away, comrade!'

And indeed, a few moments later, I already had the license in my hand, along with a letter to the owner of the apartment in which a room was allocated for me. The owners of the apartment were Uzbeks. I got a furnished room that seemed to me like a palace.

* * *

From that moment on, I lacked nothing. I got acclimated to Tashkent and became very friendly with the homeowners, who treated me with kindness, typical of Uzbeks. They are the best hosts in the world! Even when they harbor hatred for a person within their home, they treat him with kindness as if he was a good friend.

The day after the visit to the president, I went to the law faculty secretariat, where they immediately accepted me as one of the students and sent me to the university warehouse. There they gave me a new suit, shirt, and shoes. After I changed my clothes and removed the layer of filth that had accumulated on my body over the past few days, I felt like a different person.

Since then, I have visited the lectures every day between 8 a.m. and 1 p.m. Each of us also got a job in the afternoon in order to not burden the city. I was sent to work in a factory for bombs and grenades; As deputy manager of the worker's diner, where 2,500 people ate.

I felt that I had gradually regained my strength. I had plenty of food; Sometimes, I would even bring various groceries to friends whose situation was not as good as mine.

This is how things continued until the end of the semester. Then, instead of the long-awaited vacation, we were sent in groups to work the land.

On the farm I was sent to, I was given the opportunity to get to know the lives of the Uzbeks up close. For us Europeans, there were many new and strange things about them.

The Uzbek peasants do not usually master the Russian language, especially not the old generation. They still wear their national clothes, embroidered with colorful flowers. They don't like to work. Instead, they sit in their tea houses at all hours of the day and evening and sip boiling tea, without sugar. This allows them to bear the terrible heat that prevails in this region.

Sometimes I would be inclined to think that the Uzbeks are deathly afraid

[Page 215]

of manual labor. Women and children work in their place in the fields. They have no shortage of the latter: every Uzbek has several wives, who live peacefully among themselves. During my entire stay at the farm, I did not encounter any instance of competition or quarrels between the women.

The Uzbeks are a God-fearing and ritual-loving people. They hold the circumcision ceremony when a boy reaches the age of thirteen. The boy is then brought to the community's elders, and the revelry that follows the ceremony lasts for three days and three nights. Apart from the wedding, this is the most important ceremony in their lives.

During my stay at the farm, I had the chance to see an Uzbek wedding ceremony to which all the area residents were invited.

According to tradition, the bride is not allowed to meet her groom from the morning on. The latter fasts during the day, and the couple would meet only during the marriage ceremony. The congregation elects a sort of committee of five elderly women. They prepare a special room for the couple, and stand guard so that no one enters it. The young couple must spend the wedding night in this room, and the next day the women enter the room and check the sheets to see if the bride was indeed a virgin. If not, the young husband may annul his marriage and return his wife to her parent's house.

While the couple is in their room, the guests spend time outside, around a fire, and eat pilaf (a national dish made of rice, meat, and oils). The food is in a large bowl, and everyone must dip their hand and shove the rice in their mouth – otherwise, they will be considered an enemy of the family.

* * *

In such conditions – in the city during my studies and on the farm during my vacation – I lived until 1944.

I thought of my beloved parents, my sister, and Marisha always and everywhere. One painful question tormented me: are they still alive? Finally, I learned that the Red Army liberated our district. I immediately contacted the local authorities by phone, and after a few days of expectation, I received a telegram from my sister: she is alive and well and lives in Rivne.

I laughed, cried, jumped like a madman, ran to everyone I knew, and told them the wonderful news I had received. I thought I had no one left in the world – and my sister was there, alive and waiting for my return!

I began to arrange my papers frantically. And soon after, everything was ready; with a beating heart, I set off.

[Page 216]

I'm sitting on the train and can't believe my eyes. Through the train car's windows, the sandy fields of Uzbekistan and Kazakhstan pass before my eyes. I hear a locomotive horn, and the train enters the tunnel. Even before I have adjusted to the darkness, we are outside again, and a city unfolds before my eyes. I still don't know if all of this is happening in reality or if I'm dreaming: have I already left Tashkent, from the heart of Asia, and am I on my way home? Will I soon see my hometown, where I spent my best years, where I left everything dear to me?

My patience is running out. I travel for a day, two days, three, twelve. Finally, the train enters the Ukrainian lands. Snow-covered fields lie on both sides of the track – and my heart feels a pinch. Memories surface, the childhood games with snowballs, the enchanted rides on a sled pulled by a pair of horses, the skiing I loved so much. As if to anger me, it all reminds me of days that are forever gone…

The sixteenth day. We arrived in Kyiv. The train station is completely destroyed, but the traffic is as heavy as ever. We were told that we would stay here for about 24 hours. So, I go out to the platform – maybe I'll see a familiar face here…

There is no one. I wander from train car to train car, peering into the faces of passers-by, straining my ears to pick up snippets of conversation, but all in vain. The hours slowly go by. I'm tired.

The next day the train leaves from Kyiv. Home!

On January 5, 1945, at 11:30 a.m., the train arrives at Rivne. I get off the train – and I don't recognize my city. Everything here is ruined, barren, and abandoned. Not a soul in sight.

And is this Rivne, the city where I had my happy childhood, the town that was always buzzing with life? Now it is in a state of gloomy silence, like after a dead man's funeral.

I pick up my things and go to the address my sister mentioned in her letter. Approaching the place, I no longer control my nerves. My heart beats strongly as if it wanted to leap out of my chest, and my legs give out on me. For a moment, I fear I won't have the strength to reach the door.

With a trembling hand, I knock on the door: "Come in!" I hear from inside.

Inside the room a young girl sits, writing something. As I come in, she raises her head and looks at me. Asiya! My little sister Asiya!

We fall into each other's arms, cry, laugh, and kiss each other. I am not ashamed of my running tears. Asiya was a little girl

[Page 217]

when I last saw her–and now I hold a seventeen-year-old maiden in my arms.

When we calmed down a bit, we started telling each other about our past years. We didn't have much time; the news of my coming spread, and I still haven't had time to look at Asiya to my heart's content. The room was filled with people. The visits and conversations continued until late in the evening. Finally, the last of the guests left, and I was given the opportunity to chat freely with Asiya.

That night I slept on white and fragrant sheets for the first time since I left Tashkent. It took twenty-five days to get from distant Asia to Rivne.

The next day I went to Mizocz to look for the place where my old parents' house used to be. Much to my surprise, I found out that the house was standing strong – one of the few that survived in town – and that the dairy next to it also survived. However, everything seemed hopelessly neglected; No trace of our flower beds and fruit garden remained.

I entered the house trembling with excitement. I couldn't stay there long. A wave of memories flooded me, and I sobbed out loud as I went out into the street.

I almost ran away from that place and did not allow myself to look back. It was one of the hardest moments of my life. But man, as it turns out, can overcome everything. When I returned to Asiya and Rivne, I had already come to my senses and showed no sign of what had happened.

Life slowly returned to its course. The days have gone by quickly: every morning, I would stroll around to see the aftermath of the destruction with my own eyes. Every day I would hear new details about the murder of my people by the Ukrainians, about the destruction of entire cities and villages.

Finally, after three months of sitting in Rivne, I decided I had nothing more to look for there. I applied to move to Poland, and it was approved in a short time. I felt that I could no longer stay on this land, soaked in the blood of my innocent parents and relatives.

My next stop: Lodz, the largest and most vibrant city in post-war Poland. A few days later, I got an excellent job at the military attorney's office. My job entails wearing an army uniform with three stars – but I prefer to stay in civilian clothes for safety reasons. Members of the fanatical partisan organization A.K.[7] are still roaming about.

The work gives me new strength. The depression of the last few months is gradually passing. My lifestyle now resembles the one I had before the war:

[Page 218]

dances, theaters, movies. I try to forget the hardships and tragedies I experienced in these unhappy years.

I also try to forget Marisha – but I cannot do so. I was convinced she had perished along with the others, but her memory never left my heart. A kind of voice that I could not subdue told me that I must not forget her, just as I must not forget my parents.

One day, while walking with Asiya on the main street of Lodz, I hear a woman's voice behind me calling, "Ignatz!" I don't linger, thinking it was meant for someone else.

"Ignatz!" The voice repeats.

I turn back…

Marisha! Giant hammers start pounding in my head, and some kind of strange mist appears before my eyes. If it weren't for Asiya supporting me, I would have surely fallen on the pavement. I felt my mouth was wide open – but I could not utter a single sound from my numbed throat.

I managed to recover with a great effort. I wanted to take her in my arms, crush her mouth with my lips – but the squeeze of Asiya's hand on my arm reminded me that we were on the street…

I invite Marisha to my apartment, which is nearby. A moment later, we sit in my room, deep in comfortable armchairs. My sister Asiya leaves us alone and goes out to make something to drink.

I look at my Marisha and see the years that have passed, reflecting on her face. With a heavy heart, I note that my beloved had changed a little. Those great braids that I loved so much are gone. The perfect figure that aroused the girls' envy had also gone away. In the picture that was kept in my heart, Marisha always wore her silk dress, made according to the Paris fashion – and now I see before me a ragged and tired girl with the hardships of war etched on her face.

However, all this does not diminish my joy even in the slightest. My Marisha is with me again, after I believed for so long that she was no longer alive – and my happiness knows no bounds. I thirstily drink her words. And Marisha says:

She was in Warsaw during the bloody uprising. She had fake documents, and no one knew about her being Jewish. After the suppression of the rebellion, she was sent to forced labor in Vienna, and with the liberation of Poland, she arrived in Lodz.

[Page 219]

Asiya calls us to the table. We taste the coffee and cakes she made, talk for a bit longer – and then Marisha gets up and says she has to go. Livelihood matters, she explains to me. She has to support herself somehow…

I accompany her home and memorize her address. As we part separate ways, I get the feeling that she was treating me with deliberate coldness, as if she wanted to drive me away.

Why? Maybe she's married and didn't want to tell me about it, or maybe engaged – or maybe she just doesn't love me anymore? Questions, unanswered questions…

That night I can't sleep. Marisha's image was constantly in my mind's eye. At two past midnight, I turn on the light on the bedside table and force myself to read a book. Thousands of thoughts swirl in my mind, keeping me restless. I wait impatiently for the morning.

After breakfast, I go to the city and buy high-heeled shoes and a lovely dress. Then, loaded with packages, happy as a child, I run to Marisha's house.

The door is opened by a chambermaid who asks me why I was there. "Can I see Miss Marisha?" I'm asking.

"Please, here's her room." The maid disappears into the darkness of the corridor. I knock on Marisha's door.

She is alone and sitting at the table. Busy writing.

We shake hands like two strangers. I hand her my packages.

"For me?" she asks.

"I brought you some little things," I say. "Why, you can't look so neglected. You must become the Marisha I knew once again – both on the outside and in your soul."

"Ignatz… I am so glad you care for me, but please understand, I cannot accept these things without paying you for them – and I have no money…"

My heart was saddened. I feel that something is hidden behind her hesitation.

"Marisha," I implore her, "I don't understand you. Haven't we known each other since childhood, you were a classmate – and my friend for many years. But let's not talk about that – even if you were just a girl from my town, I would still feel a moral obligation towards you."

The diplomatic tone I used achieves its purpose. Marisha takes my presents and thanks me from the bottom of her heart. We exchange notes, talk

[Page 220]

About different topics – and finally, I turn to leave without talking to her about the most important thing to me – the intense love I have for her.

Before leaving, I invite her to an evening showing at the cinema, but she refuses, saying she has no free time in the evening. We, therefore, talk about meeting tomorrow afternoon at her apartment.

I decide to talk to her openly. The unclear situation we are in is not to my liking.

The next day, at 3 p.m., I show up at Marisha's. This time I don't waste time. After a short introduction, I ask for her hand.

Marisha bursts into terrible tears.

"Ignatz!" Where were you a few weeks ago? I thought about you all these years and waited for your return, not even for a moment did I believe that you were not alive. But some time ago, my faith grew weak. I met a man who fell in love with me – and we've been engaged for two weeks!"

Everything is clear to me now. I hear her sobbing and know that it's not too late. I feel that if I implore her repeatedly, Marisha will have a change of heart.

But I can't do that. I still have a shred of self-respect left in me, for I didn't stop thinking about Marisha despite all the disasters that happened to me. Many girls wanted me – but I remained loyal to Marisha. If her love is stronger than mine, I say to myself, she must come to me.

"Marisha! I have already told you about what has happened to me in recent years," I tell her, "However, I would like to add this: always, wherever I was, I remembered and loved you. I love you now and will love you in the future. My feelings for you will never change: I'm the same as before the war and will remain so in the future."

I breathe deeply and continue: "And now. I don't know if we will meet again one day. So, farewell – and accept my sincere good wishes for your new path."

"Ignatz!" Marisha tries to stop me. "Wait… Don't go yet." Her lips are trembling: she wants to say something more, but her throat won't let her.

"I'm very sorry, Marisha. But I don't have any more time to spare." Standing on the doorstep, I add: "Tomorrow, I will get my documents in order and leave for Krakow – and from there, I will continue to The Land of Israel." "As you see – we are going our separate ways."

"Goodbye!"

Translator's Footnotes:

1. Dnipropetrovsk, now Dnipro, city in Ukraine on the Dnipro River, 290 miles SE of Kyiv
2. Kuybyshev, now Samara, city in Russia on the Volga River, 875 miles ENE of Dnipro.
3. Bezymyanka, town on the outskirts of Kuybyshev.
4. Stalingrad, now Volgograd, city on the Volga River 465 miles SW of Kuybyshev (Samara).
5. Tashkent, cpital of Uzbekistan, 1,680 miles ESE of Volgograd.
6. Yuldash Akhunbabaev, a founding father and first head of state of the Uzbek Soviet Socialist Republic (Wiki)
7. Armia Krajowa (Home Army), a resistance movement in German-occupied Poland in World War II. Aligned with the Polish government-in-exile, it was disbanded by the Soviet government.

[Page 221]

How I Made Aliya
The Story of Noah Stein, the First Immigrant from Mizocz

As Recorded by Reuven Melamed

Translated from Hebrew by Ofir Horovitz, Eiden Harel Brewer and Noa Etzyon

It was in 1920; I worked then in the city of Ostroh as a blacksmith. One day I terribly missed mom, dad, and home so I decided to go to Mizocz for the Sabbath. I finished my work early, packed my things, and turned to go home, a 30-kilometer walk.

After a few hours of walking, I realized that I would not be able to make it home in the early hours of the night and decided to stay in Village N. with an acquaintance, a Jewish blacksmith.

The blacksmith hosted me nicely and offered me a job working for him, with better conditions and salary than those I had in Ostroh.

As I was considering his proposal, his wife arrived from a nearby city where she had been staying for family matters. She told us that the city was in turmoil, and that everyone was talking about a group of male "pioneers" who were all educated, from privileged families and rich homes, and were in the city on their way to Eretz Yisrael, where they would work as simple laborers. The woman added that in the city, people claim that throughout Russia, groups of "pioneers" were organizing to train themselves here, for work "there," and that students were learning to become blacksmiths, carpenters, builders, etc.

While making dinner, the woman did not stop talking about the "pioneers". The entire night we talked about the unusual fellows and Eretz Yisrael, and when I went to bed, I was unable to fall asleep due to excitement. I thought to myself, if students are learning to become blacksmiths, it means that the blacksmith profession is a good thing in Eretz Yisrael, and as an experienced blacksmith, even the students cannot compete with me. And secondly, being in Eretz Yisrael, seeing the Western Wall, the Cave of Patriarchs, and Rachel's Tomb, it is a huge thing, so I made the decision to also make aliya to Eretz Yisrael. I fell asleep feeling that I made a wise decision.

I got up in the morning and began researching what one needs to do to make it to Eretz Yisrael. They told me that I need to talk to the Eretz Yisrael office. But the office only accepts students (that is what I thought at the time) and what am I? A student? Surely, they will mock me. And as my embarrassment grew, it brought me to despair.

On my way home I could not stop thinking about Eretz Yisrael and, suddenly, I remembered that two people from our city, Alter Nemirover and Hershel Shpanover, had visited

[Page 222]

Eretz Yisrael a few years back, and they said that they went there through the city of Odessa. But now Odessa is beyond the border…

Without any other alternatives, I decided to cross the border into Odessa. I packed my few things, made snacks for the road, and set out one evening. After a few days, I managed to cross the border one night. I traveled by night and during the day I hid in the forests or the fields. When I was hungry, I would take a risk and enter a house in the village to ask for bread and water. However, I was not always close to a village, and so I had nights when I was starving and dehydrated.

Once, after several days without food, I entered a farmer's house and asked for bread while tearing up. The farmer gave me a whole loaf, and I swallowed it in one piece. The farmer and his children were stunned, made the sign of the cross, and gave me another loaf so that I would leave their house. They were concerned that I might explode in their home…

This is how I traveled for several weeks until I arrived at Odessa exhausted. But once there, I found out that the route to Eretz Yisrael was closed. I was on the verge of despair. But then some nice fellow Jews told me not to lose hope and that I should try to get to the Caucasus. From there, they explained, it would not be hard to cross the border into Turkey. And from Turkey the path to Eretz Yisrael was open.

Without much thought, I left and arrived at the Caucasus and stayed close to the Turkish border. On a dark night, I tried to cross the border into Turkey and got caught.

At my interrogation, I told the Russians the truth. I told them that I was from Mizocz near Rivne controlled by the Poles. I told them that the Poles treated us badly, and that is why I wished to get to Eretz

Yisrael. I also told them that I was unemployed, poor, and without travel money, and therefore I travelled from town to town to get to my destination.

They did not believe me and my story. They suspected that I was a prominent spy. So, they transferred me into a big prison where many notable prisoners were kept, among which were high army officers, noblemen, and industry owners and such.

After a week of interrogations, they transported everyone in my prison cell along with prisoners from other cells onto a train. On the way, as the train travelled farther from the prison, I asked a colonel with a nice beard where they were taking us. He told me that we were all sentenced to death, and were being transported to the execution place…

I did not want to die, I was innocent. So, I decided to take a risk and jump from the moving train. Secretly, I removed one of the car planks, and I jumped at the first chance I got.

[Page 223]

The guards noticed that; they fired at me, stopped the train, and searched for me. However, their search failed as I was able to hide in the forest.

I hid in that forest for a few days, scared to be caught. On the third day, I left the forest and walked toward the border. I already knew the way, and I was very careful. This time I was able to successfully cross the border, but I was caught by the Turks, and they gave me back to the Russians…

Learning from my previous poor experience, this time I did not tell my interrogators the truth. I claimed to be a Turk held captive in Russia. I told them I had forgotten my name, the Turkish language, and where I was. I was then transferred back to prison where I was constantly interrogated, but I did not change my statement.

Once I was brought before an interrogator wearing a dress, meaning a woman. After several questions, to which I answered exactly as before, she told her peers: "Why are you keeping this fellow? Can't you see that he is a perfect "idiot"?"

They brought me back to prison, and two days later they made me work in the kitchen. In my role chopping wood and drawing water, I felt great. I had everything. Compared to my life in the prison cell, where I was starving and dehydrated, I was in heaven. I had enough bread, vegetables, meat, and of course water. That is how I lived for six months. I was free to walk around town anywhere I wanted.

At the end of the summer, I wanted to know when Yom Kippur was and where the nearest synagogue was. I came across several Jews and found out that Yom Kippur was commencing in the upcoming days. I arrived at the synagogue, prayed, and fasted. I was then invited to a dinner to break the fast at the house of a Jewish hotel owner.

I told my hosts everything I had been through, as well as my strong desires to get to Eretz Yisrael. The Jewish man took care of me, helping me find work at his hotel as a porter. Once I had enough money, this Jewish man got me an Italian passport. Using that passport, I was legally able to arrive in Istanbul as a tourist. There I contacted the office of Eretz Yisrael, and then I made aliya.

[Page 224]

A Lieutenant General – a Champion Collector
From the series, "The Man and his Hobbies"[1]

by Asher Ben-Oni

Translation from Hebrew by Isaac Makovsky, Joshua Metzel and Samuel Rotenberg

Yiddish songs translated by Clair Padgett

In the house of Lieutenant General Moshe Gat, I had the opportunity to connect with a document that I needed to complete a literary work. I spent three hours in the house in a pleasant conversation and I did not feel that the rooms, which were furnished with extreme modesty, gave any sign such an interesting collector lives in the house. It was only when I left the apartment that I noticed a large shipping container in the backyard of the house.

When I asked about had been or still was in the container, I was given an answer that the only items for the collection had been shipped in the container.

Without being asked, I returned to the apartment to have another glance at the mysterious collection, and I immediately acknowledged that I would need to revisit, in order to become familiar to the content of the records, the books, the documents, the works of art, the stamps, the coins, and more and more, that were found hidden in the scattered crates across the entire apartment.

In the first moments, what interested me was what kind of collection it was, what topics the collector took an interest in.

I was amazed to hear that this person who never set foot in a *cheder*[2] and who hardly knew the experience of Diaspora Jews, who had no religious experience but grew up in Israel in a strongly secular environment in villages and kibbutzim – was in fact enamored of Jewish traditions and connected to the glorious past of our people with his heart and soul, with an enthusiastic love for Israel that few share.

Lieutenant General Gat explored a lot of the world while working in the Ministry of Foreign Affairs and more recently served as the second secretary in the Israeli Embassy in Moscow. In every place he went, he searched and found items for his collection. In every place he was interested in the Jews, their artwork and their lives. And so, he accumulated – added to the other collection areas – an interesting and unique collection of Jewish records, which were commemorated by the performances of Jewish artists around the world. However, if records of famous cantors, stage actors, fashion singers, etc. are common, then Mr. Gat's collection is special because it contains very rare, if not unique records of all the Jewish artists in the Soviet Union, past and present. Although one should not underestimate the concentration of very classical and excellent works, performed by the greatest artists in the world, on many hundreds of records.

[Page 225]

Mr. Gat and his wife, Tzipora, are particularly proud – and rightly so – of the only record by Nechama Lifshitz[3] that appeared in the Soviet Union during the Jubilee celebration [in honor of] Sholem Aleichem on an LP record. According to the testimony of the Gat couple, who heard the singer in Moscow, the recorded songs were not this singer's best selections of her repertoire.

A great shame, the Jewish public is not familiar with nor ever heard the name of this young artist. She had a voice that moved hearts and shook souls. Hearing her sing is an unforgettable artistic experience that marks one's soul for days. Her voice was not just filled with emotion and distinctly Jewish characteristics, but also culture and unparalleled versatility. Her tune followed the lyrics and notes in an indescribable way. As she sings the chorus: "*Spiel, spiel, klezmer spiel, wast dach was ich wil un was ich pil.*"[4] The excitement courses through your body and in your mind's eye as if you imagined the masses going berserk in the halls of Russian cities to her songs or when she sings in her deep, velvety voice:

> "We should sing this little song together
> Like good friends, like children from one mother
> My only request is that my song
> Should be freely heard with everyone else's song."[5]

You feel distraught so your eyes start spontaneously watering from the song about "Babi Yar," where the Jews of Kyiv were killed by the depraved Hitlerists, in the voice of Nechama Lifshitz, the way she sang was a boisterous challenge against our nation's oppressors. The lyrics of the song have the power to soften a heart of stone, and the tune of Nechema's voice evoked tears of joy. Even the regular song, "*Hinech Yafa*"[6] starts with Hebrew lyrics and her Sephardic vocalizations. A simple love song caresses and excites simultaneously when it leaves her throat, exemplifying the great singer's talent.

[Page 226]

From a concert playbill of hers found by collectors and other sources, we gathered some details about the personality of this great Jewish artist. She was born in Lithuania thirty years ago. She studied in Hebrew school and belonged to the illegal Komsomol[7]. She was a great patriot for her homeland and a dedicated member of the Communist party, and with that, a proud Jew with world recognition. Her stardom as an artist began rising after the second World War.

Other rare records by Mikhoels[8] adorned the collection and his different and versatile roles in Jewish artistic theater of Moscow in his golden years caused great aesthetic pleasure to his whole audience. Incredibly rare remnants of Jewish artists' records from the good days can also be found in the collection from when Yiddish culture flourished in the Soviet Union.

Suggestion to "*Kol Yisrael*"

We suggest "*Kol Yisrael*," an Israeli radio station, approach lieutenant general Mr. Gat, and get from him the collection of records of Yiddish artists from the Soviet Union on loan, so that the listeners can listen to a special program, dedicated to the Yiddish culture that was cut down and destroyed in the Soviet Union. Maybe the Jews "from over there" will also hear the program, because after their year of peace in the jubilee celebrations, there haven't been any more Yiddish performances in the Soviet Union. We are sure that the people of Israel for their testimonies and parties will enjoy, not only Nechama Lifshitz, Mikhoels, Zuskin[9], etc. but also the lesser-known artists.

For example, the folk song "*Itziklas Chatuna*"[10] has four different versions, and different artists performed in each song in the collection.

Mr. Gat lives on 92 Tzahal Street in Tzahala, and I am guaranteed that he will make "*Kol Yisrael*" available as a part of his collection for a special concert for his listeners of this generation.

There is no doubt that our radio services will do a good service for the listeners, and they allow them to get to know of these great artists. It will give them not only spiritual pleasure, but also an impressively deep Jewish experience. In addition, it is doubtful whether even the vast library of "*Kol Yisrael*" records are 100 records of revolutionary songs, 500 records of excellent concerts performed by the most prestigious orchestras, hundreds of records of complete operas, folk songs of the people, exotics, and many more.

[Page 227]

The Collection of Dr. Sukarno

We skipped the uninteresting files of documents and articles and began to look through the art books. Here, too, a pleasant surprise awaits us; we heard; we knew, and we were familiar with many known artists. We visited many famous museums, but we were not ashamed to admit that we were not aware that the president of Indonesia, Dr. Sukarno, was, in fact, the owner of this encompassing collection that would be the envy of any museum. Additionally, in this collection, we discovered new fruits of the brush from artists whose expressive pieces captivate and mesmerize with their artistic power.

The painters Basuki Abdullah, Soedarsono, Saleh, Sudarso, Ernest Dezentje, Trubus, Herbert Hutagalung, among others, prove that many surprises awaited us from the rising east, artistically. These modern Indonesian artists, such as Ernest and Herbert, exemplify without a shadow of a doubt that these painters developed professionally in Europe and America, and their pieces signify great talent. Mr. Gat purchased some albums with complete reproductions of this collection, which were printed in Peking, the capital of China. The extremely ornate albums testified to the great ability of the Chinese printing industry.

Jewish Art

There are also works in Mr. Gat's art collection that can only maybe be found in the central libraries of the country. We recall only some of them: The Prague Ghetto. Old artistic albums of the famous Ghetto. The Kaufmann Haggadah. A published facsimile of a manuscript from the collection of Kaufmann in the Oriental of the Hungarian Academy of Sciences. The Szyk Haggadah. Reproductions of famous art in the Jewish categories, and between them non-Jewish works of art like Repin[11], Picasso, Bronislaw, Glinka[12], and also original works with a special character.

Art of China and Japan

The albums of works of Chinese and Japanese artists are charming in their colors. They discover a strange, yet interesting and wonderful world. You will be astonished as you look at a collection of a hundred small, yet interesting original pieces, which were commemorated by the heroes of the Chinese Folktale

[Page 228]

legends. The artifacts were woven from rice straw, and from tiny, thin, and delicate materials. They are painted in spectacular colors and a great pleasure to look at.

Original Historical Certificates

As part of a list in the newspaper, it would not be possible to list, even by name, all items, and various areas of Mr. Gat's collection. However, the collection of documents relating to the various actions and doings of the Haganah, of the IDF organization in the first days of the declaration of the state, and most importantly a perfect treasure trove of newspaper excerpts about the situations of Haifa before her liberation at the hands of the army, and in the first days after her liberation. If you add to this the credentials held by Mr. Gat, from the time he was a military governor of Nazareth, the deputy commander of Gadna and more, then there is an archive of great historical value.

"Meeting" With Distant Relatives

Stuck in our notes from the exhausting work of focusing around mesmerizing, interesting things, we gladly accepted the invitation of Mrs. Gat to feast to our heart's content. It is rare to meet a collector whose wife matches his eccentricity. Mr. Gat was one of the few fortunate enough to be assisted by his wife in expanding the collection, and with her, achieving distinguished accomplishments. We greatly enjoyed the delicious feast that the owner of the house prepared and we were ready to say our goodbyes. Here, another surprise awaited us. With the lights off, we watched a video about the life of mountain Jews from the Caucasus on a small white screen… We clearly saw their eager faces to meet a guest from Israel in their ancient synagogue. We saw their homes, their businesses, their wives and their children, and even though their faces appeared mute, we saw our brothers in faith and blood, in hope and resilience.

When I left the house, the Tzahala neighborhood slumbered. The moon spread a pale and foreboding light on the universe and Tel Aviv's lights gleamed from afar. The car raced on the smooth asphalt road, and the song of Nechama Lifshitz echoed in the ears.

> "A song without sighs or tears
> Sung so that everyone can hear it.
> So that everyone can see
> That I live and I sing and I know it
> More beautiful than it ever was…"[13]

Translator's Footnotes:

1. Lieutenant General Gat was born in Mizocz as Moshe Likwornik. As a child, he immigrated to Israel. This chapter was originally published as an article in the newspaper *Herut*, December 9, 1960.
2. Jewish elementary school teaching Hebrew language and religious studies.
3. Nechama Lifshitz (1927-2017), Yiddish language and later Hebrew language soprano, who came to be a key representative of Soviet Jewish culture. She emigrated to Israel in 1969. (Wiki)
4. Yiddish lyrics embedded in the Hebrew chapter. "Play, play, klezmorim, play, you know what I want and how I'm feeling."
5. This stanza was written in Yiddish.
6. "You are beautiful"
7. Youth organization of the Community Party
8. Solomon Mikhailovich Mikhoels, (1890-1948), Yiddish actor, director of the Moscow State Yiddish Theater, and chair of the Soviet Jewish Anti-Fascist Committee, murdered in 1948. (Yivo Encyclopedia of Jews in Eastern Europe.)
9. Benjamin Zuskin (1899-1952), colleague of Mikhoels, becoming director of the Moscow Stare Yiddish Theater after Mikhoel's murder. Zuskin was executed on Stalin's orders in 1952. (Wiki)
10. Itzik's Wedding

11. Ilya Repin (1844-1930), renowned Russian painter, known for his portraits of Tolstoy and other literary and artistic figures.
12. Mikail Glinka (1904-1857), Russian composer of classical music.
13. This stanza was written in Yiddish.

[Page 229]

Thoughts about the Holocaust Era

by Moshe Perliuk

Translated from Hebrew by Ofir Horovitz, Eiden Harel Brewer and Noa Etzyon

With the end of World War II, as the curtain was raised over the killing ravine, above a torn and destroyed Europe, with millions of dead, we all waited, full of concern, for news of our brothers, our people.

Each of us had hope, and was almost certain, that we would receive the happy message that our families, parents, brothers, and all our loved ones survived and were still alive. We amused ourselves with the false hope that soon we would bring them here, to Eretz Yisrael.

* * *

And then rumors of the horrors started to arrive.

One news item after another. Each one was worse than the last. We were struck with shock. People said that this could not be true! Did such a disaster really happen? … We could not believe the news. We did not want to believe it! …

Could it be? Six million European Jews were murdered. They were not executed because of the war, but because they were Jewish and victims of a satanic, elaborate, and calculated plan – a plan of genocide.

* * *

Today, 18 years after the Holocaust, we know the full extent of the disaster, all the details of the plan, and the methods of mass destruction of an entire people.

We also have in our hands the master himself, who enacted the multifaceted plan, who instituted various methods to expedite the annihilation of the millions of our brothers that he was able to capture at that time.

The *Ashmadai*[1] – Adolf Eichmann has been captured and is awaiting his trial and punishment in Israel…

As if there is a verdict commensurate with his crime – the extermination of six million people, including a million babies -- -- --

Eighteen years have passed since the Holocaust and I still do not have peace of mind. The pain has not been relieved, and the wound has not healed. You cannot escape the nightmare in which millions, including my family, were murdered because they were Jews and the Nazis decided to eliminate them.

It is only natural that I would want the same feelings to pulsate in the heart of every Jew and especially in the youth, to whom the phrase "Never forget" is directed…

Unfortunately, and shockingly, we see just the opposite. Many and especially the youth are indifferent to the extermination of a third of the people.

[Page 230]

The youth who grew up with the pre-state uprising, the War of Independence, and the Sinai War, are distancing themselves from the atrocities and annihilation of the past, which are beyond their perception and understanding.

* * *

The plan of extermination and genocide was worked out thoroughly and scientifically and carried out not once, not with an atomic bomb, but throughout the years of the war. The extermination was carried out in different ways and in many places. To this end, the notorious concentration camps worked like factories: Buchenwald, Dachau, Chelmno, Treblinka, Majdanek, Bergen-Belsen, Auschwitz, and dozens of other places, surrounded by electrified fences and containing extermination methods such as gas chambers, crematoria, and the like.

Hundreds of thousands were killed inside the death trains and masses, more masses were led like sheep to the slaughter and shot near the graves they dug for themselves.

Tens of thousands were killed in hundreds of other ways. There were those who died by throwing themselves on an electrified barbed wire fence, some by hanging and strangling, some while undergoing medical experiments or while amusing the killers. Hundreds of thousands of babies perished in carriages or sacks into which they were collected and crammed. An entire industry was established, an industry that produced soap made from the fat of the murdered and mattresses composed of their hair.

* * *

How is it possible, the youth ask, that six million did not stand up against their oppressors, did not revolt, and did not try to fight for their lives? And if they were already condemned to die, why not take down their enemies with them ("let their souls die with the Philistines")? And here comes their well-known call "Nothing like this will happen to us!"

* * *

Why did the masses go to die like sheep to the slaughter?

The answer may be given by historians, scientists, researchers, and experts. Deep psychological motives operated here. The mass passivity had a multifaceted background. Such as: illusion, which stems from excessive optimism, deep faith, as well as objective reasons, such as the geographical environment, Gentile hatred, and above all the method of numbing, which was strictly enforced by the Nazis. All of the above and other reasons, require study and research and are waiting to be explored.

[Page 231]

* * *

We will try to provide a partial answer to the question that until now others have not tried to address.

Does going "like a sheep to the slaughter" really reflect the situation? Today we know that it does not. Following the information that came to us and the details given to us by the survivors who were on the verge of the pit or the gas chambers, it is clear that the victims should not be underestimated and that they did not go toward death like sheep to the slaughter

* * *

Let us restore the conditions the unfortunates were in and the measures taken by the murderers.

There is no doubt that if the Nazis and their aides had started the act of assassination and killing immediately after the occupation began, a different reality would have obtained. I do not doubt that the response would have come immediately. All the Jews of Europe, including the victims of Mizocz, would have organized defenses, built fortifications and barricades, and no one would have been captured alive by the murderers. Once again, the warrior spirit of the Maccabees and the Bar Kochba warriors would have excelled. On these barricades there would have been warriors: men, women, and children.

The Nazis knew what was awaiting them and the methods they used proved that they did not underestimate the heroism and courage of the Jews, members of the "inferior" race. Only thus, perhaps, does it make sense that the "actions" began only after two, three, or more years – after the occupation. This period of time was needed for them to complete the numbing process which they began immediately with the occupation and continued little by little, step by step.

In the first days after the occupation, they tried to be kind and, in many places, justified the transfer of the Jews to the ghetto out of concern for their safety and a desire to protect them from the Ukrainians, Lithuanians, etc.

Inside the protected ghettoes, the Jews were given internal rule, by appointing ghetto councils and police, establishing autonomous services, and the like. The deficiencies discovered in the supply of food and more were justified by the difficulties arising from the conditions of the war.

The second phase was to send the Jews to work, some to remote labor camps and some to daily work, to which they went out in the morning and returned in the evening. As a result, many families were broken and all those who were taken out of the ghettos, supposedly to work, never returned from the camps where they found their death in various ways. Another proof of the method of numbing was the fact that the main concern of the Nazis was that the ghettos would not have any knowledge about the extermination camps.

[Page 232]

However, people in the ghetto found out from time to time when a Jew managed to escape from the killing places and returned to the ghetto to warn the rest. But the escapees were hanged in front of all the ghetto residents for being communist agents who spread panic and false news. At best, the escapees were labeled by the Jews themselves in the ghetto as liars for maliciously spreading false stories.

By removing the residents slowly in small groups, under the pretext of productive work, they managed to eliminate even a huge ghetto like Lodz, Warsaw, etc. And the few insurgents left in the Warsaw ghetto that did try to revolt did so only after they knew that these transports were not headed to labor camps but to the gas chambers and crematoria.

On the other hand, in ghettos like Mizocz whose residents were fated not to die in crematoria but by mass killing in a huge pit, the Nazis continued the method of numbing until the very last minute. Until the Jews finally found themselves trapped inside a tangled net and mocked by Ukrainian guards who served as bloodthirsty watchdogs.

The meetings and accessibility within the ghetto on the part of the Nazis and especially on the part of their loyal slaves – the Gentiles became more frequent. By splitting the families, humiliating and suppressing their spirits gradually and systematically, the desensitization became a holocaust – so that one day it was possible to concentrate the surviving residents on their last journey–to the *Umschlagplatz*[2].

* * *

The Jewish people excel in their optimistic nature, in their energy, in their desire to live, and in their strong and deep faith that the people of Israel will live forever.

It is this national awareness that has saved our people from extinction and maintained its existence for two thousand years of exile. Hence the illusion and assurance that even the Nazis would not be able to carry out the genocide of our people. This belief particularly grew following the methods of desensitization that the murderers used.

The Diaspora Jews also believed in the morality of the world and that there were people who would set out to fight the Nazi devil. Their hopes rose with news regarding the victories of the countries in Western Europe. They secretly listened to London radio broadcasts and expected help from the wide world.

The Jews of the ghetto did not know and could not have known that international morality had collapsed irreparably. And that even the people who were accepted as Righteous Among the Nations turned their hearts to stone when it came to saving European Jewry from the clutches of the murderers. Even if we explore and discuss the issue, we can barely scrape the surface of its complexity. Moreover, it is very doubtful whether it is permissible to criticize the victims, without personally having gone through the same situation in its entirety. The description of the inhuman conditions, as given in this list, is far from complete and is only the tip of the iceberg.

[Page 233]

Those who have not gone through the hardships themselves and have not been in hell can hardly understand the spirit of the unfortunate victims, who in my eyes are pure and holy heroes.

* * *

The continuous painful history of our nation, which has endless chapters of grief, added another chapter – the largest and bloodiest among all the chapters of history. The chapter on the destruction of a third of the people. This period deserves to be called not just the most tragic period but also one of the most heroic ones in the history of our people. If we ever discover and collect all the details about the steadfastness and endurance of the tortured victims, including the rebellions that broke out in the ghettos, the heroic deeds of the Jewish partisans, etc., perhaps we can reach a different conclusion. One that contradicts and does not justify the contempt with which Israeli youth relate to the Diaspora that was destroyed. No doubt the attitude will change towards our millions of brothers who were shot, burned, suffocated, and destroyed after terrible torture and "brainwashing" that lasted not hours but years, will no doubt change.

Translator's Footnotes:

1. "The prince of demons" in Jewish lore. Versions of the same can also be found in Islamic, Christian, Greek and Zoroastrian legends.
2. Umschlagplatz, a German term for collection point used during the Holocaust to denote the holding areas adjacent to railway stations in occupied Poland where Jews from ghettos were assembled for deportation to Nazi death camps. (Source: Wikipedia)

The Last Jew of Mizocz Has Arrived in Israel

by David Dratva

Translated from Hebrew by Naomi Sokoloff

Weak, old, and broken, I returned to Mizocz from the prison labor camp where I spent six and a half years for the crime of serving as the manager of a large agricultural institution. They sentenced me to ten years of hard labor and I was released early because of poor health. After I recovered a little, I moved with my family to Poland and from there we came to Israel.

We were the last Jews who had remained in Mizocz, and with our departure the city remained "Judenfrei" – "free" of Jews and Judaism.

The Jews had built Mizocz, established factories, developed industry, workshops, and commerce. The entire town was full of hardworking, productive Jews; happy and joyful young people; and vibrant Jewish life.

I came back to Mizocz after the war because I loved the place, I was fond of the townspeople, and I was connected through dear memories to every inch of its soil. There I suffered at the time of the Polish regime, there I rose to prominence during the time of the Soviet regime, and there I also had my share of disappointments and bitterness. Now I'm in Israel. Among the remnants of my family, among Jews. I am content with my lot, glad to be a citizen of a Hebrew state, a regular citizen suffering neither deprivations nor discrimination on account of being Jewish.

[Page 234]

We will not resurrect the Jews of Mizocz and Derman. Mizocz itself has been erased and no trace remains of its Jewishness. Only in our hearts the pain continues to gnaw and sadness remains. My brethren from Mizocz, let us join together and be strong in our faith: the Jew-haters wanted to destroy us, to wipe us off the face of the earth, and look, we have established our state and it is flourishing and developing, gathering in the far-flung members of our nation and drawing them near, giving them security, a happy life, and promising our people's existence forever.

I have grown old, but happy in the knowledge that my children arrived at a safe harbor, and that my grandchildren will grow up in the bosom of our free homeland. This is our consolation: building and developing the homeland. Through the ingathering of our exiles and the flourishing of our culture, we take revenge on our enemies and deprive them of rejoicing in our catastrophe.

Impressions and Memories of My Childhood in Mizocz

by Adah Fishfeider-Teichner

Translated from Hebrew by Naomi Sokoloff

We were four children in my home. Three of us with our parents and my older sister Rivka, who lived in Zdolbuniv with her husband. I remember our house from the time when I was a little girl and went to the kindergarten that was then at the Kornik house. Papa was a prominent, wealthy merchant who traded in grain, seeds and hops. As I recall, our entire extended family was in the grain trade; my sister's husband Yakov Perliuk and several employees also helped in the business. Our house was filled with all sorts of people. Some came to sell and some to announce prices. Some came to receive money and others just to visit. Because my father was among the individuals who exported grain by train. In a big warehouse we had a special machine for cleaning the hops, the likes of which there were only a few in the entire region of Volhynia. Mr. Meisles worked for us as the bookkeeper and he had a special office. There was always a lot of traffic next to our house: farmers from all the surrounding area in their wagons, laborers, merchants, and agents, and there was a lot of noise. We were rich and things at home were very good.

I started to go to the public school and my brother Michael went to study in the Gymnasium in Rivne.

Over time, Papa got into trouble in business and lost a lot of money, which impacted him for the worse and he developed a heart ailment. After that, our situation deteriorated. Papa spent a lengthy period of time in the city, Lviv, for medical treatment. After that he returned home. For a year he hardly left his bed and finally he died.

This was the summer of 1938. I remember that fateful day as if it were today.

[Page 235]

Mama woke me from my sleep and said to hurry and notify the doctor who lived in Derman Street. My sister Sonia was not at home. She had gone to visit our older sister in Zdolbuniv. Even though I was a little girl then, I understood the seriousness of the situation and ran with all my might to the doctor. When he arrived, Papa was dying.

A year after Papa's death, it was necessary to say goodbye to Mama, to my relatives, to people dear to me, and to my hometown. The war broke out. Already in the first days, the echoes of German explosions reached Mizocz. Mama packed a few belongings and, together with Aunt Manya Fishbein and her daughters, we left to go to acquaintances in the village of Zalissia. We were there till the Russians entered Mizocz.

We came back to Mizocz and started a new life. Everyday there were meetings with speeches, free movies, crowds gathering, and rumors. We children were everywhere. We filled the meeting halls, even though we didn't understand much of what was said there, and we came to the cinema, we wandered about among the soldiers, and the main thing we learned was to stand in line.

Everyone stood in line. From the early morning hours, the lines started winding in front of all the stores. People bought everything. Even things they didn't need, for fear that there would not be any when need arose.

Slowly, but steadily, new establishments arose: offices, factories, stores, warehouses and others. Many people were thrown out of their houses, which were nationalized. Others fled for their lives, and there were also others who were promoted and became managers and high officials. My brother Michael passed a special course and worked as an accountant in an economic institution. He lived in constant fear and expectation of being fired as the son of a rich man. Mama was fearful, too, and lost sleep, afraid they would expel us from our house since we had once been wealthy. However, they didn't touch us, and to our sorrow the days arrived when we left the house and everything in it of our own accord and wandered to far-off places. Germany had attacked Russia, and already on the third day of the war the Germans took a stand next to Mizocz and the Russians withdrew. My brother Michael fled with his friends inside Russia and my sister Sonia decided to move and take me with her. She took with her a bag on her shoulder, and I, a satchel in my hand. We said goodbye to Mama and the aunts and set out. The roads were crowded with refugees who had fled, some on foot and some in wagons. Some on bicycles and some in cars. We begged those with vehicles to give us a ride, but they didn't even pay attention to our pleas. Everyone was self-preoccupied. At last, someone heeded our request and put us on a wagon for a short while. Walking and riding, we arrived tired, after great difficulties, in Shepetivka. There we

[Page 236]

entered the train station to get on a train and flee. In the station, to our surprise and joy, we found our brother Michael with his friends from Mizocz. Together with them we got on the refugee train and started to travel to the interior of the country. I remember how Yitzchak Gelman quarreled with Sonia for bringing me on such a hard journey, and all the time we were together he never stopped talking about it. On the way we met many townspeople from Mizocz and we all managed to stay at a *kolkhoz*, a collective farm.

Our situation in the *kolkhoz* was very bad. We were simply starving there. We sold all of the few valuables we had, and when this, too, ran out, we decided to travel somewhere else. My sister asked the others from Mizocz to come with us, but they said that the situation was similar everywhere, and they had no desire simply to wander about. And so, we parted from our townspeople and set out to find happiness in a different place. In that *kolkhoz*, the one we left, Yitzchak Port, Yitzchak Gelman, the Sizak brothers, and others died. They died despite several of them having money; there was nothing to buy with it. We found this out after the war from some of the few who got out of that *kolkhoz* alive. At the end of the war, we found out that all of our family, to the last one, was destroyed and the town demolished to its foundations; from all the dear places, no trace remained. Nonetheless, I wanted very much to once again see the place I was born and had spent happy days. However, fate wished otherwise. In the train returning to Poland which was supposed to go by way of Zdolbuniv, we said we would delay and take a detour to Mizocz. But for some reason the train changed direction and left for Poland by way of Belarus. And so, I did not have time to revisit the place I was from, where I had been happy and had suffered and in which all my dear ones met their deaths.

[Page 237]

Figures, People, and Personalities

[Page 237]

[Page 238]

This is a memorial!

And you, Mizoczian, while looking through this section:

Remember!

Pass before the eyes of your soul the images of the precious names
of those who are of your own flesh and blood.

They will return and live before you and their memories will be etched in your heart.

The horrific crime of their destruction, themselves having committed no sin, shall be
remembered.

God will avenge their blood, and their spirits
will be bound in the bond of life. Amen.

[Page 239]

Memorial for Mizocz

by Yoseph Koppelman

Translated from Hebrew by Corey Feuer

I will remember Mizocz and mourn with a bitter soul
The great tragedy and burning pain that
Depleted us so very much Woe, woe to us
Woe, woe to all of us. Wicked strangers destroyed
The lives of our parents, brothers, sisters
Better were the deaths by sword than deaths by hunger
Their defiled, bloodstained hands knew no mercy
Every teenager, old person, and infant
None escaped from the claws of the predator
What was their sin and what was their crime
Saintly souls, virtuous and pure
They were put in squalor and filth
While they were still fluttering between life and death, their tombs
were covered
Terror gripped every Jew who heard it
I screamed a scream like a shofar regarding why
Such a terrible tragedy happened?! Gentiles saw and became quiet
A silent quiet

May the souls of all the villains who drank the blood of our holy martyrs be obliterated from the face of the earth.

May their souls be bound up in the bond of everlasting life.

"They will rest peacefully in their graves and arise to their destinies at the end of days."

[Page 240]

The Holy Rabeinu Natan Netta Lerner,
May God Avenge his Blood

Translated from Hebrew by Corey Feuer

Rabbi Natan Netta inherited the seat of the rabbinate of Mizocz from his father-in-law, the rabbi Michael Lerner of blessed memory, not because he was a family member and married to the late Rabbi's daughter, but rather by virtue of his greatness with regards to Torah and mitzvot.

The rabbi had a hunched back from the constant sitting he did with the Talmud and his fingers were raised slightly from excessive page-turning of the books which he studied.

[Page 241]

Not once was he seen engaging in small talk; if he was not praying, he was busy with his studies or if not studying, he was writing books.

In the world of scholars in Poland, he was considered an authority for his great eruditeness in Talmud and for his expertise in rabbinic literature. His love of Zion knew no bounds, and at almost every memorial conducted during his time on the 20th of Tamuz in the memory of Dr. Herzl, he would appear wrapped in a tallit, sermonizing on the great deceased man.

In one of these sermons, he declared enthusiastically, "Herzl's not dead! Herzl lives! The righteous in their deaths are called living."

I remember his emphasis when praying the Shema "so that you will remember the day of your departure from the land of Egypt". That means from slavery to freedom, from a life of exile to a life of sovereignty, and my life breath grew faint within me." He was always ruminating on how to reach the land of Israel; he loved Israel and his soul longed for her. However, the impure hand brought forward his death and he reached his end in the proximity of his community in the mass grave in the Sosenki forest.

The Teacher David Koppelman
of Blessed Memory

by Reuven Melamed

Translated from Hebrew by Corey Feuer

From far away Warsaw, he was brought to Mizocz by the rich Tekser family, and with his arrival came a revolution in the education of the younger generation in the town. In Mizocz, like in every town in the Pale of Settlement those days, the children were educated in "chederim" [rooms], where they received Torah from the mouths of educators and small children. The learning of Tanakh, Hebrew, or grammar was forbidden and only a few select youths would read secretly from the literature of *Haskalah* [Jewish enlightenment] and learn Hebrew and grammar on their own.

The office of the teacher Shmuel David Koppelman of blessed memory was called "Cheder HaMetukan" [modernized cheder] and was completely different in its appearance, structure, and design, from all of the other "chederim" that were established in the town. Koppelman himself was also different from the rest of the educators in the area, not only in his job description, (Moreh, and not Melamed) but also in his character and behavior. He was an ultra-orthodox Jew who kept mitzvot both mild and severe, refined in his dress, respectable, and amicable. He had a broad, general education, well-versed in Judaic studies, his knowledge of Tanakh was great and he was superior in Talmudic study. Beyond that, he was knowledgeable in pedagogy and was a gifted educator. Every resident of the town – including his teaching competitors – treated him with respect and sought his company. To be Koppelman's student was considered a great honor, and all the

[Page 242]

parents worked hard to have their children be educated by him, as the tuition for studying with Koppelman was much higher than tuition for the other "chederim".

Koppelman's students stood out not only in their knowledge but also in their conduct. Belonging to the group of Koppelman's students entailed good behavior and meant that the student willingly took upon himself quite a few obligations.

His lessons were heard with great interest and attention, as the man understood the soul of the child and knew how to draw his attention with adequate explanation appropriate for the child's level of understanding. Therefore, the lessons were not a burden on the children but, rather, the children went with great desire to Koppelman's classes.

It was no wonder then that all his students excelled in their knowledge in both religious studies and secular studies. Many were jealous of him, and some among the town's scholars tried more than once to ensnare him, setting traps of one type or another for him in Talmud, Tanakh, or in Midrashim, but they always failed in their efforts. I remember how angry I was at my grandfather, Reb Velvl Melamed of blessed memory – who was an erudite man, very smart, knowledgeable, and clever – at his efforts to thwart my teacher. To my great joy and the heartfelt joy of all his students, however, our teacher Koppelman always had the upper-hand.

[Page 243]

One time, two young men from the land of Israel came to our town to stay with their aunt Hinda from the village of Spasov. They were graduates of the Hebrew high school "Herzliya", and of course spoke fluent Sephardi Hebrew. There was no dearth of Jews knowledgeable in Hebrew in the town. But Sephardi pronunciation, however – 'where does that come from'? Those who were envious of Koppelman spoke of the hearts of the youths who were brought to him in order to test his knowledge and to cause him to fail.

They entered the "cheder" in the middle of studies and promptly started to perform the task assigned to them. To their astonishment, however, they immediately switched from being the testers to the tested. Koppelman, in all his cleverness, understood that they were sent by his opposers to test him, and he embarrassed the arrogant young men. Instead of a failing and ignorant "educator", they stood before an intelligent teacher, a man of extensive knowledge and with good information on the happenings both in the land of Israel and the Diaspora. With difficulty and great embarrassment, they quickly walked out of the "cheder" and acknowledged their failure.

I was at the time a student in the lower grade, and I did not properly understand the debate being conducted amongst them that was conducted entirely in Sephardi Hebrew, but I do remember the joy that overcame the students of the upper grades in seeing the victory of their beloved teacher.

Koppelman was agitated and tired after this encounter, and only a faint smile of satisfaction hovered over his face. His wise and educated wife brought him a cup of tea and said complainingly: "Why did you insult two young men from the land of Israel?". He answered her question with another: "How dare two brats like them come and try to insult me in front of my students with questions that it seemed to them I would not withstand?". She looked at him for an extended period with obvious affection and then left. She had been convinced.

To me Reb David Koppelman was not only a teacher, but also a mentor, guide, and father figure. Since my father traveled to America when I was a child, I learned not only the Torah from him but also how to behave and how to think, as I was a frequent visitor in his household and friends with his son Solomon who was the same age as me.

He was perfect in my eyes, and my dream was to be like him when I grew up…

I excelled in school, as I always managed to turn in my homework on time and in order so that I would not lose the favor of my teacher who I loved and respected more than anything else.

In 1917, when the revolution broke out and the tyrannical rule of the Romanovs was overthrown, great happiness overcame the entire Jewish community. The participation of the Jews in the demonstrations of joy was large and sincere, and the enthusiasm transcended every boundary. Everyone believed that

[Page 244]

better days were really coming for the entire world and for the Jewish people residing in it. Unfortunately, Koppelman did not share in this happiness. On the contrary, quiet grief spread across his face, and his heart worried for what was to come. In hints he would tell us, his students, that this happiness is alien to us and that the results of the revolution remain unknown. "Rejoice not, Israel, as other nations do," he would say to us when he saw how enthused we were by the revolution and its instigators.

Only now in hindsight do I see and appreciate the hesitations of this wise man. On the other hand, he received news of the Balfour Declaration with unimaginable joy. He then gathered his students and sermonized to them on the great value of this declaration for our people. He could not control his spirit while speaking, he was excited, he performed the Shehecheyanu blessing and declared that this was a day of hope for him, and that we should rejoice and be happy for it. In the early days of the new Polish government, he fell ill and died young, during what were still the best of his years. His memory will be kept in the hearts of all his students until their last breaths.

The Koppelman family takes leave of their son Yosef on his departure for Israel

[Page 245]

Shmuel Gantzberg
of Blessed Memory

Translated from Hebrew by Corey Feuer

Shmuel Gantzberg was the glory of the town. Short of stature, skinny and weak-bodied, but still attracting attention with his appearance that bore marks of nobility. He established in the area the first Zionist party, the "Hitachadut" [Union] party, and organized the best local youth within the Zionist movement.

He received his post-secondary education in Odessa, knew languages and was very broadly educated. With the establishment of the Yiddish press in Rivne, he started writing in the newspapers of the provincial towns and was considered among the best journalists in the provincial towns. He also taught for a while in Rivne and was active in the "Tarbut" movement in Poland.

He lived in Mizocz with his parents, his brother, and also his sisters in the ghetto, and he met his demise along with the people of the city for whom he labored, whom he guided, and whom he prepared for Zion. May his soul be bound up in the bond of life.

Shlomo Koppelman
of Blessed Memory

Translated from Hebrew by Corey Feuer

He was one of the leaders of the Zionist movement in Mizocz. As son of the teacher Koppelman, from his childhood he suckled along with his mother's milk love for his people and for the homeland, and from his youth he was active in the Zionist movement.

[Page 246]

From the establishment of the JNF in Mizocz up until the bitter end of the Zionist activity, he served as the power of attorney for the JNF's board, was a board member of the "Hitachadut" party and was among the prominent figures in the movement in general.

He educated the future generation of activists and in his devotion served as an example to all.

According to reliable information, he successfully saved himself on the day of the destruction of the ghetto and fled into the forests. However, a short time later he was caught by Ukrainian rioters and was executed in the cruelest of ways. His corpse served as food for birds of prey and for the animals of the forest, and a few townspeople managed to bury his remains. May these words be a memorial on his unknown grave and his soul shall be bound up in the bond of life.

Reb Yitzhak Berez

Translated from Hebrew by Corey Feuer

He came to Mizocz from the city of Alexandria along with the industrialization of the town, in the last decade of the nineteenth century. He built a big, beautiful house outside of what was at the time the center of the town and next to the house he erected his factory for the production of wool and coarse woolen fabrics for the farmers.

His appearance stood out, his wisdom, knowledge, and connections, amid the backward area; although

[Page 247]

he grew a long beard, kept tradition, and was among the permanent worshippers at the Beit Midrash, he was tolerant of the winds that began to blow in the area of the Jewish moshav; he advocated for general education, explained the value of modern life and made an effort to provide his children with a general education together with their traditional Jewish education.

Yitzchak Berez and his wife Chasya

The man loved life and lived it to the fullest. His mischievousness and pranks were famous throughout the area. His sayings and jOchs earned him a reputation and many years after his death, the Mizoczians still got joy out of them.

Because of his public status, his intelligence, and his generosity, everyone loved him, and they forgave his antics to which they fell victim, even the most distinguished community members.

After his death, his sons inherited leadership of the factory. They brought to it changes in the spirit of the times and made decent livings. The Shoah befell even the Berez family. Only the son Tovyah remained after it, as he had gone up to Israel before the war, along with some grandchildren who had miraculously survived

Reb Yechiel the Butcher of Blessed Memory

by A"BA

Translated from Hebrew by Corey Feuer

The slaughterer, mohel, hazzan, engraver, embroider, and inventor Reb Yechiel the Butcher, of blessed memory, was born before his time. There is no doubt that this man was born to greatness, and were he to receive

[Page 248]

a proper education, train in the academy of arts or study medicine, he would have achieved remarkable things and became world-famous.

He had a poetic soul, a natural instinct for beauty, and a tendency to explore the unknown.

When he noticed in a Jewish house, or even in a house of a foreign nobility, a beautiful rug and specially embroidered or interestingly knitted curtains, he would spend hours upon hours there in order to copy the patterns, imitate them, or at least feast his eyes on items.

[Page 249]

As a mohel he was an artist in his profession, and doctors would marvel at his agility, his understanding of hygiene, and his ability. They would say that had he studied medicine, he would have been an outstanding surgeon. When he was embroidering a parochet for the Torah ark, sculpting a tombstone, or painting "Know before whom you stand", it was impossible not to be impressed by the beauty of his craftsmanship.

He never learned how to read sheet music and never received a musical education, but he had a strong and pleasant voice, a natural understanding, and a fondness for popular melodies and religious tunes. He knew cantorial passages and learned each new rendition with amazing ease. When necessary, he also created melodies of his own.

The lions that he would embroider onto the carpets also decorated the walls of the Christian nobility, and his works even attracted many interested customers from outside of Mizocz.

Reb Yechiel was known for his tight-fistedness, however when it came to an expensive chisel, a special pocketknife, a necessary saw, or tools for his experiments, he spared no expense.

He worked in silver and gold, combining and mixing different materials without having any knowledge of chemical formulas or theoretical physics.

He had perfect manners. He was always clean and polished, cheerful and agile, witty with eyes wide-open. Many were jealous of him, plotted against him, and suspected him of not following religion, but he just went on living how he lived. An appreciator of art, he continued chasing after beauty and loving life.

Some years before the Holocaust, Reb Yechiel Reznik the butcher fell ill and never recovered. Only then were those against him and those who fought him quiet; only then did they learn to value and to admire the man. The whole town attended his funeral, and everyone mourned his loss, and they understood that the town had lost an asset of great value.

The Grandmother Leah Reznik

by Chaya

Translated from Hebrew by Corey Feuer

I never once saw my grandmother, Leah Reznik, idle. Her hands were always occupied with work. After finishing regular housework, she loved to embroider and knit. She had hands of gold, and her embroidery was renowned. In the summer, it was customary of her to weave warm socks and winter sweaters for all her grandchildren. And in the winter, she would embroider napkins, tablecloths, scarves, and other gems. In the last two decades of her life, she abstained from certain foods. Nowadays we refer to this lifestyle as dieting. Be that as it may, she always worked because she never fell ill; she was always healthy and full of life.

[Page 250]

In addition to her family, she also cared for the needs of the general public. She especially loved the mitzvah of "anonymous giving". She used me and my brother Yaakov for distributing necessities among the needy, and following her instructions, we would without being seen bring aid and relief to the houses of the needy.

Each and every Sabbath, in the afternoon, she would sit for hours and hours and read tales of the weekly parsha from "Tseno Ureno". She often times would also tell me the stories of the Torah. She cherished her grandchildren above all else, and I spent more time with her then I did at my parents' house.

The message from the Ministry of Immigration in Poland came to me incidentally on Saturday. The next day, I had to leave Poland. I immediately started packing my belongings with haste. Grandma also came in to participate in the packing. I remarked to her that she should not help me, as she needed to maintain the sanctity of the Sabbath. She responded to me, however, that the land of Israel was not any less holy than Shabbat, and she continued to help.

When it was time for us to part, I saw for the first time in my life twinkling tears in the eyes of Grandma and Grandpa. They sensed that we would not see each other again. Grandpa was privileged and died in his bed, in his house, of natural causes. However, my precious grandmother, humble and God-fearing, met her end in the mass grave of the saints of Mizocz at the hands of those savage animals – the Germans and the Ukrainians.

May God avenge her blood and may her soul be bound in the bond of life.

[Page 251]

Yitzhak Port

by Chaya Reznik (Altman)

Translated from Hebrew by Corey Feuer

He was among the prominent leaders of Mizocz's Zionist movement. In his youth, he joined "Gordonia" and while starting as an ordinary member, thanks to his dedication, knowledge, and aptitude, he reached the movement's leadership and gained broad recognition.

He obtained his education and knowledge through his own efforts, as his poor parents were not able to give him an education, which in the Poland of their day was very expensive.

He additionally filled positions of responsibility in the executive committees of the Funds [funds like the JNF] and was active in fundraising for the Land of Israel. Yitzhak Port educated a whole generation of young people on the fulfillment of the Zionist ideal, and his educational undertakings are well-remembered by his students; "Gordonia's" wall newspaper, which he organized and valued, was of high quality and was used as a powerful tool in building the character of the movement's youths. He also dedicated lots of time and work to the local hakshara group.

He secretly also wrote essays, articles, stories, and poems. More than once, I enjoyed hearing him read his beautiful work. In addition to his ability to extract stories from his pen, he knew how to play the violin, was gifted in organizational skills, and knew how to endear himself to anyone with whom he came into contact.

[Page 252]

He was a modest person, always shy. His head bustled full of plans, and his love for Zion knew no bounds. His life's dream was to make it to the Land of Israel. Due to the precarious condition of his health, however, the doctors forbade him to leave for "hakhshara" [training to go to the Land], and he made plans to reach his longed-for destination in other ways.

When Hitlerite Germany attacked Russia, he fled with the retreating Red Army and hoped to reach the Land of Israel through Russia. He could not, however, withstand the hardships of the war, and he died in the wilderness of Soviet Asia. May he be bound up in the bond of life.

My Father's House

by Rachel (Ilka) Brisker-Nemirover

Translated from Hebrew by Corey Feuer

There was a tradition in our family according to which one of the family members must always be living in Mizocz and continuing the family business. My parents lived in Lutsk from the day they married. But since my father was his parents' only child, he returned to Mizocz in order to keep the tradition and continue the chain. Already in his youth he showed an inclination towards public work and politicking; at the age of thirteen [the age of bar-mitzvah], he convinced his parents, who were rich, to allocate one thousand rubles from their fortune towards the establishment of a charity fund in the town, and when he grew up, my father Yonah Bar Altar Nemirover, or as he was nicknamed in the town, Yonah Feigeles (named after his mother Feyga) was among the most prominent community organizers. Thanks to his wisdom, his handsome and proud outward appearance, his courage, and his connections, he protected the town's Jewish residents in times of war and riots, at the risk of himself and his family. As a loyal and trustworthy community leader, He did not ever want to reveal to the authorities any lawbreaking or violations of the authority's orders, and he was once almost hanged because of this and was miraculously saved thanks to a Gentile who owed him a favor.

Through the power of his intense will, he performed every difficult and impossible thing: when the town's "mikvah", which was religious and traditional, was damaged, and the people suffered from it, Dad raised the funds and the mikvah was restored; when a "gemilut chesed" fund was needed, Dad did not rest until the fund was established. Often, different needy people who had not yet paid off their previous loans came and requested an additional loan. He had no choice but to pay for them from his pocket, and he did not refuse them another loan. When the youth movement branch "HaShomer HaLeumi" [the National Guard] was not able to operate because of a lack of licensing and a lack of means, Dad intervened, obtaining a license and supported with a charitable hand the work of the branch. My mother, Hinda, who was a naturally modest and quiet woman, did not get involved in public affairs, but she had a

[Page 253]

warm and sensitive heart and a wide-open hand. The city's poor people, such as Srulenio, Henele, Helem and others regularly dined with us, and when needy people would come from outside of the town, Mom would often give them her children's food. My parents were an exemplary couple.

They were devoted and faithful to family and children and empathized with others' troubles. During the Hitlerite conquest, Dad did not let go of public service, and thanks to him and his friends, there were no instances of moral corruption in Mizocz, and until the ghetto's final destruction, the Jews lived relatively quietly.

May these few words be used as a monument in the holy memory of my parents, who perished along with the rest of the community in Mizocz, and may their names be blessed forever.

The Wound that Will Never Heal

by Liza Nemirover-Shtelong

Translated from Hebrew by Corey Feuer

More than twenty years have passed since World War II broke out. Since then, the world has changed, as have its inhabitants. The murderous Hitlerite regime has been vanquished, and almost all its founders and initiators have been wiped out. The ruins of the war have been restored, nations have been rejuvenated and the State of Israel established, and it is developing and gathering the remaining of our people. However, I cannot understand how is it that all of Europe stood on the blood of our people and did not

[Page 254]

stop the Germans from its extermination? To this day, I still cannot grasp how they transported millions of our brothers like lambs to the slaughter with the tacit approval of the whole world.

The memory of my family, and the sight of my beloved town, Mizocz, never escaped my memory even for a day. My father and teacher Reb Yonah Nemirover, may God avenge his blood, who never did harm to anyone, and for all his life faithfully dealt with the needs of the public. He who supported the needy with a generous hand and who provided relief and assistance to anyone who turned to him, why was he murdered by impure villains, when several of them were assisted by him during regular times. And my mother, the unforgettable Hinda? Mild-mannered, a devoted mother and wife, a comrade and friend to all of the neighbors and the relatives, who never harmed anyone, did only good and righteous deeds, why was she murdered with cruelty of a wild animal?

The Nemirover family

What sin did my older sister, Tyofe, her husband Eliezer Goldstein, and my sisters Sonya and Devorah commit, that they were murdered at the peak of their flourishing. And what crime did my only brother Michael – the splendor of our home, who excelled not only in his virtue and attributes, but also in his captivating beauty and pleasant behavior – commit so that the thread of his life was severed in its midst?

Can we really forget and reconcile ourselves with this?

[Page 255]

Up until my last day on earth, the memory of my town, of its people, roads, and scenery will never leave my memory nor my soul!

Instead of a tombstone atop their unknown grave, it is my desire to mention the names of some of the members of my widespread family; Deborah Bonis, my father's sister, her husband Shmuel and their children Sonia and Malka. She was a great public activist, chairperson of the Women's League for the Working Land of Israel, and a member of every public and Zionist association. He was a philanthropist with a big heart and a wide-open hand. My aunt Mina, my father's second sister, her husband Beryl Wachs, and their children, Sonia, Malka, Newma, and Yonah. My old aunt, Elta Melamed and her girls: Golda and her husband Shimon Gerber, Leia and her son Lyube, Rachel and her husband Gershon Mossman and their daughter Zina, Mina and her husband Joseph Shubkes and their two children, Dora and her husband Fibel Goldberg.

My old uncle Reb Moshe Melamed and his son Laivish Melamed, Laivish's wife Leah, and their children. Laivish was counted among the pre-eminent public activists in the town and did a lot for the Zionist movement, the youth, and the funds.

May the souls mentioned in this list of mine and the souls of all the other martyrs of the Mizocz community be bound up in the bond of life along with all the saints of Israel.

Us survivors will never forget the horror and in the building of the free homeland in our ancient land, we will erase the shame and the pain.

In Memory of my Parents

by Asher

Translated from Hebrew by Corey Feuer

My father, Reb Yaakov Samson son of Asher Tsvi Gilberg, was fondly remembered by the residents of the town many years after his death. Yankl R. Ashers was a well-known name in the town. His pedigree was skyhigh, and that very fact was enough in those days to endow him with adoration, respect, and glory. The reputation of his father Reb Asher of blessed memory reached vast distances: his wealth, his factories, his learnedness and good deeds, his generosity, his standing proud even before counts and ministers, the opulent customs in his court, and the fact of his being the employer of almost every one of the town's residents; him and his offspring were endowed with respect and glory. After his death, his heirs lost their wealth. The multiple factories, the production plants, the court, the houseware, and the expensive furniture were sold and dismantled, and the children dispersed afar. Only my father and his brother Yeshayahu the teacher stayed in the area. However, their family reputation was remembered even in their descent,and everyone treated them with respect. My memory of my father

[Page 256]

is hazy. I was about nine years old when my father died. Several of his actions and deeds are etched in my memory forever. He was rich in natural talents in all sorts of different fields; he knew how to play several instruments – especially violin – without ever having learned them. He had hands of gold and he knew how to fix all sorts of complex machines, and he also knew how to put together engines and machines by himself. He made things from wood and from metal, from charcoal and from glass. A painter and a sculptor, a jeweler and a weaver. He learned by himself the craft of watchmaking and made a living from committeet in his final days. He was an expert artisan in his profession, and even the town's count would bring him antique clocks to fix that even excellent professionals had trouble repairing. When I grew up, I came to understand that he had a poetic soul and a propensity for art. He left behind a collection of delicate artistic pieces made from silver, gold, and ivory, of which only a few ended up in my possession. The bulk of it was "taken" by friends or sold by my mother. I understood his delicate taste when I started to familiarize myself with tableware, sculptures, wooden carvings, and lots of other things I found when I grew up left in the house. He was cheerful, very physically healthy, and hungry for life. He loved nature, his profession, and spending time travelling. He would take me with him on short trips and would explain everything to me. I do not know much about his character or his tendencies apart from what I have been told by people who knew him. He married a beautiful young maiden at the age of forty –my mother, Leah, daughter of Reb Yitzaak Fliter. They had four children, three boys and one girl. I was nine and my younger brother Zev was less than a year old when my father fell ill and died. My mother was left with four children without the means to live. At first, we made a living from selling objects my father had accumulated, but afterwards my mother recovered and started herself a business. In her widowhood, my mother proved herself to be a capable woman, courageous and talented in her knowledge in how to get by. She sacrificed herself for the members of her household and made sure they were never lacking anything. She was a model housewife, good of heart like no other. She was sensitive to other people's hardships and always ready to help in times of trouble. Because of her excellent qualities, she succeeded in getting remarried to a financially secure bachelor even though she was the mother of four children. My stepfather, Joseph Arbitorer, treated us like a father dedicated to his children. We loved him and he us, and in this served as an example for all. He and my mother had a single son. During the holocaust which befell our people, everyone was killed. Only my brother Zev and I were left. The memory of my parents will not exit my heart until my last breath.

[Page 257]

Reb Yitzaak Fliter and his wife Esther

by Baruch Fliter and Zev Gilberg (their grandchildren)

Translated from Hebrew by Corey Feuer

Reb Yitzaak Fliter was considered to be one of the most admired figures in the town and was familiar to everyone. As a doctor, he was very popular with the people of the town, and he was considered among the rural population surrounding the town to be an expert like no other.

Yitzchak Fliter and his wife Esther

He did not have an advanced medical education. The official title that he carried was that of medic. Thanks to his enormous experience and his diligence in his medical work, his opinions were thoroughly considered even by the certified doctors that would periodically come to town. When the town grew and several doctors with academic degrees settled in town, he nevertheless maintained his position and status, and the residents – Jews and Christians alike – continued to need him. He was a very religious Jew, a man with an imposing figure, wealthy and decisive in his opinions. He faithfully dealt with the public's needs and was trusted by all people. Saturdays' kiddushes, which were held regularly at his house, attracted not just his many family members, but also many friends and acquaintances. During holidays, they would go on for hours and turn into feasts. He of course had opinions of all public affairs, and the rabbi and important homeowners of the town were regular houseguests. By his side helping was his wife – Esther.

[Page 258]

She was the treasurer of the Committee for the Benefit of the Orphans and was active on behalf of the Yeshiva Committee, collecting donations and valuables for the benefit of the yeshiva boys. Their many sons, daughters, and grandchildren all lived in Mizocz or in the area. Their house was big and spacious, and it stood out in the town. During the time of Petliura's government, the local Ukrainians protected the house and prevented it from being harmed. During the Hitlerite occupation, Yitzaak became very weak and went blind. However, despite this, and despite his old age, he held on and even treated the Ghetto residents. He prepared medicines himself from plants. during Aktion, he hid with his wife in a storeroom. The Ukrainian murderers discovered them, and while being cruelly beaten, they were taken to the plaza of the Death March. They died in a mass grave in pits in the Sosinsky Forest. May their souls be forever bound in the bond of life.

Baruch Fliter

by Baruch

Translated from Hebrew by Corey Feuer

My uncle Baruch Fliter was a simple Jew – simple in the best sense of the word. He was an active public activist and was well-known in the town. He loved to busy himself with the needs of the general public and he got involved with the political parties in town. When a fire brigade was established in the area, he was chosen as commander and served in the role up until the Holocaust.

Baruch Fliter

All his children were members of the youth movement Beitar, and he himself eventually became attached to the movement and was active in Brit HaChayal. He served as power of attorney for the Tel-Chai Foundation board, and

[Page 259]

he took an active role in the town's public life. The war hit him like a ton of bricks. His eldest son Yaakov was taken to the Red Army, and he traveled with it to Russia. This negatively impacted Baruch and his wife Feiga and the two fell permanently ill. During the expulsion to the death march, they did not leave their house, and they were shot at home in their bed. Of this family remained only the eldest son, who migrated at the time to Russia, and who made the couple ill with their worry for him. May his soul be bound up in the bond of life.

Itzchak Schochet the Teacher

by Arbi

Translated from Hebrew by Corey Feuer

He arrived in Mizocz in the early twenties at the invitation of a few homeowners. It was intended for him to fill the place of the teacher Koppelman, who had just died. Young, full of vigor, tall, and handsome – he immediately gained high standing and recognition. His wife, Tehila of the House of Halperin, delicate and cultured, helped beside him, and their house became a meeting-place and place of recreation for the local intelligentsia. He established a generation of students for whom Hebrew was their common tongue. In his house, they spoke Hebrew, and his daughter Hadasa knew no other language. He eventually left teaching and opened a business selling books and writing instruments. Since his mind was dedicated to Zionist and Jewish politics and to spiritual things, and because he was not a good fit for sales, he closed the business after a while.

A number of years before the Holocaust, he joined the Revisionist movement, moved to Warsaw, and went to work in the head office of the Tel-Chai Foundation. With the outbreak of the war and the conquest of Poland and its division by Germany and Russia, his son Binyamin (Nyuma) came to Rivne from Warsaw in order to meet with close family from Russia. He told them that his father had an American visa, and that the family was thinking of heading there soon. They did not manage to get out in time, however. The entire family perished in the Warsaw ghetto; some died of hunger and some from disease, some in extermination camps and some in labor camps.

May his soul be bound in the bundle of life.

[Page 260]

Siyuma (Sammy) Oliker

by Ben

Translated from Hebrew by Corey Feuer

From a culturally assimilated environment and a life of comfort and pleasures, he joined the Zionist movement, and upon his arrival became not only among the most active in his area but also initiated individuals and groups who until his arrival had stood distant from and been indifferent to Zionism.

In the beginning of his Zionist career, he was active in the youth groups, especially the youth branch of "The National Guard". He later became fascinated with the Revisionist ideology and joined the local Beitar youth branch. From then on, he changed beyond recognition. All his time, his many talents, his money, and his thoughts went towards the movement. The Beitar youth branch, under Siyuma's leadership, reached the rank of perfection in every sense of the word, and it counted among the largest and greatest in the whole country. He embodied every commandment of the movement; he participated in courses and central seminars and received the title of "Madrich" [counselor]. He later headed various military training courses, which were organized on behalf of the Warsaw Commission. He learned Hebrew, became accustomed to physical labor, and made aliyah around two years before the outbreak of the war.

In Israel he was destined to work in the factories of the Dead Sea. The climate and the exhausting work, which he was not used to, destroyed his health, and he fell ill for an extended period of time. Since then, he never recovered, and he did not return to good health. He made do in Jerusalem and worked for Leumit Health Care Services, with frequent disturbances because of his illness. In 1958, he died at the age of 55 years. Of blessed memory.

[Page 261]

Reb Yeshayahu Mayer Kotel
of blessed memory

by Chaya Goldman–Kotel

Translated from Hebrew by Yitschok Tzvi Margareten

My father – Mr. Yeshayahu Mayer Kotel was a known name in Mizocz and the vicinity. As a well doing and honest businessman whose business dealing were exceeded the town borders and went till the capital city Warsaw and even past the country borders. He was also accepted by the government and was liked and honored not only by Jews but also by the peasants in the vicinity.

The Kotel Family

Our house was open to all. Paupers who went begging at doors ate there to satiation. Needy received support and loans. And for a poor bride, our house took care of from bringing her to the wedding till creating a livelihood for her husband. My mother of blessed memory and we the children helped with giving charity and support to the needy.

Despite his many businesses, father was integrated in community work and gave much of his time for community needs. He was the Gabbai in the Shul of the Trisk Chassidim and a great activist in the founding fund. He worried for the traditional and religious education and head of the Trisk Chassidim. The Trisk Rebbe, when he came to our town, **he** was always hosted by us.

[Page 262]

The biggest and nicest room in our home was given over to him and the whole house became public property for the chassidim. During the days of the Rebbe's stay in Mizocz, became a holiday for the chassidim. Our home what then full of song and joy. The meals continued unabated and Torah and and chassidic songs filled the house.

The meal on Shabbat eve, was especially joyful and combined with chassidic dancing with the Rebbe's participation. Father used to take off his shoes, and dance on the tables with white socks till exhaustion. His children went in his ways. We were all raised in a traditional religious spirit and we were connected to the Zionist movement.

With the destruction of Mizocz, our house and our family fate was destructed as too as the fate of all martyrs. Should the memory of my family members be blessed and bound in everlasting life.

In Remembrance of the Schwarzman Family

by Eliezer Schwarzman

Translated from Hebrew by Naomi Sokoloff

My father, R. Aharon (z"l)[1] was a traditional Jew and he worked from morning till night to provide for his family. My mother, Golda, ailing all her days, had her hands full caring for her six children.

These parents always took care to give their children a good education. They employed the best teachers in town for us, and we lacked for nothing. When the children got older, they helped the parents. The sons helped Papa in the grain trade, and the daughters helped Mama in managing the household. We were a family rooted in Judaism, a dedicated, hard-working, extensive, and productive family; I alone remain, the last and only remnant of that family. All were murdered by the degenerate murderers. May their souls be bound up in the bonds of life.

Translator's Footnote:

1. Of blessed memory. R' stands for "Reb", a title equivalent to "Mr."

In Remembrance of the Tentzer Family

by Braindel Schwarzman-Tentzer

Translated from Hebrew by Naomi Sokoloff

Grandma Batya had three sons: Herschel, Moshe, and my father, Yehuda. Grandma was widowed in her twenties, and so it fell on her to make a living to support the children. She knew how to prepare them to pursue a profession. When they married and stood on their own feet, Grandma devoted herself to helping others in need and especially loved providing support for orphans. My father Yehuda died in the prime of his life, in 1930, and my mother, Slova, remained alone with three small children. She rallied for the sake of her children, worked hard, and fulfilled their needs. They lacked for nothing. During the Holocaust, they all perished, mother, my brother Gershon, and my sister Bracha. May their memory be blessed.

[Page 263]

Kaddish[1]

On the unknown grave of my parents --
Zalman bar Yitzhak Fliter and Leah bat Baruch (née Schwarzgorn)

by Baruch, son of Zalman and Leah Fliter

Translated from Hebrew by Naomi Sokoloff

My mother used to call me affectionately, "*kaddish mayner*" (my *kaddish*). She devoted her life to her children; they kept her busy and preoccupied her thoughts, and her highest hopes were for them. *Kaddish!* Neither my parents nor I were granted a proper Jewish burial for them with a *kaddish* recited over their graves.

Zalman Fliter and his wife Leah (née Schwarzgorn), murdered in the Holocaust

* * *

Everyone loves their parents, respects them, and cherishes and remembers them forever. Almost everyone thinks that their mother or father was more devoted than all the other parents in the world. However, I am not exaggerating when I say that my mother could truly serve as a model, not only in her dedication to her children, but also in her understanding of how to attend to their future and strengthen them to protect them from harm or trial.

I remember when I was a small boy. I became ill and needed an operation. Mama neglected the house, her husband, and all other matters, sitting for entire weeks by my side in the hospital until I recovered from surgery.

When I got older and had acquired some education, Mama began to attend to my future. We were not so wealthy, but Mama knew how to save here and there and made it possible for me to study in Rivne, to acquire a profession that would stand me in good stead for when I would need to support myself. And she did not only take care of her own family. As a hard-and-fast rule, every Thursday she fed at least three indigent people.

[Page 264]

* * *

We were five children in the house. The apartment was not spacious but it was adequate. Warmth and love prevailed there. My parents were working people and happiness prevailed in our home.

In the evenings – especially on winter evenings – the house was full of guests. And when space at our place was tight, they would spill into the second wing of the house. Grandpa and Grandma lived there.

Next to tables laden with tea, pastries, fruit, and beverages, they would pass the time in lively conversation, games of dominoes, chess, lotto, and sometimes also cards,[2] and so on. Grandpa's house held great attraction not only for the children and many grandchildren, but also for relatives, friends, and acquaintances. The house was always abuzz with guests. Among the regular guests I remember R. Yona Nemirover and leaders of the social work in which Grandma was active.

I remember all this with pain and sadness, because I will never again sit in the midst of this large and dear family; not only were the people slaughtered, but no trace of the household remains…

* * *

My parents, who so loved their children, did not live to take joy and comfort in their achievements. I was not granted the chance to remember them in the form of a grave or monument. I have no hope that I will ever be able to visit or prostrate myself on their grave, for no one knows where they are buried or how they met their end.

May these words of mine serve as a modest monument in their memory and for me as a small comfort for the pain that will never ease.

Yitgadal veyitkadash shmei rabah…[3].

Translator's Footnotes:

1. There is reference here also to games called 501"My Landlord" and "Oko."
2. The opening words of the prayer, the mourner's *kaddish*.

My Father R. Shmuel Eisengart,
May God Avenge his Blood

by Ida

Translated from Hebrew by Naomi Sokoloff

My father. Those two words contain a multitude of delicate feelings. Boundless love, deep respect and great longing for my father, my teacher, who was murdered at the hands of degenerate demons in his 57th year, when he was father to three daughters and grandfather to a granddaughter. His noble image is tied inextricably to the happy days of my childhood and it accompanies me till today. Although he made a living from commerce, he was given above all to the life of the spirit and educating the children. In actuality, mother ran the business. He, as a

[Page 265]

teacher by profession, knew how to impart to us a national, liberal, religious education, noble virtues, and a desire to learn. I do not remember even a single instance in which Papa punished us with flogging. And if sometimes he did raise a hand against a child, he immediately lowered it with a smile on his

The Eisengart family

lips, and instead scolded with a wagging finger. …He knew Hebrew and Russian well, but he stumbled a bit in the Polish tongue. However, more than once he put us to shame with his vast, thorough knowledge of Polish literature. He was a scholar who loved books, possessed understanding, and had a knack for teaching; he was a devoted family man and a man involved in the community. I saw him cry for the first time when Ukrainians went on a rampage against the Jews of Mizocz. "Papa, why are you crying?" I asked him then. And he answered in a voice choked by tears, "Woe is me that this it has come to this for you." In the ghetto he was forced to clean the street next to the hall of the local council. At his age and in his state of health – the work was too much for him. I therefore tried several times to do the work for him. But he always objected fiercely, got angry, and prevented me from helping. In 1938 he became very sick and almost died. At that time, I couldn't imagine how I would overcome such a blow if, God forbid, he were to leave

[Page 266]

this world, and then my father perished and with him also the entire family and I am still alive, as in yesteryear…For I received the commandment to live from Papa. And in the continuation of this splendid chain of an ordinary Jewish family, I see the will of my father, whose memory will be kept in my heart forever. May his memory be blessed and bound up in the bonds of life.

**Memorial plaque in honor of the Zalman Fliter family
and the Shmuel Eisengart family murdered in the Holocaust**

An Eternal Flame in Memory
of the Progeny of Chone the Rabbi of Mizocz
And they are: Hayyim Yossi Gelman, Batyah Wohlman, Sima and Nechama (z"l)

by Shmuel Mandelkorn, from Melinov

Translated from Hebrew by Naomi Sokoloff

Just as Joseph the Righteous pleaded with his brothers before his death in Egypt, "carry my bones up from this place with you",[1] so the victims of the Holocaust asked before their deaths, *"gedenkt unz, nemt nekome far unz"* (remember us, avenge our blood).

[Page 267]

Their request echoes in our ears without cease. And, for good reason, each one of us thinks about it and endeavors to perpetuate the memory of our martyrs, devoting our time, energy, and resources.

And just as it is commanded us, till the end of all generations, to tell the story of the exodus from Egypt, and "whoever increases the telling is praiseworthy",[2] so it is our obligation to write down and put into a book every detail of the Shoah, of the people, the communities, and the like. Every kind of commemoration of the martyrs is sacred work. Monuments, grave stones, memorial plaques, books, and so on are important for the entire Jewish people. Those who make them, produce them, inscribe them, and edit them will be blessed. Commemoration has double meaning: a) "so that you will remember what the German Amalek did to you"[3]; b) through the act of commemorating we pass before our eyes all the martyrs, and it is as if they are alive. Maybe this is the explanation of the verse, "who revives the dead with an utterance"[4]. That is to say, when we recall the name of the deceased, he is alive in our eyes. Therefore, even here, "whoever increases the telling is praiseworthy" because in reviving the dead we are dealing with no trifling matter.[5]

My uncle R. Hayyim Yossi Gelman (z"l) numbered among the most important householders in Mizocz. He was an erudite Jew, a well-versed scholar who regularly devoted hours to Torah study; he was a prosperous and successful merchant, who loved order and was fond of nature and whose house excelled in its cleanliness and well-tended gardens. No trace of him or his household remains. He, his wife, his only son, and his daughter-in-law – they died the death of martyrs. Of some small consolation to me are Aunt Batya's children, who stayed alive. From them came two daughters in Israel. Tovah Scheinfeld in Kibbutz Mishmar Hasharon and her sister Leah in Jaffa. Two more daughters live abroad and all have raised Jewish families. My mother, Nechama (z"l) had three sons and all of them are in Israel, and they, too, have raised families and continue the family line. I want to conclude with the saying and the blessing, "He will swallow up death forever and may we not have further grief."[6]

Translator's Footnotes:

1. A reference to Gen. 50:25.
2. Words from the Passover Haggadah.
3. A reference to Deuteronomy 25:17. In Jewish tradition, "Amalek" has come to stand for all mortal enemies of the Jews.
4. From the Seven-Faceted Blessing (*bracha ahat me'en sheva*).
5. The "we are dealing with no trifling matter" appear in Aramaic, not Hebrew: *"ka askinan, velav milta zutarta hi"*. They are quoted from the Talmud.

6. Traditional words of condolence offered to someone who has been bereaved.

Golda Moshe-Hayyim Yusis (z"l)

by Reuben

Translated from Hebrew by Naomi Sokoloff

Who in Mizocz did not know Golda Moshe-Hayyim Yusis? What a marvelous character this squat, stocky woman was! Every Thursday she would go from door to door of the houses in Mizocz and gather charitable contributions; despite the fact that she fasted that day, she went to all the homes, so as to collect the most donations.

In the evening – after breaking her fast – she would arrange the coins in packets, and the eldest of her grandchildren would run to the houses of the needy with the phrase

[Page 268]

she had put in their mouths: "Grandma asked me to repay the debt and say thank you." The needy would accept the packets with a smile and run quickly to arrange their purchases for the Sabbath.

She used to participate in every funeral and sincerely shared the sorrow of the deceased's family.

Before her death she asked the prominent people of the town to study Mishna by her bed, and her final wish was honored. May her memory shine and be remembered among all the names of those who came from Mizocz.

Berko Iosilevich Street

by Chaya Murak

Translated from Hebrew by Naomi Sokoloff

Zeivel Murak and his Wife

I was born and raised in Berko Iosilevich Street, in the house of my father, Zeivel Murak, the shoemaker. All the residents of the street, my parents among them, were simple, honest, working people, content with their lot. Papa related to everyone with respect and a pleasant countenance, a smile always on his lips, and he was happy.

[Page 269]

I was an only daughter, loved and pampered. I loved Mizocz and the young people there very much. As a member of "Gordonia" I used to spend time at the club and meet with youth from other organizations. We all dreamt of and worked on behalf of the Jewish homeland, and it saddens the heart that most of those young people were murdered and it was not granted them to arrive here. May their memory be blessed.

Acknowledging the Feldman Family

by Moshe Feldman

Translated from Hebrew by Naomi Sokoloff

My family in Mizocz was extensive. Many uncles and aunts, both from my father's side and my mother's, cousins and other relatives who together numbered eighty people.

Papa's house numbered eight people. Papa and Mama and six children. I was the eldest among the children. My father, R. Menachem Mendel used to work hard, toiling from dawn till dusk in commerce. A number of years before the Shoah he succeeded in solidifying our circumstances and we became prosperous. As for Mama Hannah, her hands were always full with work: the living conditions in the house were difficult, but exemplary order reigned throughout. The house was neat and the children clean, well-taken care of, and carefree. Mama especially cared about the education of the children and was happy when they succeeded in their studies.

Our home was traditional. Sabbaths and Jewish holidays left an impression on me, even till today. And how great was the pain and how piercing the sorrow, that out of all the family only my brother Yeshayahu and I remained. All the rest met their end in the pit, in the mass grave of the Mizocz martyrs. May their souls be bound up in the bonds of life.

A Soul in the Breizman Family,
May God Avenge His Blood

by Sarah Biber-Lukick

Translated from Hebrew by Naomi Sokoloff

My brother-in-law Levi Breizman, member of a very extensive family in Mizocz, and his wife Etti, the daughter of R. Menachem Mender Biber (z"l), the author of the books *Yalkut Menachem* and *Mazkeret Ligdolei Ostroh*,[1] were an exemplary couple. Their big, beautiful house which stood at the entrance to the city in Polish Street was one of the most splendid in town and open to everyone. My brother-in-law Levi was a modest, honest man and a successful merchant. On account of his many businesses, his house was always bustling

[Page 270]

with people: merchants from the biggest cities in the country, villagers from the surrounding area, local business people, workers, and agents or people in need of his favors. When fairs were held, at the house they would boil water in a large samovar and put it on a big table laden with bread, jam, and schmalz, and everyone who entered could eat to his heart's content. My sister Etti and her mother-in-law Hena Eidel used to serve the guests themselves. Etti, who was a nurse by profession, acted also in everyday life like a good sister[2] to everyone who turned to her. Mr. Shmuel Eisengart, who lived in their apartment, used to speak with my sister only in Hebrew, and he testified that she had complete proficiency in that language.

Levi Breizman and his family

Gladly and willingly they would offer their spacious house for use by the local committee of the Jewish National Fund, or for organizing the traditional *minyan*[3] for *Simchat Torah*[4], and of course they would also prepare the *kiddush*[5] for the worshipers. Both of them related to me and my sister Rivka like devoted, loving parents, and perhaps even more than that.

In the terrible catastrophe that befell our people at the time of the war, they met their deaths together with all the members of our holy community. May their memory be blessed and their souls bound up in the bonds of life.

[Page 271]

**The Perliuk family with their daughter-in-law Hinda (wife of Moshe)
when she visited in Mizocz**

Translator's Footnotes:

1. Menachem's Treasury [Compilation] and The Great Ones of Ostroh: A Memento.
2. A play on words. In Hebrew the same word means both "nurse" and "sister".
3. Prayer quorum, a congregation of at least 10 adult Jews
4. A holiday celebrating the completion of the annual cycle of public readings of the Torah and the beginning of the new cycle.
5. Referring to blessings and refreshments after the prayer service.

[Page 271]

Without Graves...

by Moshe Perliuk

Translated from Hebrew by Naomi Sokoloff

To the memory of
My father – Hayyim
My mother – Zelda
My sisters – Leah, Hinda, and Shaina
My brother-in-law – Yitzchak and my sister's son – Yacov
Who perished in the Shoah.

My dear parents and sisters did not have a grave.

Nor a monument – a marker of mute, silent stone

For the lives that were and no longer are,

For the lives that were lost in the valley of slaughter even as they were blossoming.

For my father and mother– the best, most honest, intelligent people; the most loyal and devoted of parents, for my sisters who perished in their youth – my heart secretly cries without cease.

[Page 272]

The murderers saw to it that even the smallest consolation would not remain for those who survived and stay mired in grief, forever broken.

I have lost hope that I will ever be able to throw myself onto the graves or headstones of my dear ones.

My great sorrow would move even the cold stone, if there were one, to speak – my language would be understood and it would listen to me talk.

A grave and a headstone – my dear ones were not granted even that – not even a trace remains ---

But in my heart, which bleeds, I guard the memory of them and will, until my last breath. May their souls be bound up in the bonds of life.

**Celebration in the home of Chaim Perliuk in honor of
the visit of Hinda (wife of Moshe) in Mizocz**

Our Mother Sarah Goldberg (née Trochler)

by Kayla and Mordechai

Translated from Hebrew by Naomi Sokoloff

At a young age she married our father, Leibush, who was a scholar and ritual slaughterer from a respected family in the town of Kaniv. Still in the bloom of her youth she was widowed, and we lost our father. With difficulty, Mama barely supported her family till she buckled under the weight of that burden. A number of years after that, she married Shlomo Finkel and gave birth to three more children.

At the time the ghetto was being liquidated, she managed to escape with her husband, together with the Kurtz and Mendelssohn families from among the refugees. After eight days of hiding she went out to look for

[Page 273]

food, was caught, and killed. We learned this from Mrs. Kurtz. The others of this group in hiding were all killed, too, and only Mrs. Kurtz remained alive.

Sarah Goldberg (née Trochler)

Mama was fifty years old when she died. Her life was devoted to the family. She dreamt of getting *nachas*[1] from her children, but was not granted this. May her memory be blessed and her soul bound up in the bonds of life.

**From right to left: Yitzchak Leiber, Shabbetai Golob (lives in Israel),
Asher Sudobitzky and Borya Sizak**

[Page 274]

Memorial in honor of the Kopit family and the Tzirkel family murdered during the Holocaust

Translator's Footnote:

1. The special joy that comes from taking gratification in and being proud of one's children's accomplishments.

[Page 275]

In Remembrance
of Our Little House that was Destroyed

by Nachum Zeev bar Yerachmiel Kopit

Translated from Hebrew by Naomi Sokoloff

At the edge of town, hidden among dense trees, surrounded mostly by greenery, stood our small house. Our house was small, and poor in appearance, but honesty and happiness prevailed within its walls. In that house I was born and raised and I lived there with my brother and two sisters, may G-d avenge their blood, and I never left till the bitter end. My parents were simple people, honest and upright. Above all they valued the commandments of charity and hospitality. Accordingly, every embittered or needy person found in our house a sympathetic ear, a meal, and support. Our house being close to the synagogues in town, villagers were eager to stay there when they came to town for the Days of Awe, *yohrzeit*[1] or holidays; also when a village orphan needed to study Torah in town, we took care of all his needs. When the Germans desecrated the *Beit Midrash*,[2] father risked his life to save the Torah scroll from their degenerate hands. He cried like a child then, and was consoled because from then on there was no doubt in his heart that the hand of G-d would deal with those evil doers and they would never be cleared of their crimes in doing harm to our people's sanctuaries.

On the day the ghetto was liquidated, Papa – a pious Jew – remembered to don his prayer shawl and lay *tefillin*[3] and recite the confession while walking to the killing pits. Mama, in contrast, in her last moments focused on smuggling the youngsters out past the ghetto walls. She almost succeeded in her task; only her first granddaughter, Tsipkeleh – whom we all cherished – did she not succeed in saving. [Tzipkeleh] perished together with my parents and the entire sacred community.

Till my last breath, engraved on my heart will be the memory of our little house and its dear inhabitants. May my small, modest account here serve as a monument to their lives and as a respectful remembrance of them.

Translator's Footnotes:

1. The anniversary of a death, to be marked with memorial prayers.
2. Tradition House of Study
3. Phylacteries

[Page 276]

In Remembrance
of My Brother Yosef Wolfman, z"l

by his sister, Tova

Translated from Hebrew by Naomi Sokoloff

At a young age it befell him to become the guardian of a big family. Papa died, and we remained without means or livelihood. Yosef took on the heavy burden of providing for the family and did so honorably. He was very successful in business and the family lacked for nothing.

Yosef Wolfman and his sister Rachel

Even though he was the only provider and the only male in the house, he was never haughty. All his earnings he gave to Mama and he trusted her in all ways. When the older sisters came of age, he married them off respectably. A number of years before the Holocaust he married a woman much younger than himself, and a son was born. The match didn't work out and he separated from his wife a short time before the German-Russian war broke out. At the time of the killings he managed to flee to the forest and took with him his son, his prayer shawl, his *tefillin*, and an axe. According to what the survivors recount, he perished at the hands of the Ukrainians. In the forest he aided and helped his brothers in sorrow. Heroically, he more than once defended those in hiding and saved them. His faith in the G-d of Israel gave them courage and instilled hope in the hearts of the survivors. At the end, he was felled by a bullet. May his memory be blessed.

[Page 277]

On the Grave of Our Friends
Michael Nemirover and David Gantzberg

by their friends: Yosef Karni and Yacov Gelman

Translated from Hebrew by Naomi Sokoloff

Two friends had sons.

One was born on Hanukkah and his name was Michael Nemirover, and the second was born on Shavuot and his name was David Gantzberg. The two of them were educated together from childhood. They were pampered and cared for like two expensive, ornamental trees in a garden. When they got a little older, they parted ways. Michael was a member of "Hashomer Haleumi" and David was in "Gordonia," but they maintained their childhood friendship and stayed connected with ties of mutual affection.

David

Michael

The two of them numbered among the most splendid young men of our town. They bore the charm and grace of nobility and they were exemplary in their conduct and virtue.

We remember the last moments of parting from them. We had been recruited into the Red Army and they stayed in Mizocz. Michael somehow sensed that we would not see each other again, and he said, it's such a pity I can't go with you. David was lying on his bed with a broken ankle and crying as we left. Michael met his end in the mass pit of the martyrs of Mizocz. David healed and was recruited to the army and died a hero's death at the front lines of the Red Army in Kalinin.

We worked together with them on behalf of Zion. We dreamt of continuing to work in Eretz Israel on behalf of our people. But fate wished otherwise. They were not even granted a Jewish burial. May these words be an eternal flame on their unknown graves. May their souls be bound up in the bonds of life.

[Page 278]

My Parents, Yitzchak and Rivka Yasin

by Esther

Translated from Hebrew by Naomi Sokoloff

My parents were simple, honest people. Papa was a tailor and earned his living with the work of his hands. Mama was a good homemaker, devoted to her children and husband and friends and all the neighbors. My parents deprived themselves[1] to obtain education for their children.

On Sabbaths and holidays the house was filled with joy and light, happiness and gaiety. Papa was an optimist by nature, he loved life and always believed in good days to come. Even during the dark days of the ghetto, he did not lose faith and was sure the reign of evil would meet its downfall. But he and the members of my family did not live to see that downfall; they perished together with all the Jews of Mizocz on the day the ghetto was liquidated. May their memory be blessed.

Translator's Footnote:

1.   Literally, they took from their own mouths.

In Remembrance
of the Family of Eliahu Oliker

by Yona

Translated from Hebrew by Naomi Sokoloff

Papa, R. Eliahu Oliker, was a very pious Jew and he gave his many children a religious education.

We lived at the edge of town in a small, modest house, and we were all happy. Papa was proud of his family and his children. He succeeded in marrying off all of them and took much joy and gratification in them. On the night of the Passover *seder*, we would all gather at his house and his happiness knew no bounds. Paper never grumbled and he never complained against G-d. He always said, whatever G-d wills is good. In the ghetto, mother was very worried for the children and lamented our bitter fate, but Papa accepted even the suffering and remained certain in his belief that G-d would not abandon His people. But all my extensive family perished and I remained alone. May their souls be bound up in the bond of life.

[Page 279]

Additional Family Photographs

Captions Translated by Nathen Gabriel

**Esther Yasin's parents
(Yitzchak and Rivka Yasin, names added by
translator)**

[Page 280]

The Weltfreint family from Katowice

The family of Moshe Yosi Fishfeider

[Page 281]

The family of Tzvi Sizak

The family of Yosef ben Gedalyahu Kornik

[Page 282]

Mottel Sizak and his wife

Shlomo Sizak and his wife

[Page 283]

Chaim Breznerand his wife Chaya

Meir Berez and his wife Roza

[Page 284]

Right to left: Chaim Brezner, his wife Chaya, their daughter Asya and Meir Berez

The family of the sister of Mamtzia Gelman, Sarah Schulman

[Page 285]

The Sudobitzky family at the wedding of Reizel to Yakov Mizocz

The father of Tzippora Sudobitzky–Holtzker

[Page 286]

The family of Yosef Mizocz

The Koppelman family

[Page 287]

Avraham Scheinfeld and his wife Feiga

Wolf Neiman and his wife Chaya

[Page 288]

Avraham Golob and Bluma Golob

Chana Braunstein wife of Moshe Kuninar(?)

[Page 289]

Buzi Mizocz

Pinchas Fishfeider

Lipa son of Yosef–Zalman Sudgalter

Dr. Liebster

[Page 290]

Avraham son of Lipa Sudgalter, Risi Kneplier, Yakov son of Chaim Kneplier

Demonstration in a refugee camp in Germany demanding free immigration to Israel

[Page 291]

A committee of the Mizocz landsmanshaft in Israel and editorial board of the book

Seated from left to right: Reuven Melamed, Chaya Altman, Asher Ben–Oni, Liza Shtellung, Moshe Feldman
Standing from left to right: Baruch Fliter, Yakov Gelman, Yosef Karni, Moshe Perliuk, Nachum Kopit and Mordechai Scheinfeld

[Page 292]

**Asher Ben–Oni speaks at a memorial for the martyrs of Mizocz
Next to him Reuven Melamed**

[Page 293]

Acknowledgement

It is our pleasant obligation to express here our thanks and acknowledge the editor of this
book, our comrade Asher Ben-Oni, who not only initiated the publication
of the book, but worked diligently to spur on the contributors, and from crumbs of testimony
and fragmented reports, construct an eternal monument to the city of
our birth – Mizocz. For this, may he be blessed.

The Committeee of the Organization for Former Residents from Mizocz

The Editorial Board of the Mizocz Book

[Pages 294-314]

List of Martyrs from the Mizocz Ghetto

Original transliteration by Beryl Baleson
Revised for this edition by Bella Hass Weinberg

Family name(s)	First name(s)	Gender	Marital status	Additional family	Remarks	Page
א Alef						
APPEL	Moshe	M				294
APPEL	Aniya	F				294
APPEL	Lazer Eliezer	M				294
APPEL	Baruch	M				294
ABRACH	Abraham	M				294
ABRACH	Kayla	F				294
ACKERMAN	Ephraim	M				294
ACKERMAN	Rachel	F				294
ACKERMAN	Aharon	M				294
ACKERMAN	Tziza	F				294
AVNER	Mordechai	M				294
AVNER	Zlata	F				294
AVNER	Sarah	F				294
EISENGART	Shmuel	M				294
EISENGART	Pesiya	F				294
EISENGART	Deborah	F				294
	Gittel	F	married		maiden name: EISENGART	294
	Abraham	M	married		Wife's maiden name	294

				EISENGART. Father David	
	Hana	F		Mother's maiden name EISENGART. Father Abraham and mother Gittel	294
ARBITORER	Joseph	M		Mother's maiden name EIŞENGART	294
ARBITORER	Leah	F			294
ARBITORER	Zvulun	M			294
ERLICH	Abraham	M			294
ERLICH	Shaindel	F			294
ERLICH	Shlomo	M			294
ERLICH	Bila	F			294
ERLICH	Israel	M			294
OLIKER	Moshe	M			294
OLIKER	Eliyahu	M			294
OLIKER	Heniya	F			294
OLIKER	Ze'ev	M			294
OLIKER	Pesiya	F			294
OLIKER	Asher	M			294
OLIKER	Moshe	M			294
OLIKER	Yosef ben Gedalyahu	M			294
OLIKER	Nahum	M			294
OLIKER	Tzirel	F			294
OLIKER	Ita	F			294
OLIKER	Asher	M			294
OLIKER	Abraham	M			294
OLIKER	Figa	F			294
OLIKER	Chernale	F			294

OLIKER	Abraham	M				294
OLIKER	Raizel	F				294
OLIKER	Abraham	M				294
OLIKER	Yehiel Baruch	M				294
OLIKER	Leah	F				294
OLIKER	Yacov	M				294
OLIKER	Bobtziya	F				294
OLIKER	Bentzion	M				294
OLIKER	Asher	M				294
OLIKER	Isaac	M				294
OLIKER	Raizel	F				294
OLIKER	Itziya	F				294
OLIKER	Moshe	M				294
OLIKER	Pnina	F				294
OLIKER	Pesach	M				294
OLIKER	Sarah	F				294
OLIKER	Hillel	M				294
OLIKER	Nusiya	F				294
ASHKENAZI	Moshe	M				295
ASHKENAZI	Haya Sarah	F				295
ASHKENAZI	Isaac	M				295
ASHKENAZI		M			Child	295
OCHS	Billa	F				295
OCHS		F			Mother's name Bila	295
IDSIS	Tzvi	M	married		Name of spouse – Faiga	295
IDSIS	Faiga	F	married		Name of spouse – Tzvi	295

	Muma	F	married	husband	maiden name IDSIS. Mother Faiga	295

ב Bet

BERKOVSKI	Rabbi Shimon	M				295
BERKOVSKI	Leah	F				295
BERKOVSKI	Michael	M				295
BAT	Kalman	M				295
BAT	Pearl	F				295
BAT	Yacov	M				295
BAT	Israel	M				295
BAT	Leah	F				295
BAT	Maniya	F				295
BAT	Soniya	F				295
BAT	Hana	F				295
BONIS	Shmuel	M				295
BONIS	Deborah	F				295
BONIS	Malka	F				295
BONIS	Soniya	F				295
BORNSTEIN	Moshe	M				295
BORNSTEIN	Ethel	F				295
BORNSTEIN	Tzvi	M				295
BORNSTEIN	Arye	M				295
BORNSTEIN	Abraham	M				295
BORNSTEIN	Diniya	F				295
BORNSTEIN	Shaindel	F			Maiden name KRAINDIS	295
BARINSTEIN	Yacov	M				295
BARINSTEIN	Zissel	F				295
BARINSTEIN	Roza	F				295

BERNSTEIN	Arye	M				295
BERNSTEIN	Yacov	M				295
BREZNER	Hayyim	M				295
BREZNER	Haya Sarah	F				295
BREZNER	Asiya	F				295
BERMAN	Tama	F				295
BERMAN	Buzi Yekutiel	M				295
BERMAN	Yacov	M				295
BERMAN	Hana	F				295
BERMAN	Hayyim	M				295
BELFER	Yacov	M				295
BELFER	Anika	F				295
BELFER	Rachel	F				295
BELFER	Aba	M				295
BARINSTEIN	Hana	F				295
BROIDA	Rachel	F				295
BROIDA	Rivka	F				295
BROIDA	Miriam	F				295
BROIDA	Batya	F				295
BROIDA	Buzi	M				295
BROIDA	Tzvi	M				295
BERCHASH	Rivka	F			Maiden name FLITER	295
BERI	Isaac	M				295
BERI	Sarah	F				295
BERI	Hayyim	M	married	2 children		295
BERI		F	married	2 children	Name of spouse – Hayyim	295
BORK	Joseph	M				296
BORK	Elka	F				296

BORK	Tzvi	M				296
BORK	Asher	M				296
BORK	Pearl	F				296
BORK	Rivka	F				296
BICKS	Tzvi	M				296
BICKS	Haya Sarah	F				296
BICKS	Buzi	M				296
BROTZKY	Yacov	M				296
BROTZKY	Hana Rivka	F				296
BROTZKY	Moshe	M				296
BROTZKY	Fraida	F				296
BROTZKY	Avigdor	M				296
BRIZMAN	Levi	M	married		Name of spouse – Ita	296
BRIZMAN	Ethiya	F	married		Name of spouse – Levy	296
BRIZMAN		M			Father Levy and mother Ita	296
BRIZMAN		F			Father Levy and mother Ita	296
BRIZMAN	Joseph	M				296
BRIZMAN	Hana Sarah	F				296
BRIZMAN	Netta	F				296
BRIZMAN	Hayyim	M	married	2 children		296
BRIZMAN		F	married	2 children	Name of spouse – Hayyim	296
	Gittel	F	married	husband & 2 children	Maiden name BRIZMAN	296
BRIZMAN	Hayyim	M				296
BRIZMAN	Fradel	F				206
BRIZMAN	Hinda	F				296

BRIZMAN	Mordechai	M	married	3 children	Name of spouse – Haya	296
BRIZMAN	Haya	F	married	3 children	Name of spouse – Mordechai	296
BRIZMAN	Godil	M	married			296
BRIZMAN		F	married		Name of spouse – Godil	296
BRIZMAN		M			Father Godil	296
BEREZ	Moshe	M				296
BEREZ	Pracha	F				296
BEREZ	Isaac	M				296
BEREZ	Mair	M				296
BEREZ	Roza	F				296
BEREZ	Zoia	F				296
BIRENBAUM	Doctor Mordechai	M			Authorised refugee	296
BELFER	Shalom	M	married		Name of spouse – Tova	296
BELFER	Tova	F	married		Name of spouse – Shalom	296
BELFER		M			Father Shalom and mother Yova	296
BRAUNSTEIN	Sarah	F				296
BRAUNSTEIN	Ze'ev	M				296
BRAUNSTEIN	Shalom	M				296
BRAUNSTEIN	Figa	F				296
BRAUNSTEIN	Hana	M				296
BRAUNSTEIN	Gittel	F				296
BRAUNSTEIN	Mordechai	M			Mordechai had a sister. There is nothing about her	296
BRAUNSTEIN	Deborah	F				296
BRAUNSTEIN	Figa	F				296

BRAUNSTEIN	Musiya	M			296
BRAUNSTEIN	Haya	F			296
BRAUNSTEIN	Rivka	F			296
BRAUNSTEIN	Asher	M			296
BRAUNSTEIN	Raizel	F			296
BRAUNSTEIN	Haya	F			296
BRAUNSTEIN	Yonah	M			296
BRAUNSTEIN	Soniya	F			296
BRAUNSTEIN	Isaac	M			296
BERNSTEIN	Yacov	M			296,297
BERNSTEIN	Baila	F			296,297
BERNSTEIN	Batya	F			296,297
BERNSTEIN		M		child	296,297
BERNSTEIN		F		daughter	296,297
BERNSTEIN		M		child	296,297
BERNSTEIN	Betzalel	M			297
	Ephraim	M		from BERNSTEIN family	297
	Ethel	F		from BERNSTEIN family	297
	Sincha	M		from BERNSTEIN family	297
	Miriam	F		from BERNSTEIN family	297
	Yenta	F		from BERNSTEIN family	297
BERNSTEIN	Abraham	M	one child		297
BERNSTEIN	Malka	F	one child	Maiden name LANGER	297

BIOALSKY				Refugees from KONSEK 12 people	297

ג **Gimmel**

GUSACK	Melech	M			297
GUSACK	Deborah	F			297
GUSACK	Roza	F			297
GUSACK	Fira	F			297
GOLDBRENNER	Tzvi	M	married	Refugee from Bilgoraj	297
GOLDBRENNER		F	married	Refugee from Bilgoraj. Name of spouse – Tzvia	297
GERSTEIN	Yacov	M	married	Name of spouse – Bluma	297
GERSTEIN	Bluma	F	married	Name of spouse – Yacov	297
GERSTEIN		M		Father Yacov and mother Bluma	297
GERBER	Golda	F			297
GERBER	Shimon	M			297
GERBER	Luba	F			297
GERBER	Valla	F			297
GREENBERG	Joseph Hayyim	M			297
GREENBERG	Hava	F			297
GREENBERG	Yehiel	M			297
GREENBERG	Meir	M			297
GREENBERG	Tzvi	M			297
GREENBERG	Abraham	M			297
GREENBERG	Rachel	F		Maiden name KOPPELMAN	297
GREENBERG	Mina	F			297

GREENBERG	Sarah	F				297
GOLBERTON	Hayyim	M	married		Name of spouse – Bina	297
GOLBERTON	Bina	F	married		Name of spouse – Hayyim	297
GOLBERTON	Bracha	F	married	2 children		297
GOLBERTON	Miriam	F				297
GOLBERTON	Haya	F				297
GREENBERG	Isaac	M				297
GREENBERG	Leah	F			Maiden name PERLIUK	297
GREENBERG	Yacov	M				297
GUZ	Menucha	F			Maiden name PERLIUK	297
GERMAN	Liova	M				297
GLEIT	Figa	F				297
GLEIT	Isaac	M				297
GLEIT	Rivka	F				297
GREENBAUM	Sarah	M			Mother of Haya SCHINDELHAUS	297
GANDELMAN	Tzvi	M	married			297
GANDELMAN		F	married		Name of spouse – Tzvi	297
GANDELMAN		M			a child. Father Tzvi	297
GANTZBERG	Yehoshua Dov	M				297
GANTZBERG	Sarah	F				297
GANTZBERG	Shmuel	M				297
GANTZBERG	Abraham	M				297
GROSMAN	Abraham	M				298
GROSMAN	Leah	F				298
GROSMAN	Peretz	M				298

GROSMAN	Bella	F				298
GROSMAN		F			A girl not clear whom her parents were	298
GANTZBERG	Sima	M				298
GANTZBERG	Tzifa	F				298
GANTZBERG	Nahum	M				298
GROSMAN	Shmuel	M	married		Refugee from Bilgoraj	298
GROSMAN		F	married		Name of spouse – Shmuel	298
GROSMAN	Moshe	M				298
GROSMAN	Haya	F				298
GROSMAN		M			A boy – origins are not clear	298

ד Dalet

DORDICK KATZ	Yehoshua	M		one child		298
DORDICK KATZ	Sarah	F		one child		298
DORDICK KATZ	Menachem Mendel	M				298
DORDICK KATZ	Nioniya	F		one child		298

ה Hey

HALPERIN	Binjamin	M	married	3 children	Name of spouse – Leah	298
HALPERIN	Leah	F	married	3 children	Name of spouse – Binjamin	298
HONIGSFELD	Shpesil	M	married		Refugee from Bilgoraj	298
HONIGSFELD		F	married		Name of spouse – Shefsil	298
HONIGSFELD	Mordechai	M				298
HONIGSFELD	Tzvi	M				298

ו Vav

WELFMAN	Joseph	M				298
WELFMAN	Batya Rivka	F				298
WELFMAN	Gershon	M				298
WELFMAN	Rivka	F				298
WELFMAN	Isaac	M				298
WELFMAN	Yacov	M	married	2 children	Name of spouse – Rachel	298
WELFMAN	Rachel	F	married	2 children	Name of spouse – Yacov	298
WELFMAN	Reuben	M	married	one child		298
WELFMAN		F	married	one child	Name of spouse – Reuven	298
WILLSTEIN	Abraham	M				298
WILLSTEIN	Rachel	F				298
WILLSTEIN	Yacov	M	married			298
WILLSTEIN		F	married		Name of spouse – Yacov	298
WILLSTEIN	David	M				298
WILLSTEIN	Joseph	M				298
WASSERMAN	Joseph	M				298
WASSERMAN	Billa	F				298
WASSERMAN	Isaac	M				298
WEISBERG	Yehuda	M				298
WEISBERG	Batya	F				298
WEISBERG	Rachel	F				298
WELTFREINT	Emanuel	M			Refugee from Katowicz	298
WELTFREINT	Faiga	F			Refugee from Katowicz	298
WEINER	Reuben	M				298

WEINER	Sarah	F				298
WEINER	Shmuel	M	married		Name of spouse – Haya	298
WEINER	Haya	F	married		Name of spouse – Shmuel	298
WEINER	Isaac	M				298
WEINER	Aharon	M				298
WEINER	Zissel	F				298
WEINER	Haniya	F				298
WEINER	Lipa	M				298
WEINER	Aharon Laiv	M	married	one child		298
WEINER		F	married	one child	Name of spouse – Aharon Lev	298
WEINER	Hayyim	M	married	one child		299
WEINER		F	married	one child	Name of spouse – Hayyim	299
WEINER	Lev	M				299
WEINER	Yenta	F				299
WEINER	Isaac	M				299
WEINER		F			a child	299
WEINER	Asher	M				299
WEINER	Figa	F				299
WEINER	Abraham	M				299
WEINER	Moshe	M				299
VASICHER	Abraham	M	married	one child	Name of spouse – Rivka	299
VASICHER	Rivka	F	married	one child	Name of spouse – Abraham	299

ז　Zayin

SEIFMACHER	Asher Zelig	M				299
SEIFMACHER	Kraina	F				299

SEIFMACHER	Shmuel	M				299
ZIAFMACHER	Figa	F				299
SILBERSTEIN	Yishayahu	M				299
SILBERSTEIN	Miriam	F				299
SILBERSTEIN	Raizel	F				299
SILBERSTEIN	Gittel	F				299
SILBERSTEIN	Elka	F				299
SILBERSTEIN	Moshe	M				299

ט Tet

TELLER	Hava	F				299
TELLER	Rachel	F				299
TEPPER	Isaac	M				299
TEPPER	Slava	M				299
TRACHTENBERG	Sarah	F	married	2 children		299
TRACHTENBERG		M	married	2 children	Name of spouse – Sarah	299
TRACHTENBERG	Mordechai	M				299
TRACHTENBERG	Sarah	F				299
TRACHTENBERG	Hana	F				299
TRACHTENBERG	Eliyahu	M				290
TENTZER	Batya	F				299
TENTZER	Slovi	M				299
TENTZER	Bracha	F				299
TENTZER	Gershon	M				299
TENTZER	Moshe	M				299
TENTZER	Yenta	F				299
TENTZER	Gershon	M				299
TENTZER	Baruch	M				299
TENTZER	Baruch	M				299
TENTZER	Bracha	F				299

TENTZER	Yehuda	M			299
TENTZER	Tzvi	M			299
TENTZER	Zelda	F			299
TENTZER	Gershon	M			299
TENTZER	Billa	F			299
TENTZER	Daliya	F			299
TEKSER	Mordechai	M			299
TEKSER	Billa	F			299
TEKSER	Benny	M			299
TEKSER	Asher	M			299
TROCHLIER	Michael	M			299
TROCHLIER	Baila	F		Maiden name SHTREIMAL	299
SHTREIMAL	Kayla	F			299
TROCHLIER	Fruma	F		Maiden name PERLIUK	299
TROCHLIER	Abraham	M			299,300
TROCHLIER	Susiya	F			299,300
TROCHLIER	Isaac	M			299,300
TROCHLIER	Tzvia	F			299,300
TROCHLIER	Michael	M			299,300
TROCHLIER	Billa	F			299,300
TROCHLIER	Veliya	M			299,300
TROCHLIER	Bila	F			299,300
TROCHLIER	Isaac	M			299,300
TROCHLIER	Hadassah	F			299,300
TROCHLIER	Tzvi	M			299,300
TROCHLIER	Miriam	F			299,300
TROCHLIER	Baruch	M			299,300
TROCHLIER	Fraidel	F			299,300
TROCHLIER	Roza	F			299,300

TROCHLIER	Baruch	M				299,300
TROCHLIER	Hana	F				299,300
TROCHLIER	Tuvia	M				299,300
TROCHLIER	Mamtziya	M				299,300
TROCHLIER	Figa	F				299,300
TENHOLTZ				whole family	Refugees from Bilgoraj. Son was policeman	300
TRELOVSKY	Simcha	M	married			300
TRELOVSKY		F	married		Widow of Rabbi LERNER. Name of spouse – Simcha	300

׳ Yod

YASIN	Isaac	M				300
YASIN	Rivka	F				300
YASIN	Raizel	F				300
YASIN	Rachel	F				300
YASIN	Tzipora	F				300
YASIN	Pinchas	M				300
YASIN	Leah	F				300
YASIN	Etiya	F				300
YASIN	Yacov	M				300

כ Kaf

KAGAN	Tzvi	M				300
KAGAN	Leah	F				300
KAGAN	Tova	F				300

ל Lamed

LERNER	Rabbi Nathan Netta	M				300

LERNER	Rachel	F			300
LERNER	Abraham	M			300
LERNER	Shaindel	F			300
LERNER	Zahariya	M			300
LIPOVITZKY	Arye	M			300
LIPOVITZKY	Liza	F			300
LIPOVITZKY	Yacov	M			300
LIPOVITZKY	Nusiya	F			300
LIPSHITZ	Arye	M			300
LIPSHITZ	Haya	F			300
LIPSHITZ	Rivka	F			300
LIPSHITZ	Tova	F			300
LIPSHITZ	Bentzion	M			300
LAUFER	Kayla	F	2 children		300
LAUFER	Isaac	M	2 children		300
LAUFER	Esther	F			300
LAUFER	Sarah	F			300
LAUFER	Yehezkel	M	married	Name of spouse – Miriam	300
LAUFER	Miriam	F	married	Name of spouse – Yehezkel	300
LAUFER		M		a child. Father Yehezkel and mother Miriam	300
LAUFER	Hayyim	M	married	Cemetery guard	300
LAUFER		F	married	Name of spouse – Hayyim	300
LAUFER	Asher	M			300
LAUFER	Aharon	M			300
LAUFER	Gittel	F			300
LAUFER	Hirshel	M			300

LEVIN LIVANDER	Moshe	M			Son in law of Ephraim the dumb from the cemetery	301
LEVIN LIVANDER	Haya	F			Son in law of Ephraim the dumb from the cemetery	301
LEVIN LIVANDER	Motti Hirsh	M			Son in law of Ephraim the dumb from the cemetery	301
LUSTIK	David Aharon	M				301
LUSTIK	Faiga	F				301
LUSTIK	Pesiya	F				301
LUSTIK	Bracha	F				301
LUSTIK	Malka	F				301
LUSTIK	Esther	F				301
LUSTIK	Moshe	M		2 children		301
LUSTIK	Shlomo	M				301
LIODOMIRSKY	David	M				301
LIODOMIRSKY	Golda	F				301
LIODOMIRSKY	Mordechai	M			born 1927	301
LIODOMIRSKY	Shlomo	M			born 1931	301
LEIBER	Tzvi	M				301
LEIBER	Vechna	F				301
LAVONSKY	Mordechai	M				301
LAVONSKY	Gnesiya	F				301
LAVONSKY	Haya	F				301
LANGER	Zissel	F				301
LANGER	Joseph	M				301
LANGER	Lipa	M				301
LANGER	Binjamin	M				301
LANGER	Haya Susiya	F				301

LANGER	Yehoshua	M			Ritual slaughterer	301
LANGER	Rachel	F				301
LANGER	Esther	F				301
LANGER	Miriam	F				301
LIKWORNIK	Susil	F				301
LIKWORNIK	Yehiel	M				301
LIKWORNIK	Tova	F				301
LIKWORNIK	Taliya	F				301
LIKWORNIK	Abraham	M				301
LIKWORNIK	Mantzy	F				301
LIKWORNIK	Raizy	F				301
LIKWORNIK	Isaac	M				301
LIKWORNIK	Soniya	F				301
LIKWORNIK	Moshe	M				301
LIKWORNIK	Gushka	F				301
LIKWORNIK	Michael	M	married			301
LIKWORNIK		F	married		Name of spouse – Michael	301
LIKWORNIK	Arye	M				301
LIKWORNIK	Haya	F				301
LIKWORNIK	Hana	F				301
LIKWORNIK	Abraham	M				301
LIKWORNIK	Esther	F				301
LIKWORNIK	Hana	F				301
LIPPEN	Yacov	M				301
LIPPEN	Rachel	F				301
LIPPEN	Gisiya	F			a daughter from Rachel's first husband	301

מ Mem

MINDLIN	Ganiya	F				301

MELAMED	Deborah	F			301
MELAMED	Fruma	F			301
MELAMED	Leah	F			301
MELAMED	Laivish	M			301
MELAMED		M		a child	301
MENDYUK	Slava	M			301
MENDYUK	Rachel	F			301
MENDYUK	Mordechai	M			301
MARGALIT	Mandil	M			302
MARGALIT	Hava	F			302
MARGALIT	Yonah	M			302
MARGALIT		F		a child	302
MIRMELSTEIN	Moshe	M			302
MIRMELSTEIN	Esther	F			302
MIRMELSTEIN	Rachel	F			302
MIRMELSTEIN	Yenta	F			302
MILLER	Shmuel	M			302
MILLER	Haya	F			302
MILLER	Zaivel	M			302
MOCHIN	Aharon	M			302
MOCHIN	Braindel	F			302
MOCHIN	Joseph	M			302
MOCHIN	Moral	M			302
MOCHIN	Deborah	F			302
MOCHIN	Mesiya	F			302
MOCHIN	Tzipora	F			302
MOCHIN	Sender	M			302
MOCHIN	Pesiya	F			302
MOCHIN	Yehuda	M			302
MOCHIN	Rivka	F			302

MOCHIN	Moshe	M				302
MOCHIN		M			a child	302
MURAKOVITZ	Abraham	M	married	3 children		302
MURAKOVITZ		F	married	3 children	Name of spouse – Abraham	302
MULMAN	Ephraim	M				302
MULMAN	Pearl	F				302
MULMAN	Bentzion	M				302
MULMAN	Yochevet	F				302
MULMAN	Joseph	M				302
MULMAN	Yoel	M				302
MULMAN	Heniya	F				302
MULMAN	Asher	M				302
MEILIER	Eliezer	M				302
MEILIER	Haya	F				302
MEILIER	Baruch Lev	M				302
MURAK	Zvulun	M				302
MURAK	Maika	F				302
MURAK	rachel	F				302
MEDNIK	Gershon	M				302
MEDNIK	Rivka	F				302
MEDNIK	Hana	F				302
MEDNIK	Mesiya	F				302
MEDNIK	Raitzia	F				302
MOSSMAN	Gershon	M				302
MOSSMAN	Rachel	F				302
MOSSMAN	Zina	F				302
MIZOCZ	Zailik Buzi	M				302
MIZOCZ	Bat Sheva	F				302
MIZOCZ	Tzvia	F				302

MIZOCZ	Mordechai	M				302
MIZOCZ	Joseph	M				302
MIZOCZ	Krisiya	F				302
MIZOCZ	yacov	M	married		Name of spouse – Raizel	302
MIZOCZ	Raizel	F	married		Name of spouse – Yacov	302
MIZOCZ		F			Father Yacov and mother Raizel	302
MIZOCZ	Moshe	M				302
MIZOCZ	Yishayahu	M				302
MIZOCZ	Asher	M				302
MIZOCZ	Mordechai	M	married	One child		303
MIZOCZ		F	married	One child	Name of spouse – Mordechai	303
MIZOCZ	Meir	M	married	One child	Name of spouse – Figa	303
MIZOCZ	Figa	F	married	One child	Name of spouse – Meir	303
MEISLITSCH	Chaitziya	F				303
MEISLITSCH	Mordechai	M				303
MEISLITSCH	Aniya	F				303
MEISLITSCH	Tuviya	M	married	one child		303
MEISLITSCH		F	married	one child	Name of spouse – Tuviya	303
MEISLITSCH	Moshe	M	married	one child	Name of spouse – Mila	303
MEISLITSCH	Meliya	F	married	one child	Name of spouse – Moshe	303
MEISLITSCH	Faivel	M	married		Name of spouse – Babale	303
MEISLITSCH	Babela	F	married		Name of spouse – Faivel	303
MEISLITSCH	Abraham	M			Father Faivel and mother Babale	303

MEISLITSCH	Laivish	M			Father Faivel and mother Babale	303
MALGALTER	Reuben	M			Ritual slaughterer	303
MALGALTER	Hana	F				303
MALGALTER	Tzvi	M				303
MALGALTER	yacov	M				303
MALGALTER	Deborah	F				303
MALGALTER	Faivish	M				303
MALGALTER	Joseph David	M			Ritual slaughterer	303
MALGALTER	Esther	F				303
MALGALTER	Yishayahu	M			dumb	303
MALGALTER	Michael	M				303
MALGALTER	Golda	F				303

ב Nun

NUDLER	Tzvi	M				303
NUDLER	Leah	F				303
NUDLER	Rivka	F				303
NUDLER	Shimon	M				303
NUDLER	Hana	F				303
NUDLER	Isaac	M				303
NEMIROVER	Yonah	M				303
NEMIROVER	Hinda	F				303
NEMIROVER	Sarah Soniya	F				303
NEMIROVER	Deborah	F				303
NEMIROVER	Michael	M				303
GOLDSTEIN	Tziofa	F	married		Maiden name NEMIROVER. Name of spouse – Laizer	303

GOLDSTEIN	Laizer	M	married		Name of spouse – Tziofa	303
NAGEL	Isaac	M	married		Name of spouse – Losiya	303
NAGEL	Lusiya	F	married		Maiden name FINKEL. Name of spouse – Isaac	303
NOIACHS	Asher	M				303
NOIACHS	Rivka	F				303
NOIACHS	Liosiya	F				303
NEIMAN	Ze'ev	M				303
NEIMAN	Haya	F				303
NEIMAN	Raizel	F				303
NEIMAN	Ethel	F				303
NEIMAN	Zissel	F				303
NEIMAN	Ital	F				303
NEIMAN	Mottel	M				303
NEIMAN	Haya Susil	F				303
NEIMAN	Udi	M				303
NULMAN	Israel	M				303
NULMAN	Dov	M				303
NULMAN	Meniya	F			a girl	303
NULMAN	Yacov	M				303
NULMAN	Sima	F				303
NULMAN	Hana	F				303

ס **Samech**

SUDHALTER	Yacov	M				304
SUDHALTER	Haya Sarah	F				304
SUDHALTER	Nehemiya	F				304
SUDHALTER	Deborah	F				304

SPEKTOR	Isaac	M	married		Name of spouse – Tzvia	304
SPEKTOR	Tzvia	F	married		Name of spouse – Isaac	304
SPEKTOR		F			Father Isaac and mother Tzvai	304
SPEKTOR	Hainech	M	married		Name of spouse – Shaindel	304
SPEKTOR	Shaindel	F	married		Name of spouse – Hainech	304
SPEKTOR		F			Father Hainech and mother Sahindel	304
SIZAK	Gershon	M				304
SIZAK	Sarah Soniya	F				304
SIZAK	Tzvi	M				304
SIZAK	Mordechai	M				304
SIZAK	Soniya	F			Not clear whose wife Soniya is	304
SIZAK	Tahala	F				304
SIZAK	Joseph	M				304
SIZAK		M			a child	304
SIZAK	Shlomo	M				304
SIZAK	Golda	F				304
SIZAK	Tahala	F				304
SIZAK	Rachel Leah	F				304
SKOLNIK	Nathan Netta	M				304
SKOLNIK	Lipsha	F				304
SKOLNIK	Yonah	M				304
SKOLNIK	Menachem Mendel	M				304
SKOLNIK	Tziofa	F				304

SKOLNIK	Herzl	M				304
SUDOBITZKY	Asher	M				304
SUDOBITZKY	Ital	F				304
SUDOBITZKY	Yacov	M				304
SUDOBITZKY	Shifra	F				304
SUDOBITZKY	Binjamin	M				304
STELTZKY	Meir	M	married		Name of spouse – Rachel	304
STELTZKY	Rachel	F	married		Name of spouse – Meir	304
STELTZKY		F			Father Meir and mother Rachel	304
SIMES	Isaac	M				304
SIMES	Rachel	F				304
SIMES	Figa	F			Sister of ISAAC	3o4
STARTZ	David	M				304
STARTZ	Batya	F				304
STARTZ	Meliya	F				304
STARTZ	Bila	F				304
STARTZ	Pesiya	F				304
SEGAL	Mordechai	M	married		Refugees from Warszawa	304
SEGAL		F	married		Refugees from Warszawa. Name of spouse – Mordechai	304
SEGAL	Antek	M			Refugees from Warszawa	304
SEGAL	Henka	F			Refugees from Warszawa	304
SEGAL	Isaac	M	married	one child		304
SEGAL		F	married	one child	Name of spouse – Isaac	304

פ Peh

PECKENTER	Raizil	F				304
PECKENTER	Zelig	M				304
PECKENTER	Shifka	M				304
PECKENTER		M			a boy	304
FIRER	Arye	M				304
FIRER	Tema	F				304
FIRER	Hava	F				304
FIRER	Abraham	M				304
FISHFEIDER	Tova	F				304,305
FISHFEIDER	Moshe Joseph	M				304,305
FISHFEIDER	Bluma Leah	F				304,305
FISHFEIDER	Michael	M				304,305
FISHFEIDER	Tuviya	M				304,305
FINKEL	Aniota	F				305
FINKEL	Hava	F				305
FINKEL	Shlomo	M	married	3 children	Name of spouse – Sarah	305
FINKEL	Sarah	F	married	3 children	Name of spouse – Shlomo	305
PORT	Arye	M				305
PORT	Faiga	F				305
PORT	Tova	F				305
PORT	Esther	F				305
PORT	Isaac	M				305
FLEISCH	Baruch	M				305
FLEISCH	Hasiya	F				305
FLEISCH	Pesach	M				305
FLEISCH	Shaindel	F				305

FLEISCH	Mordechai	M			305
FLEISCH	Leah	F			305
FLEISCH	Rivka	F			305
FLEISCH	Betzalel	M			305
FLEISCH	Isaac	M			305
PERLMUTTER	Abraham	M			305
PERLMUTTER	Gittel	F			305
PERLMUTTER	Kila	F			305
PERLMUTTER		F		a girl	305
PERLMUTTER	Deborah	F			305
PERLMUTTER	Nachman	M			305
PERLMUTTER	Mendel	M			305
PERLMUTTER	Hasiya	F			305
FIDELMAN	Aba	M			305
FIDELMAN	Choma	F			305
FIDELMAN	Sioma	M			305
FIDELMAN	Poliya	F			305
PINCHASOVITZ	Shmuel	M			305
PINCHASOVITZ	Figa	F			305
PINCHASOVITZ	Duniya	F			305
PINCHASOVITZ	Joseph	M			305
FISHER	Joseph David	M		not clear whose children they are	305
FISHER	Shmuel	M			305
FISHER	Maika	F			305
FINKELSTEIN	Shlomo	M			305
FINKELSTEIN	Sarah	F			305
FINKELSTEIN	Meir	M			305
FINKELSTEIN	Rachel	F			305
FINKELSTEIN	Mordechai	M			305

FINKELSTEIN	Tzipora	F				305
FISHMAN	Tzvi	M				305
FISHMAN	Dov	M	married		Name of spouse – Duniya	305
FISHMAN	Duniya	F	married		Name of spouse – Dov	305
FISHMAN		M			a boy	305
PRESSMAN	Binjamin	M				305
PRESSMAN	Hayyim	M				305
PRESSMAN	Yehudit	F				305
PERLIUK	Yacov	M				305
PERLIUK	Rivka	F			maiden name FISHFEIDER	305
PERLIUK	Buriya	M				305
PERLIUK	Liova	F				305
PERLIUK	Aba	M				305
PERLIUK	Hayyim	M				306
PERLIUK	Zelda	F				306
PERLIUK	Hinda	F				306
PERLIUK	Shaina	F				306
PERLIUK	David	M				306
PERLIUK	Pearl	F				306
PERLIUK	Laiv	M				306
PERLIUK	Pesach	M				306
PERLIUK	Gittel	F				306
PERLIUK	Sima	F				306
PERLIUK	Pearl	F		whole family		306
PERLIUK	Ethel	F	married		Husband of Ethel	306
PERLIUK		F			Mother's name Ethel	306

PERLIUK		F		Mother's name Ethel	306
PERLIUK	Aharon	M			306
PERLIUK	Haniya	F			306
PERLIUK	Raizel	F			306
PERLIUK	Batsheva	F			306
PERLIUK	Pnina	F			306
FINKER	Shlomo	M			306
FINKER	Udi Malka	F			306
FINKER	Yacov	M			306
FINKER	Gittel	F			306
FINKER	Mendil	M			306
FINKER	Jodeph	M			306
FINKER	Hana	F			306
FINKER		F		a boy	306
POLIAKOV	Sarah	F			306
POLIAKOV	Dovrish	M			306
POLIAKOV	Rivka	F			306
FELDMAN	Ze'ev	M			306
FELDMAN	Sarah Faiga	F			306
FELDMAN	Yishayahu	M			306
FELDMAN	Aidel	F			306
FELDMAN	Tzvia	F			306
FELDMAN	Pearl	F			306
FELDMAN	David	M			306
FELDMAN	Netta	F			306
FELDMAN	Miriam	F			306
FELDMAN	Isaac	M			306
FELDMAN	Pesiya	F			306
FELDMAN	Tzvia	F			306

FELDMAN	Menachum Mendel	M				306
FELDMAN	Hana	F				306
FELDMAN	Tzvia	F				306
FELDMAN	Sarah	F				306
FELDMAN	Gittel	F				306
FELDMAN	Pearl	F				396
FELDMAN	Shimon	M				306
FELDMAN	Shaina	F				306
FELDMAN	Sarah	F				306
FELDMAN	Hana	F				306
FELDMAN	Yishayahu	M				306
FELDMAN	Pearl	F				306
FELDMAN	Moshe	M	married	2 children	Name of spouse – Hana	306
FELDMAN	Hana	F	married	2 children	Name of spouse – Moshe	306
FUCHS	Yonah	M				306
FUCHS	Michael	M				306
FUCHS	Menucha	F				306
FUCHS	Ethel	F				306
FUCHS	Figa	F				306
FUCHS	Soniya	F				306
FUCHS	Ethel	F				306
FUCHS	Zissel	F				306,307
FUCHS	Hayyim	M				306,307
FUCHS	Moshe	M				307
FUCHS	Haya	F				307
FUCHS	Figa	F				307
FUCHS	Sarah	F				307
FUCHS	Yacov	M				307

FUCHS	Haya	F				307
FUCHS	Ethel	F				307
PRESSMAN	Dov	M				307
PRESSMAN	Hana	F				307
PRESSMAN	Esther	F				307
PRESSMAN	Abtaham	M				307
PRESSMAN	Joseph	M				307
FUCHS	Nunack	M				307
FUCHS	Leah	F				307
POLISHUK	Mordechai	M				307
FOIGELSTEIN	Joseph	M	married	2 children	Son in law of Yehoshua KATZ. Name of spouse – Faiga	307
FOIGELSTEIN	Faiga	F	married		Maiden name KATZ. Father Yehoshua. Name of spouse – Joseph	307
FLITER	Doctor Isaac	M				307
FLITER	Esther	F				307
FLITER	Baruch	M				307
FLITER	Faiga	F				307
FLITER	Dov	M				307
FLITER	Zalman	M				307
FLITER	Israel	M				307
FLITER	Mumtziya	F				307
FLITER	Harzl	M				307
FLITER	Rachel	F				307
FLITER		M			A boy born in the ghetto	307
FLITER	Shmuel	M				307
FLITER	Hana	F				307

FLITER	Meliya	F				307
FLITER	Bracha	F				307
FLITER	Abraham	M				307
FLITER	Hava	F				307
FLITER	Reia	F				307
FLITER	Zalman	M				307
FLITER	Leah	F				307
FLITER	Gittel	F				307
FLITER	Israel	M				307
FLITER	Abraham Bar	M				307
FLITER	Zelta	F				307
FLITER	Israel	M	married	one child	Father Avraham Dov. Name of spouse – Menucha	307
FLITER	Menucha	F	married	one child	Name of spouse – Israel	307
FLITER	Joseph	M			Father Israel and mother Menucha	307
FLITER	Zelta	F			Father Israel and mother Menucha	307
FLITER	Shmuel	M				307
FLITER	Hayyim	M				307
FISHBEIN	Aba	M				307
FISHBEIN	Faiga	F				307
FISHBEIN	Joseph	M				307
FISHBEIN	Tzeitel	F				307
FISHBEIN	Faivel	M				307
FISHBEIN	Moshe	M				307
FISHBEIN	Yehuda	M				308
FISHBEIN	Maniya	F				308
FISHBEIN	Taivel	M				308

FISHBEIN	Soniya	F				308
FISHBEIN	Ina	F				308

𝐱 Tzadik

ZUKERMAN	David	M				308
ZUKERMAN	Bila	F				308
CHERNIETZKY	Shabtai	M				308
CHERNIETZKY	Alter	M				308
CHERNIETZKY	Rachel	F				308
CHERNIETZKY	Batya	F				308
CHERNIETZKY	Tzvi	M		two children	not clear to whom the children belong	308
CHERNIETZKY	Abraham	M	married	one child		308
CHERNIETZKY		F	married	one child	Name of spouse – Abraham	308
CHERNAVKSY	Joseph	M	married	2 children	Name of spouse – Golda	308
CHERNAVKSY	Golda	F	married	2 children	Name of spouse – Joseph	308

𝐏 Kof

KOPIT	Yerachmiel	M				308
KOPIT	Tzirel	F				308
KOPIT	Levi	M				308
KOPIT	Kayla	F				308
KOPIT	Miriam	F				308
KOPIT	Gisiya	F				308
KOPIT	Meir Arye	M				308
KOPIT	Roiza	F				308
KOPIT	Joseph	M				308
KOPIT	Elka	F				308
KOPIT	Isaac	M				308

KOPIT	Moshe	M				308
KOPIT	Israel	M				308
KOPIT	Eliezer	M				308
KOPIT	Yehudit	F				308
KOPIT	Ita	F				308
KOPIT	Bentzion	M	married	2 children		308
KOPIT		F	married	2 children	Name of spouse – Bentzion	308
KOPIT	Sarah	F				308
KESTENBAUM	Yacov	M				308
KESTENBAUM	Sarah	F				308
KESTENBAUM		F			apparently the mother of YACOV	308
KRISIK	Zelig	M				308
KRISIK	Raizel	F				308
KRISIK	Shmuel	M				308
KRISIK	Chumka	F			Maiden name SPIELFOGEL	308
KRISIK	Leah	F				308
KRISIK	Taivel	M				308
TEKES	Rachel	F	married		Maiden name KORNIK. Name of spouse – Aharon	308
TEKES	Aharon	M	married		Name of spouse – Rachel	308
TEKES	Golda	F			Father Aharonand mother Rachel	308
GREIAR	Tama	F	married		Maiden name KORNIK. Name of spouse – Isaac	308
GREIAR	Isaac	M	married		Name of spouse – Tama	308

GREIAR	Tzila	F			Father Isaac and mother Tama	308
KORNIK	Miriam	F				308
KOPPELMAN	Poea	F				308
KOPPELMAN	Arye	M				308
KOPPELMAN	Shlomo	M				308
KOPPELMAN	Miriam	F				308
KOPPELMAN	Shmuel	M				308
KRAKER	Soniya	F				308
KRUG	Pinchas	M	married		Name of spouse – Sarah	309
KRUG	Sarah	F	married	one child	Name of spouse – Pinchas	309
KESSEL	Asher	M		one child		309
KESSEL	Itka	F				309
KESSEL	Taniya	F				309
KESSEL	Iziya	F				309
KASHUK	Isaac	M				309
KASHUK	Yuliya	F				309
KASHUK	Raizel	F				309
KASHUK	Shimon	M				309
KASHUK	Fraida	F				309
KASHUK	Zvulun	M				309
KASHUK	Uliya	F				309
KASHUK	Saliya	F				309
KASHUK	Eliezer	M				309
KOTEL	David	M				309
KOTEL	Mordechai	M				309
KOTEL	Rachel	F				309
KOTEL	Zisiya	M	married			309

KOTEL		F	married		Name of spouse – Zisiya	309
KARP	Hayyim	M				309
KARP	Tova	F				309
KARP	Yacov	M				309
KARP	Ethel	F		one child		309
KNIEVER	Rivka	F				309
KNIEVER	Aidel	F		one child		309
KERVIETZ	Binjamin	M				309
KERVIETZ	Leah	F				309
KERVIETZ	Ze'ev	M				309
KERVIETZ	Hana	F				309
KUPPERMAN	Abraham	M				309
KUPPERMAN	Yenta	F				309
KUPPERMAN	Yishayahu	M				309
KALIMEIR	Abraham	M				309
KALIMEIR	Soniya	F				309
KALIMEIR	Bentzion	M				309
KALIMEIR	Yochevet	F				309
KALIMEIR	Nahum Nuniya	M	married	and family		309
KALIMEIR		F	married	and family	Name of spouse – Nahum Maniya	309
KLUGEN	Joseph	M				309
KLEINMAN	Berel	M	married	one child		309
KLEINMAN		F	married	one child	Name of spouse – Berel	309
KLEINMAN	Aharon	M	married	2 children	Name of spouse – Maniya	309
KLEINMAN	Nmaniya	F	married	2 children	Name of spouse – Aharon	309
KLOTZMAN	Wolf	M				309

KLOTZMAN	Miriam	F				309
KLOTZMAN	Haya	F				309
KLOTZMAN	Eliyahu	M				309
KLOTZMAN	Israel	M	married	one child	Name of spouse – Fraida	309
KLOTZMAN	Fraida	F	married	one child	Name of spouse – Israel	309
KAGAN	Tzvi	M				309
KAGAN	Miriam Leah	F				309
KAGAN	Tova	F				309
KAGAN	Ita	F				309
KOJFMAN	Shlomo	M				310
KOJFMAN	Raizel	F				310
KOJFMAN	Aba	M				310
KOJFMAN	Gittel	F				310
KATCHKE	Bandet	M				310
KATCHKE	Israel	M				310
KATCHKE	Haya Mirel	F				310
KATCHKE	Rachel	F				3130
KATCHKE	Figa	F				310
KATCHKE	Ethel	F				310
KATCHKE	Moshe	M				310
KATCHKE	Malka	F				310
KATCHKE	Figa	F				310
KATCHKE	Haya	F				310
KATCHKE	Rivka	F				310
KATCHKE	Hayyim Michael	M	married	one child	Name of spouse – Menucha	310
KATCHKE	Menucha	F	married	one child	Name of spouse – Hayyim Michael	310
KLOTZ	Reuben	M				310

KLOTZ	Pearl	F				310
KLOTZ	Abraham	M				310
KLOTZ	Vitiya	M				310
KLOTZ	Hana	F				310
KLOTZ	Pearl	F				310
KLOTZ	Michael	M				310
KANTOR	Moniya	M				310
KANTOR	Biela Rachel	F				310
KANTOR	Buzi	M				310
KANTOR	Tuviya	M				310
KANTOR	Asher	M				310
KANTOR	Batya	F				310
KANTOR	Asher	M				310
KANTOR	Fruma	F				310
KANTOR	Braindel	F				310
KANTOR	Abraham	M				310
KANTOR	Mumah	F				310
KANTOR	Fifa	M	married	2 children	Name of spouse – Faiga	310
KANTOR	Faiga	F	married	2 children	Name of spouse – Fifa	310
KOPAIKIS	Shlomo	M				310
KOPAIKIS	Frieda	F				130
KOPAIKIS	Mordechai	M				310
KOPAIKIS	Tzirel	F				310
KOMERIVKA	Meir Arye	M			Policeman in the ghetto	310
KOMERIVKA	Rivka	F			Maiden name BRIZMAN. Father Hayyim	310

ר **Resh**

ROSENBAUM	Yonah	M				310
ROSENBAUM	Shaina	F				310
ROSENBAUM	Udiya	M				310
ROSENBAUM	Ita	F				310
ROSENBLATT	Braindel	F				310
ROSENBLATT	Meir Arye	M				310
ROSENBLATT	Guta Rachel	F				310
RIDNER	Fraida	F				310
RIDNER	Shlomo	M				310
RIDNER	Batsheva	F				310
RIDNER	Tzvi	M				310
RIDNER	Moshe	M				310
REVER	Moshe	M				310
REVER	Yehudit	F				310
REISENBERG	Rivka	F				310
REISENBERG	Baba	F				310
ROTSCHNEIDER	Shmuel	M				311
ROTSCHNEIDER	Menucha	F				311
ROTSCHNEIDER	Daitel	F				311
ROTSCHNEIDER	Ethel	F				311
REZNIK	Leah	F				311
REZNIK	Tzvi	M				311
REZNIK	Chesha	F				311
REZNIK	Gnesiya	F				311
REZNIK	Mordechai	M				311
REZNIK	Moshe	M				311
REZNIK	Yacov	M				311
REZNIK	Bila	F				311
REZNIK	Bila	F				311

REZNIK	Fraidel	F				311
REZNIK	Asher Isaac	M				311
REZNIK	Chiniya	F				311
REZNIK	Raizel	M				311
ROSENSTEIN	Tzizia	F				311
ROSENSTEIN	Ze'ev	M				311
ROSENSTEIN	Mrliya	F				311
ROSENSTEIN	Tzvi	M				311
ROSENSTEIN	Ita	F				311
ROSENSTEIN	Tzve	M				311
ROSENSTEIN	Ita	F				311
ROSENSTEIN	Tzvi	M				311
ROSENSTEIN	Yacov	M				311
ROSENSTEIN	Leah	F				311
ROSENSTEIN	Asher	M				311
	Joseph	M			to the family ROSENSTEIN	311
	Miriam	F			to the family ROSENSTEIN	311
	Asher	M			to the family ROSENSTEIN	311
RUDMAN	Moshr	M				311
RUDMAN	Soniya	F				311
RUDMAN	Tacov	M				311
RUDMAN	Joseph	M				311
ROSENBLATT	Berel	M				311
ROSENBLATT	Ethrl	F			Maiden name PERLIUK	311
ROSENBLATT	Maniya	F				311
ROSENBLATT	Yacov	M				311
ROSENBLATT	Gisiya	F				311

ROSENBLATT	Nehama	F				311
ROSENBLATT	Eliyahu	M	married	2 children	Name of spouse – Faigel	311
ROSENBLATT	Faigel	F	married	2 children	Name of spouse – Eliyahu	311
ROSENBLATT	Abraham	M	married		Name of spouse – Rickel	311
ROSENBLATT	Rickel	F	married		Name of spouse – Abraham	311
ROSENBLATT		M			a boy. Father Abraham and mother Rickel	311
ROSENBLATT	Braindel	F				311
ROSENBLATT	Ze'ev	M				311
ROSENBLATT	Abraham	M				311
ROSENBLATT	Moshe	M				311
ROSENBLATT	Haya	F				311
ROSENBLATT	Susil	F				311
ROSENBLATT	Rivka	F				311
ROSENBLATT	Tzvi	M				311
ROSENBLATT	Gittel	F				311

ש **Shin**

SHUBKES	Joseph	M	married	2 children	Name of spouse – Malka	311
SHUBKES	Malka	F	married	2 children	Name of spouse – Joseph	311
SHUBKES	Jeniya	F			teacher	311
SCHAPIRA	Joseph	M				312
SCHAPIRA	Susil	F				312
SCHAPIRA	Luniya	M				312
SCHAPIRA	Jeniya	F				312
SCHAPIRA	Asher	M				312
SCHAPIRA	Duba	F				312

SHMIRGOLD	Abraham	M				312
SHMIRGOLD	Braindel	F				312
SHTIVEL	Aba	M				312
SHTIVEL	Leah	F				312
SHTIVEL	Sarah	F				312
SHTIVEL	Leva				the name and gender are not clear	312
SHTIVEL	hayyim	M				312
SHTIVEL	Baruch	M				312
SHTIVEL	Hana	F				312
SHTIVEL		F			a girl	312
SCHENRIK	Moshe	M				312
SCHENRIK	Rachel	F				312
SCHENRIK	Ita	F				312
SCHENRIK	Shimshon	M				312
SCHENRIK	Sarah	F				312
SCHENRIK	Yacov	M	married			312
SCHENRIK		F	married		Name of spouse – Yacov	312
SCHENRIK		F			Father Yacov	312
SCHENRIK	Shmuel	M	married			312
SCHENRIK		F	married		Name of spouse – Shmuel	312
SCHENRIK	Aharon	M				312
SCHENRIK	Faigel	F				312
SCHENRIK	Faisi	M				312
	Batya	F	married		Maiden name SCHENRIK. Name of spouse – David	312
	David	M	married		Name of spouse – Batya	312

SCHENRIK	Mendel	M	married	and family		312
SCHENRIK		F	married	and family	Name of spouse – Mendil	312
SCHENRIK	Saniya	M		and family		312
SHINMAN	Adla	F		one child		312
SHINMAN	Haya	F				312
STEIN	Batya	F				312
STEIN	Tzvi	M				312
STEIN	Rizel	F				312
STEIN	Shlomo	M	married			312
STEIN		F	married		Name of spouse – Shlomo	312
STEIN	Mordechai	M				312
STEIN	Bracha	F				312
SCHENRIK	Mordechai	M				312
SCHENRIK	Rivka	F				312
SCHENRIK	Eliezer	M				312
SCHENRIK	Baruch	M				312
SCHENRIK	Bracha	F				312
SCHENRIK	Zenbil	M				312
SCHENRIK		M			a boy	312
SCHENRIK	Mendel	M				312
SCHOR	Abraham	M	married	2 children	Name of spouse – Bila	312
SCHOR	Bila	F	married	2 children	Name of spouse – Abraham	312
SHTZERBATY	Abraham	M				312
SHTZERBATY	Hana	F				312
SHTZERBATY	Gittel	F				312
SCHWARZGORN	Moshe	M				312
SCHWARZGORN	Baruch	M				312

SCHWARZGORN	Gittel	F				312
SCHWARZGORN	Etsther	F				312
SCHINDELHAUS	Haya	F			Maiden name GREENBAUM. Mother Sarah	313
SCHINDELHAUS	Isaac	M				313
SCHINDELHAUS	Shlomo	M				313
SCHINDELHAUS	Shmuel	M				313
SCHINDELHAUS	Moshe	M				313
SCHINDELHAUS	Gittel	F				313
SCHINDELHAUS	Eliyahu	M				313
SCHINDELHAUS	Aniya	F				313
SCHINDELHAUS	Nuneck	M				313
SCHINDELHAUS		M			a boy	313
SCHAG	Yehoshua	M				313
SCHAG	Haya Gittel	F				313
SCHAG	Hayyim	M				313
SCHAG	Rachel	F				313
SHEMESH	Yacov	M				313
SHEMESH	Tzvia	F				313
SHEMESH	Moshe	M				313
SHEMESH	Hilik	M				313
SCHEINFELD	Abraham	M	married		Father Herzl	313
SCHEINFELD		F	married		Name of spouse – Abraham	313
SCHEINFELD	Abraham	M				313
SCHEINFELD	Figa	F				313
SCHEINFELD	Yonah	M				313
SCHEINFELD	Mendel	M				313
SCHEINFELD	Lipa	M				313
SCHEINFELD	Bila	F				313

SCHINDELETZKY	Meir Arye	M			313
SCHINDELETZKY	Rachel	F			313
SCHINDELETZKY	Rivka	F			313
SCHWARZGORN	Aharon	M			313
SCHWARZGORN	Golda	F			313
SCHWARZGORN	Shmuel	M			313
SCHWARZGORN	Hinda	F			313
SCHWARZGORN	Dov	M			313
SCHWARZGORN	Taivel	M			313
SCHWARZGORN	Pesiya	F			313
SHPANOVER	Tzvi	M			313
SHPANOVER	Rachel	F			313
SHPANOVER	Yacov	M			313
SHPANOVER	Shaindel	F			313
SHPANOVER	Esther Rachel	F			313
SHPANOVER	Aharon	M			313
SHPANOVER	Faiga	F			313
SHPANOVER	Ethel	F			313
SHPANOVER	Michael	M			313
SHPANOVER	Hana	F			313
SHPANOVER	Abraham	M			313
SHPANOVER	Pinchas	M			313
SHPANOVER	Figa	F			313
SHPINKA	Mattel	M		from ALESKA famiky	313
SHPINKA	Chernila	F			313
STEFER	Hana	F			313
STEFER	Kutziya	F			313
STEFER	Rachel	F			313
STEFER	Rivka	F			313

STEFER	Yosef ben Gedalyahu	M				313
STEFER	Bentzion	M				313
STEFER	Bluma	F				313
STEFER	Mindel	M				313
STEFER	Baruch	M				313
STEFER	Tzvia	F				313
STEFER	Tzvi	M	married	2 children	Name of spouse – Ita	313
STEFER	Ita	F	married	2 children	Name of spouse – Tzvi	313
STEFER	Joseph	M				314
STEFER	Esther	F				314
STEFER	Rivka	F				314
STERNBERG	Eliezer	M				314
STERNBERG	Faiga	F				314
STERNBERG	Yochevet	F				314
STERNBERG	Brindil	F				314
STERNBERG	Isaac	M				314
STERNBERG	Zahava	F				314
STEINSCHNEIDER	Yehoshua	M	married		Name of spouse – Deborah	314
STEINSCHNEIDER	Deborah	F	married		family of Tzizia ROSENSTEIN. Name of spouse – Yehoshua	314
STEINSCHNEIDER		M			Father Yehoshua and mother Deborah	314
SCHULDINER		M	married	one child	Refugees from Bilgoraj. Mother Pesiya	314
SCHULDINER		F	married	one child	Refugees from Bilgoraj	314

SCHULDINER	Pesiya	F		Refugees from Bilgoraj	314
SHTZERBATY	Abraham	M			314
SHTZERBATY	Hana	F			314

[Page 315]

List of People from Derman', (Ustenskoye Pervoye) Who Were Annihilated in the Mizocz Ghetto in 1942

Original transliteration by Beryl Baleson
Revised for this edition by Bella Hass Weinberg

Family name(s)	First name(s)	Gender	Additional family
FISHBEIN	Hayyim	M	
FISHBEIN	Batya Rivka	F	
BERENSTEIN	Asher	M	
BERENSTEIN	Henika	F	
BERENSTEIN	Lahuka	F	
BERENSTEIN	Nata	M	
BERENSTEIN	Baila	F	
BERENSTEIN	Batya	F	
SUDGALTER	Baba	F	
SUDGALTER	Abtraham	M	
SUDGALTER	Gittel	F	
SUDGALTER	Baila	F	
SUDGALTER	Tzipa	F	
RADITMAN	Zaivil	M	
RADITMAN	Figa	F	
RADITMAN	Baiba	F	
RADITMAN	Fraidale	F	

MIZATSH	Faivish	M	
MIZATSH	Sarah Faiga	F	
PERETZMAN	Mattil	M	
PERETZMAN	Sunny	F	
PERETZMAN	Manny	F	
PERETZMAN	Roiza	F	
KNEPLIER	Hayyim	M	
KNEPLIER	Hasiya	F	
KNEPLIER	Yacov	M	
KNEPLIER	Gadil	M	
KNEPLIER	Zelick	M	
KNEPLIER	Moshe	M	
GATZENZANEN	Braindel	F	
GATZENZANEN	Zalman	M	
GATZENZANEN	Midal	M	
BERENSTEIN	Mali	F	
BERENSTEIN	Ita	F	
BERENSTEIN		F	
GATZENZANEN	Netta	F	2 children
GATZENZANEN	Maniya	F	3 children
DRATVA	Baila	F	
DRATVA	Rachel	F	

LAST NAME INDEX

Surname translation for English-language edition by Bella Hass Weinberg

A

Abdullah, 185
Abrach, 127, 128, 149, 150, 264
Ackerman, 264
Aharon, 119
Akhunbabaev, 173, 180
Aleska, 309
Alter, 126
Altman, 3, 43, 44, 45, 209, 261
Anda, 109
Appel, 264
Arbitorer, 215, 265
Arlosoroff, 15, 138
Asch, 13
Asher, 144
Ashers, 214
Ashkenazi, 266
Atlas, 13
Avner, 264

B

Bachan, 19
Bakast, 13
Bandera, 98, 157
Bandorenka, 60
Baraz, 98, 160
Barinstein, 267, 268
Bat, 133, 267
Bayer, 100
Belfer, 268, 270
Ben Baruch, 150
Ben-Oni, 1, 93, 104, 136, 263, *Also see Gilberg*
Ben–Zion, 47
Berchash, 268
Berenstein, 311, 312
Berez, 21, 203, 204, 249, 270

Beri, 268
Berkowski, 54, 267
Berman, 5, 27, 94, 136
Bernstein, 127, 128, 271
Bialik, 13
Biber, 152, 231
Biber-Golick, 152
Biber-Lukick, 231
Bicks, 80, 269
Bioalsky, 272
Birenbaum, 270
Bonchkovsky, 97
Bonis, 21, 123, 213, 267
Bork, 268
Bornstein, 267
Branstein, 55
Braunstein, 12, 42, 68, 71, 84, 152, 257, 270
Braz, 5, 99, 165
Breizman, 123, 231, 232
Brezner, 128, 249, 268
Breznerand, 248
Brinstein, 119
Brisker-Nemirover, 210
Brizman, 152, 269, 270, 302
Broida, 268
Broinowski, 81
Bronislaw, 185
Bronka, 96
Bronstein, 5
Brotzky, 5, 269
Buber, 141

C

Chaim the Postman, 163
Charni, 61
Chernavksy, 297
Chernietzky, 297

Chertok, 17, 18
Chukralnik, 160

D

Dayan, 14, 126, 139
Dezentje, 185
Dordick, 70
Dordick Katz, 274
Dos, 43
Dratva, 22, 191, 312

E

Eichmann, 187
Eisengart, 57, 75, 98, 127, 152, 225, 227, 232, 264, 265
Eisengart-Fliter, 75
Erlich, 27, 42, 48, 265

F

Feigeles, 210
Feldman, 3, 41, 119, 126, 128, 138, 231, 261, 293, 294
Fidelman, 13, 21, 72, 123, 291
Filianiuk, 36
Finias, 162
Fink, 142
Finkel, 8, 11, 14, 19, 26, 72, 87, 101, 139, 235, 287, 290
Finkelstein, 291, 292
Finker, 293
Fiodorov, 59, 61
Firer, 12, 38, 41, 74, 85, 290
Fishbein, 31, 192, 296, 297, 311
Fisher, 37, 291
Fishfeider, 118, 126, 246, 258, 290, 292
Fishfeider-Teichner, 192
Fishman, 292
Fleisch, 127, 128, 149, 290, 291
Fliter, 3, 8, 9, 11, 13, 16, 17, 28, 33, 41, 42, 53, 86, 88, 89, 93, 123, 136, 154, 215, 216, 217, 223, 227, 261, 268, 295, 296
FoigelStein, 14, 295
Fuchs, 294, 295

G

Gandelman, 273
Gantzberg, 6, 10, 11, 12, 57, 58, 117, 118, 119, 120, 122, 123, 126, 128, 152, 201, 241, 273, 274
Gat, 183, 184, 185, 186
Gatzenzanen, 312

Gelberg, 126, 133
Gelman, 3, 18, 22, 32, 33, 49, 54, 69, 119, 124, 126, 127, 128, 193, 228, 241, 250, 261
Gerasimchuk, 82
Gerber, 32, 33, 34, 41, 42, 213, 272
German, 273
Gerstein, 272
Geskis, 49
Giebel, 127
Gievski, 45
Gilberg, 4, 13, 14, 130, 138, 142, 161, 167, 214, 215, Also see Ben-Oni
Gleit, 273
Glinka, 185, 187
Gnipoler, 9
Golberton, 273
Goldberg, 40, 42, 214, 235, 236
Goldberg–Tzizin, 45
Goldbrenner, 21, 26, 71, 272
Goldman–Kotel, 220
Goldstein, 213, 286, 287
Golob, 237, 256
Gordin, 13
Gordon, 117, 122, 126, 127
Gorntzel, 126, 139, 149
Greenbaum, 273, 308
Greenberg, 95, 272, 273
Greiar, 298, 299
Grobe, 53, 54
Grosman, 120, 273, 274
Grossblatt, 26, 73
Gurewitz, 5, 118, 119
Gusack, 21, 70, 272
Guz, 273

H

Halbmilion, 8, 17
Halperin, 11, 218, 274
Hartstein, 99, 100
Helem, 211
Henele, 211
Herzl, 197
Hitler, 26, 53, 66, 68, 69, 77, 86, 91, 93, 108, 109, 110, 141, 144
Honigsfeld, 274
Horenstein, 5
Horowitz, 45, 93
Hutagalung, 185

I

Idsis, 13, 266
Iwanowa, 169

J

Jabotinsky, 131, 134, 141
Jasienski, 142
Jung, 53
Jurgilewicz, 109, 110

K

Kagan, 279, 301
Kalim, 32
Kalimeir, 300
Kantor, 45, 124, 127, 302
Kaput, 5, 118, 127
Karmi, 3
Karni, 241, 261
Karp, 300
Karwitzky, 5, 17, 73, 144
Kashuk, 11, 13, 16, 299
Kashuk-Szprync, 72
Kashuky, 16
Katchke, 301
Katz, 14, 161, 295
Kervietz, 300
Kessel, 299
Kestenbaum, 13, 14, 117, 298
Kestenberg, 12
Khmelnytsky, 4, 23
Kleinman, 6, 12, 13, 117, 120, 126, 152, 300
Klonitzky, 125
Klotz, 301, 302
Klotzman, 37, 300, 301
Klugen, 300
Klugman, 66
Kneplier, 259, 312
Kniever, 22, 33, 54, 300
Kojfman, 301
Komerivka, 302
Kopaikis, 302
Kopit, 3, 6, 13, 30, 84, 85, 238, 239, 261, 297, 298
Koppelman, 12, 13, 14, 16, 38, 82, 94, 117, 118, 120, 126, 152, 196, 198, 199, 200, 201, 202, 218, 254, 272, 299
Kornik, 12, 98, 118, 119, 128, 192, 247, 298, 299
Kotel, 220, 221, 299, 300
Kraindis, 267

Kraker, 299
Krashinsky, 106, 107
Kraszewska, 27
Krisik, 140, 298
Krug, 299
Krupniok, 83
Kuninar(?), 257
Kupperman, 300
Kurtz, 235
Kutchner, 64

L

Langer, 8, 16, 19, 41, 42, 85, 114, 124, 150, 271, 281, 282
Latochin, 128
Laufer, 280
Lavon, 117, 127, *Also see Lubjaniker*
Lavonsky, 281
Leiber, 237, 281
Lerner, 8, 54, 196, 279, 280
Levin Livander, 281
Liebster, 8, 14, 19, 259
Lifshitz, 183, 184, 186
Likwornik, 35, 37, 117, 118, 119, 120, 123, 126, 127, 128, 186, 282
Likwornik-Gat, 127, 128
Liodomirsky, 281
Lipovitzky, 280
Lippen, 282
Lipshitz, 38, 42, 280
Lubjaniker, 117, 122, 127, *Also see Lavon*
Lukacs, 163
Lundowski, 162
Lustik, 281

M

Makhliak, 61
Makhliuk, 61
Malgalter, 126, 127, 286, *Also see Melgater, Milhalter, Mulhalter, Yeshayahu the Mute*
Mandelkorn, 228
Margalit, 283
Matsiuk, 91
Matzak, 31
Mednik, 284
Meilier, 284
Meir, 41, 42
Meisles, 192
Meislitsch, 5, 17, 27, 106, 136, 285, 286

Melamed, 3, 12, 13, 43, 68, 69, 82, 83, 85, 117, 118, 120,
    123, 126, 152, 153, 180, 198, 199, 213, 214, 261,
    262, 283
Melamed-Nemirover, 155
Melgalter, 93, 124, *Also see Malgalter*
Mendelssohn, 235
Mendyuk, 11, 50, 61, 84, 121, 283
Mikhoels, 184, 186
Milhalter, 8, 140, *Also see Malgalter*
Miller, 72, 283
Milter, 83, 84
Mindlin, 282
Mirmelstein, 11, 13, 283
Mizatsh, 312
Mizocz, 5, 82, 124, 251, 253, 258, 284, 285
Mochin, 283, 284
Molotov, 30, 146
Moshe Rabbeinu, 9, 24
Mossman, 69, 213, 284
Mottel the Naughty, 163
Mottel the Stingy, 161
Mulhalter, 118, *Also see Malgalter*
Mulman, 9, 38, 40, 41, 128, 284
Murak, 230, 284
Murakovitz, 284
Myronov, 168, 169, 170

N

Nagel, 287
Nassias, 158
Neiman, 255, 287
Nemirover, 9, 11, 15, 21, 52, 70, 114, 122, 123, 154, 158,
    181, 210, 212, 213, 224, 241, 286
Nemirover-Shtelong, 212
Noiachs, 287
Nudler, 286
Nulman, 287

O

Oblowski, 38
Ochs, 41, 266
Ognev, 142
Oliker, 13, 15, 18, 37, 38, 39, 42, 43, 44, 80, 132, 134,
    141, 142, 163, 219, 243, 265, 266
Omanski, 105, 107
Orlovski, 39

P

Parpeniuk, 58
Peckenter, 290
Peretzman, 312
Perliuk, 3, 14, 15, 128, 135, 141, 187, 192, 233, 234,
    235, 261, 273, 278, 292, 293, 304
Perlmutter, 31, 38, 291
Petliura, 14, 16, 19, 24, 150, 216
Picasso, 185
Pickoretz, 80
Pinchasovitz, 291
Plinker, 45
Pochbula, 42, 83
Pogorilitzer, 133, 158
Polchik, 151
Poliak, 42, 47
Poliakov, 293
Polishuk, 295
Port, 118, 127, 193, 209, 290
Pressman, 292, 295

R

Rachel the Pivcher, 162
Raditman, 311
Rakovtchekhe, 88
Reisenberg, 303
Remarque, 142
Repin, 185, 187
Rever, 303
Reznik, 8, 9, 55, 118, 126, 127, 140, 207, 209, 303, 304,
    Also see Yechiel the Butcher
Ridner, 303
Riesel, 126
Romanchenko, 79
Rosenbaum, 303
Rosenblatt, 27, 35, 38, 41, 42, 43, 45, 48, 80, 136, 142,
    151, 303, 304, 305
Rosenblum, 24
Rosenstein, 31, 37, 38, 42, 304, 310
Rotschneider, 303
Rudman, 11, 21, 22, 33, 70, 304

S

Saleh, 185
Sannis, 69
Savulke, 91
Schag, 308
Schapira, 11, 13, 41, 42, 97, 305

Scheinfeld, 3, 13, 18, 126, 158, 228, 254, 261, 308
Scheinman, 20, 21, *Also see Shinman*
Schenrik, 13, 14, 154, 306, 307
Schimonowitz, 27
Schindeletzky, 309
Schindelhaus, 69, 80, 82, 273, 308
Schisel, 58, 139
Schochet, 11, 13, 14, 126, 133, 139, 218
Schor, 307
Schuldiner, 310, 311
Schulman, 250
Schwarzgorn, 119, 124, 128, 223, 307, 308, 309
Schwarzman, 222
Schwarzman-Tentzer, 222
Segal, 289
Seifmacher, 276, 277
Shemesh, 308
Shinman, 307, *Also see Scheinman*
Shmalier, 32
Shmirgold, 306
Shoham, 127, 128
Shoham-Fleisch, 148
Sholem Aleichem, 13, 183
Shpanover, 123, 181, 309
Shpinka, 309
Shtellung, 3, 261
Shtivel, 21, 31, 70, 81, 128, 306
Shtreimal, 278
Shtzerbaty, 307, 311
Shubkes, 214, 305
Silberstein, 277
Silberstien, 277
Simes, 289
Singer, 32, 33, 140
Sizak, 32, 193, 237, 246, 247, 248, 288
Skolnik, 288, 289
Soedarsono, 185
Spektor, 288
Spielfogel, 298
Srulenio, 211
Stanislaus II Augustus, 67
Stanislav, 48
Startz, 289
Stefer, 35, 309, 310
Stein, 180, 307
Steinberg, 47, 48
Steinschneider, 310
Steltzky, 289
Sternberg, 119, 126, 310
Stifer, 95
Sudarso, 185

Sudgalter, 156, 259, 311
Sudhalter, 287
Sudobitzky, 237, 251, 289
Sudobitzky–Holtzker, 252
Sukarno, 185
Svoboda, 13, 36
Szyk Haggadah, 185

T

Tekes, 298
Tekser, 5, 12, 198, 278
Teller, 12, 13, 117, 126, 277
Tenholtz, 279
Tentzer, 222, 277, 278
Tentzer-Schwartzman, 128
Tepper, 277
Toharan, 37
Trachtenberg, 43, 277
Trelovsky, 279
Trochler, 31, 42, 80, 162, 235, 236
Trochlier, 48, 69, 72, 278, 279
Trubus, 185
Tzipak, 140
Tzirkel, 238
Tzitzin, 49

V

Vasicher, 276
Vigoda, 20, 99
Vorozhnilik, 95, 98

W

Wachs, 213
Wasserman, 10, 27, 85, 96, 104, 105, 106, 107, 108, 110, 111, 142, 275
Weiner, 38, 41, 275, 276
Weinstein, 21, *Also see Willstein*
Weinzweig, 41, 97
Weisberg, 275
Welfman, 275
Weltfreint, 26, 38, 47, 96, 245, 275
Wiener, 35, 41, 42
Willstein, 275, *Also see Weinstein*
Winogradsky, 80
Wohlman, 228
Wolfman, 37, 38, 240

Y

Yarmaliuk, 69, 80

Yasin, 243, 244, 279

Yechiel the Butcher, 205, *Also see Reznik*

Yeshayahu the Mute, 137, *Also see Malgalter*

Yosef ben Gedalyahu, 120

Yusis, 154, 229

Z

Zatz, 41, 42

Zelinsky, 26

Zeltzer, 121, 127

Zhbik, 63

Zukerman, 297

Zuskin, 184, 186

סוף

www.ingramcontent.com/pod-product-compliance
Lightning Source LLC
Chambersburg PA
CBHW082004150426
42814CB00005BA/222